WOMEN-OF-FAITH PEACEBUILDERS

Women-of-faith Peacebuilders

ELISABETH PORTER

Elisabeth Porter

PP

Perspicuous Press

Contents

Preface   vii

Acronyms   ix

1 Introducing Women-of-faith Peacebuilders   1

2 Religion and Global Trends   14

3 Women-of-faith as Transformative Agents   43

4 Women-of-faith Participating in Peace Processes   73

5 Women-of-faith Building Coalitions   109

6 Women-of-faith Empowering Violated Victims   151

7 Women-of-faith Practising Just Peace   184

Conclusion   225

References   231

Published by Perspicuous Press

ISBN 978-0-6457515-1-2 (paperback)

ISBN 978-0-6457515-2-9 (ebook)

Cover Image: IStock, Credit PhotoIris 2021, Location Siberia.

Preface

All books have a story because they take a long time to write. This one began in 2016 when I was Professor of Politics and International Relations at the University of South Australia. My favourite teaching course was "Peace, Justice, and Reconciliation." Many of my students had come from war-torn nations and related personally to much of the course content. The discussions were lively, with personal anecdotes included. My students enhanced my understanding of the impact of war and the wonder of a just peace. I wrote drafts of this book in academic mode for my research output. Then the university withdrew the teaching in this field, and my position became redundant. I altered the style of the book to make it more readable. It was independently published in 2018 and published by Perspicuous Press in 2024 with minor updates.

In writing my first drafts, I benefited from a semester of time off teaching when I was granted a sabbatical. I spent my time as a Visiting Research Professor at the Queens University Belfast, in the Senator George J Mitchell Institute for Global Peace, Security, and Justice. In Chapter seven, in my discussion on apology, I acknowledge that many of the conditions I write about were taken from a summary presented at a participatory workshop I attended, which was run by Kieran McEvoy and Anna Bryson, "Who, what, where, when, why: apology and dealing with the past in Ireland," on 7 November 2016, at the Queens University Belfast.

Throughout this book, all italicized words in quotations are in italic in the original. I have also chosen to italicize words or phrases that I want to emphasize. In reference to the narratives discussed in Chapter seven, Jennifer Freeman, the Associate Director for Peace-Makers Projects, University of San Diego, granted me permission to use quotations from these narratives, communicated by email on 17 November 2016.

Drafting this book has been a solitary process of research, thinking, and writing. It is not based on fieldwork, but on an intensive scrutiny of primary and secondary literature, always looking for first-person accounts of peacebuilding by women whose faith matters to them.

I would like to thank my wonderful husband Norman, who is always a loving, affectionate, and amazing support to my work. I am abundantly grateful for the love and friendship we share.

Contact me on: lisporter55@gmail.com

Acronyms

A21 - Abolishing Injustice in the Twenty-First Century

ARLPI - Acholi Religious Leaders Peace Initiative

AWID - Association for Women's Rights in Development

BiH - Bosnia-Herzegovina

BRA - Bougainville Revolutionary Army

CATW - Coalition Against Trafficking in Women

CEDAW - Convention on the Elimination of all Forms of Discrimination Against Women

CPWR - Council for a Parliament of the World's Religions

CRSV - conflict-related sexual violence

DDR - disarmament, demobilization, and reintegration

DRC - Democratic Republic of Congo

GBV - gender-based violence

GPPAC - Global Partnership for the Prevention of Armed Conflict

IDP - internally displaced persons

IEP - Institute for Economics and Peace

ILO - International Labour Organization

IR - international relations

ISIS - Islamic State of Iraq and the Levant (or Islamic State of Iraq and Syria)

LRA - Lord's Resistance Army

LWI - Liberian Women's Initiative

MARWOPNET - Mano River Women's Peace Network

MENA - Middle East and North Africa

NAP - national action plan

NGO - non-governmental organization

nd - no date

np - no page

PNG - Papua and New Guinea

RUF - Revolutionary United Front

SAVE - Sisters Against Violent Extremism

SDGs - Sustainable Development Goals

SGBV - sexual and gender-based violence

UN - United Nations

UN Action - UN Action Against Sexual Violence in Conflict

UNDP - United Nations Development Program

UNHCR - United Nations High Commissioner for Refugees

UNIFEM - UN Development Fund for Women

UNODC - UN Office on Drugs and Crime

UNSCR - United Nations Security Council Resolution

UWOFNET - Uganda Women of Faith Network

WILPF - Women's International League for Peace and Freedom

WIPNET - Women in Peacebuilding Network

WPS - women, peace, and security

1

Introducing Women-of-faith Peacebuilders

Who are women-of-faith in the context of politics and peacebuilding? What do they do, and why do they do it? Why is a book on these women needed? In answer to that last question, I suggest that there are four main reasons.

First, because religion is playing an increasingly dominant role in global politics in ways that need to be understood, and because for many women and men, religious faith is an integral aspect of their identities, influencing their social and political involvement. Thus, understanding the connections among religion, identity, and global politics is important for comprehending contemporary international relations and global politics. Further, articulating the role that women-of-faith play in building peace highlights their distinctive contributions to the politics and practices of peacebuilding, contributions that often are hidden from the limelight.

Second, although United Nations Security Council Resolution (UN-SCR) 1325 on Women, Peace, and Security (UN Security Council 2000) is the advocacy tool utilized by UN staff, scholars, policy-makers, nongovernmental organizations (NGOs), aid and development workers, and peace practitioners, for increasing women's active involvement in decision-making on all women, peace, and security (WPS) matters, there is little scholarly work that links this significant resolution and its related sister resolutions to the role of religion and faith as it is practised in everyday life. So, I think that it is worth exploring how various countries draw on religion and faith in developing their national action plans (NAPs) on the implementation of this key resolution to see how women-of-faith can fruitfully be incorporated into, and indeed lead, decisions that enhance WPS strategies.

Third, the literature on peacebuilding stresses the importance of utilizing local traditions and indigenous peacebuilders in transforming conflict, building security, and sustaining peace. Yet, feminist scholars have, in the main, omitted paying attention to the way that women-of-faith leaders act as role models in local communities and thus have the potential to instigate social and cultural change in ways that further gender equality. What women-of-faith typically do is to work at the informal, grassroots levels, work which usually isn't reflected in high-profile reporting. For this reason, it is imperative to document what these women-of-faith are doing, and to value the differences their activities are making in local communities.

Fourth, the work of UNSCR 1325 generally is formulated in a liberal-oriented and rights-based, secular framework that sits in tension with the more relational, communal focused peacebuilding of local women. This secular focus misses the important roles that women-of-faith play in transforming conflict, challenging religious extremism and the radicalization of youth, and contributing in amazing ways to building peace with local knowledge. Thus, it is important to tease out the tensions between the communal orientation of local women-of-faith and the secular, individual-rights emphasis within the WPS community.

Before expanding on these four underlying rationales, a few clarifications are in order. It is important to note that this book is not about religion, but about *women whose self-defined faith is a prime motivator for their peacebuilding work.* I acknowledge that I have more personal knowledge of Christianity than of other faiths. It is also the case that there is more documentation of the work done by Christian women compared with that by women of other faiths. Nevertheless, I include a variety of faiths and interfaith examples in my investigation whenever possible. Two further clarifications: First, my analysis revolves predominantly around the peacebuilding practices that occur in contexts of war, post-war, and transitional justice societies, rather than in interfaith dialogue in multicultural Western nations. Second, the conceptual framework of the book is interdisciplinary in connecting peace and conflict studies, politics and international relations, the sociology of religions, and transitional justice, all within a feminist interpretive context. This framework is clarified more fully in Chapter three, but simply stated, I use a gender lens to highlight gendered inequalities and injustices that occur in everyday experiences and in global politics. This lens also helps to highlight the significant contribution to peacebuilding that women and men make.

Now, in the next section of this chapter, I expand on the four rationales outlined above.

Rationale

Religion in Global Politics

Throughout history, religious rhetoric has been used to justify so-called holy wars. We are familiar with the negative aspects of religion — those seen in interstate wars carried out in the name of defending religious beliefs, civil wars raging between groups of differing faiths, and the use of religion to curtail women's rights. But while at times religion is used to justify terrible acts of violence, at other times it provides a basis for peacebuilding. Religious differences can alienate diverse groups; yet, where there is openness to difference, religious visions of a just peace can unite people through their common aspirations. Oppressive religion destroys creative minds and stultifies human rights, while inspirational religious ideas build people up and can prompt social justice activism. After the end of the Cold War, identity-based conflicts revealed ways in which religious identity can be used to legitimize violence; yet, as will be seen in the chapters that follow, there are many religious leaders who advocate reconciliation through interfaith dialogue.

Within the discipline of international relations (IR), the rising prominence of religious actors in politics in developing and developed countries has raised a host of ethical questions about issues such as self-determination for specific groups, spurious justifications for violence committed in the name of religion, and the international responsibility to protect minority religious groups. In addition, the post-9/11 global context has elevated the profile of the impact of religion on war, terrorism, and women's rights. Wherever there is an intertwining of religion and politics, there is a great deal at stake for women regarding equality, autonomy, and bodily integrity. There are countless instances of patriarchal traditions that are justified by religious dogma that seriously limit women's involvement in public life, leadership, and decision-making. At the same time, women's rights advocates who promote universal human rights norms in the Global South often struggle with accusations of "cultural imperialism and Western-style individualism" (Razavi and Jenichen 2010: 845).

Yet, as I expand later, religion may offer emancipatory opportunities for women to demonstrate leadership in education, health care, and providing support for communities. These tensions between religion's enhancement or limitation of women's agency are teased out in the following chapters. But while I do address the ways that religion can be a driver of conflict and undermine women's potential, my chief aim in this book is to highlight ways in which women from many faith backgrounds overcome massive religious, cultural, and traditional obstacles and can *rely on their faith to build peace, improve security, foster reconciliation, and practice a just peace.*

UNSCR 1325 and Religion

Fundamental to my analysis is the global "women, peace, and security" (WPS) agenda that has emerged in response to the persistence of the international community of equality, justice, and human rights activists. The Fourth World Conference on Women held in Beijing in 1995 saw an unprecedented 17,000 formal participants and 30,000 activists come together to further gender equality and the empowerment of women. This led to the Beijing Declaration and Platform for Action, which articulates twelve areas of critical concern regarding gender inequality. These urgent needs identified are:

- the environment,
- power and decision-making,
- discrimination and violation of the girl child,
- economic empowerment,
- unequal access to education and training,
- poverty,
- violence against women and girls,
- women's human rights,
- institutional mechanisms to promote the advancement of women,
- inequalities in health care,
- the media, and
- the effects of armed conflict.

The Platform gave worldwide visibility to the need to redress gender inequalities in a systematic fashion, and it unleashed the political will to do so, reinforcing the activism of the women's movement (Gardam and Jarvis 2000). Yet, especially regarding the impact of war and armed conflict on women's security, much more needs to be done.

The lobbying of leading women's activist groups within the NGO Working Group on Women, Peace, and Security, a consensus-based coalition of fourteen significant international NGOs, reinforced the pressing need to attend to war's impact on women and girls, culminating in the historic United Nations Security Council Resolution 1325 on Women, Peace, and Security (Security Council 2000), and subsequently followed by sister resolutions 1820 (UN Security Council 2008), 1888 (UN Security Council 2009a), 1889 (UN Security Council 2009b), 1960 (UN Security Council 2010), 2106 (UN Security Council 2013a), 2122 (UN Security Council 2013b), 2242 (UN Security Council 2015), 2467 (UN Security Council 2019a), and 2493 (UN Security Council 2019b). UNSCR 1325, the first UN Security Council resolution to specifically address the impact of armed conflict on women and girls, reaffirms "the important role of women in the prevention and resolution of conflicts and in peacebuilding," and stresses "the importance of their equal participation and full involvement" in maintaining and promoting peace and security and increasing women's role in decision-making processes to prevent and resolve conflict and further peace and security.

Specifically, it calls for increased *participation* of women in peace processes; *protection* of women and girls and respect for their rights; *prevention* of gender-specific violence; and incorporating a gender perspective in peacekeeping and training, relief and recovery work, peace agreements, and the implementation of all activities relating to conflict, peace, and security. Subsequent resolutions call for the *prosecution* of violators. These resolutions bring much-needed attention to the effect of violent conflict on women and girls and the crucial need for women to be meaningful actors in all decision-making processes related to peace and security.

UNSCR 1325 does not mention religion specifically. It does, though, at note 8, call on all actors to "support local women's peace initiatives and indigenous processes for conflict resolution." I am taking this note to be of great significance in highlighting local women's peacebuilding.

And UNSCR 1888, at note 15:

> *Encourages* leaders at the national and local level, including traditional leaders where they exist and religious leaders, to play a

more active role in sensitizing communities on sexual violence to avoid marginalization and stigmatization of victims, to assist with their social reintegration, and to combat a culture of impunity for these crimes. (UN Security Council 2009a)

As is noted in Chapter six in a discussion of National Action Plans (NAPs) for the implementation of UNSCR 1325, the involvement of religious leaders in increasing women's security is crucial, certainly in sensitizing community attitudes toward the harm caused by violence against women, but also in terms of changing social structures and cultural attitudes in ways that would increase women's participation as active agents in decision-making.

UNSCR 2242, in its preamble:

> *Urges* Member States and the United Nations system to ensure the participation and leadership of women and women's organizations in developing strategies to counter terrorism and violent extremism which can be conducive to terrorism, including through countering incitement to commit terrorist acts, creating counter narratives and other appropriate interventions, and building their capacity to do so effectively, and further to address, including by the empowerment of women, youth, religious and cultural leaders, the conditions conducive to the spread of terrorism and violent extremism which can be conducive to terrorism. (UN Security Council 2015)

UNSCR 2467, in note 16c, encourage religious and traditional leaders "to play a more active role in advocating within communities against sexual violence in conflict." At note 19, it also asks these leaders "to help shift the stigma of sexual violence from the victims to the perpetrators." (UN Security Council 2019a).

The scholarship that has emerged around the WPS agenda provides a concrete body of knowledge within which to situate my exploration of how women practice a just peace in contexts where religious differences contribute to conflict, where the harm of religious extremism seems overwhelming, and where religion stifles women's ability to make decisions (see Cohn, Kinsella and Gibbings 2004; Heathcote and Otto 2014; Kirby and Shepherd 2016; Puechguirbal 2010; Tryggestad 2009; Willett 2010).

My central argument is that many women-of-faith peacebuilders, particularly those who identify with feminist values, are doing much of the work called for by UNSCR 1325 and related resolutions, despite not always being aware of the resolutions. The principles of UNSCR 1325 are now integrated into official peace and security projects as standard practice (de Jong Outdraat, Stojanović-Gajić, Washington, and Stedman 2015). Yet, many women contribute significantly to peacebuilding practices in unofficial ways that do not gain adequate recognition. As will be demonstrated, *they build peace in unique ways.*

Peacebuilding and Local Traditions

Given the stress in peacebuilding literature and practice on the importance of the *local* for myriad reasons – for example, because local people understand local needs, to avoid paternalism and neo-colonialism, and because building local capacity strengthens the chance for sustainable peace (Richmond 2009) – I seek to show that it is important to utilize all *indigenous traditions* that are working toward a just peace, including those motivated by faith. The twenty-year anniversary of the Beijing Platform for Action and the fifteenth-year anniversary of UNSCR 1325 in 2015 saw a renewed emphasis on what it means to localize the priorities of gender equality, empowerment, and women's security in promoting the voices of civil society. Hence examples given in the book deliberately highlight local, grassroots work.

While the role of women in peacebuilding, long neglected in the literature, is starting to be recognized (for example, Anderlini 2007; Olonisakin, Barnes, and Ikp 2011; Porter 2007), when the topic is women and religion, this remains "largely unexplored terrain"

(Marshall and Hayward 2010: 3). Certainly, there is scholarship on the ways that religious dynamics hamper women's public roles (Carlson 2011; Greiff 2010; Razavi and Jenichen 2010; Verveer 2016); but there is little discussion on the ways that it may be "facilitating women's full participation in peacebuilding (particularly religious dynamics *propelling* women into peacework)" (Hayward 2015: 308). Additionally, scant consideration is given to the connections among gender, women, religion, and peacebuilding. Katherine Marshall and Susan Hayward explain that the lack of attention to these connections matters, because it "has led not only to failures to understand fully the nature of conflict, but has hidden from view potential avenues for resolving conflicts, promoting post-conflict healing and reconciliation, and building sustainable peace" (2010: 4). It is precisely the highlighting of this potential that is my central aim.

Thus, it is important to document what women-of-faith are doing in local communities to build peace, explain why they are doing this work, and highlight what unique contributions they make. By providing examples of women telling their stories to explain how their personal faith acts as a motivation in their public work as community peacebuilders, my research demonstrates their *relational, communal contributions to building just peace.* This research is not gained from primary fieldwork data. Rather, I sought examples that are drawn from a broad range of geographic areas and faiths to show how women-of-faith build peace. My priority lay in sourcing *first-person narratives of women's account of how faith spurs their peacebuilding.*

Relationship of Feminism, Religion, and Secularism

A purely secular focus on women, peace, and security concerns misses the importance of religion's potential in overcoming conflict, as well as the capacity of many women-of-faith to bypass religion's restrictive dictates to transform conflict in their unique ways. Ann Tickner writes that despite the discipline of IR showing a strong resurgence of interest in religion since 9/11, "new work on religion in IR has largely ignored gender. But it is also the case that IR feminists have largely ignored religion" (2014: 128). Indeed, some feminist discourse, noting institutional patriarchy within most religions, regards religion with contempt, as an obstruction to women's equality. These views must be considered, yet I suggest that there is a real case for making connections between, on the one hand, the secular scholarly and practical world of IR, transitional justice, and WPS advocates and, on the other hand, the peacebuilding work that is being done by women-of-faith in conflict zones and post-war settings. In doing so, links between building peace, affirming gender equality, valuing religious diversity, and creating inter-faith dialogue are highlighted.

Pramada Menon acknowledges: "I think for a very long time, those of us who work within women's human rights have not really worked on issues of religion. I suspect that this has to do with our desire to appear secular" (in Balchin 2011: 72). Rama Mani also "argues for a fundamental shift in both perspective and language that includes an appreciation of spirituality in the work of women and men who operate, in varying ways, outside the conventional bounds of academia and international policies" (in Hayward and Marshall 2015: 325). The secular language of international politics obscures the fact that, in the places where most violent conflict occurs, nearly everyone looks to spiritual resources for inner sustenance. Hayward writes that secular organizations like the Institute for Inclusive Security are seeking to get more women involved in international affairs, "but the analytical and visible field of religious peacemaking is behind the curve…. It's not a matter of women not being involved in religious peacemaking – it's more a matter of their efforts not being seen, supported, or analyzed" (in Marshall and Hayward 2010: 5). The work carried about by women-of-faith is often unrecognized, but on the frontlines of conflict, women are providing care by "working to heal war-torn communities, addressing HIV/AIDS treatment and prevention, fighting poverty, defending human rights, and struggling to establish a more just and harmonious society" (Religions for Peace 2009: 5).

Key Concepts

Three recurring concepts are utilized throughout this book: women-of-faith, post-conflict, and peacebuilding. I explain these now. As intimated, "Women-of-faith have historically 'fallen through the cracks' of the scholarship and practice of religious peacebuilding and women's peacebuilding, marginalized from both fields" (Hayward 2015: 308). Hayward defines what she calls "women-of-faith peacebuilders" to be "women who have important and formative links to the religion as a source of inspiration and formation or, more practically, who use religious resources as a central component of their peace work, to be religious women peacebuilders" (2015: 308-309). Hayward also includes in this category women who work through faith-based organizations, social services, or scholarship to advance justice and peace, as well as women in secular arenas who cite their link to faith as a force that inspires and shapes their work. Fuller explanations of what it means to be a woman-of-faith appear in Chapter three. Suffice to note here that my methodology is to include examples from any woman building peace who claims the importance of faith to her work.

The term "post-conflict," used frequently within UN documents and in the IR, transitional justice, and peacebuilding literature, is in my view, problematic. It is an ambiguous term "in obscuring the insecurities people experience after the cessation of war, ignoring the gender-specific ways that women and men experience insecurity and security; and it understates the degree to which gendered violence remains in a militarized or previously violent culture" (Porter 2016: 210). Often, the presence of international peacekeepers mixing with local security forces heighten feelings of militarized security (Simić 2012). Yet, the period immediately after war has ended, when a state is in transition from violence to enhancing security and sound governance, represents a moment of great potential to work toward gender equality and justice. With these qualifications in mind, because the term "post-conflict" is in common usage, I continue to use it (although sparingly). However, I prefer to use the term "post-war" to indicate that, for many people, some conflict remains, and the effect of war lingers.

"Peacebuilding" also has specific meanings in the literature and in UN usage. Previous United Nations Secretary-General Boutros Boutros-Ghali explained that "post-conflict peacebuilding" refers to the rebuilding of infrastructures, institutions, and relationships, with an emphasis on preventing recurring conflict (1992: 5). In the IR literature, peacebuilding is seen to start "when the fighting has stopped. It is, by definition, a post-conflict enterprise" (Paris 2004: 39). While not disregarding these understandings, I argue that they miss a lot of everyday activities that occur as part of unofficial peacebuilding. In the context of peace and security, the everyday is "a culturally appropriate form of individual or community life and care" (Richmond 2009: 558). Thus, I believe that expansive views of peacebuilding are "more likely to recognize women's informal activities as peacebuilders" (Porter and Mundkur 2012: 29). John Paul Lederach also calls for peacebuilding to be considered "more than post-accord reconstruction," and to be understood in a thorough way that "sustains the full array of processes, approaches, and stages needed to transform conflict toward more sustainable, peaceful relationships" (2004: 20).

In this book, I utilize a broad definition of peacebuilding, developed in my earlier works:

> I argue that peacebuilding involves all processes that build positive relationships, heal wounds, reconcile antagonistic differences, restore esteem, respect rights, meet basic needs, enhance equality, instil feelings of security, empower moral agency, and are democratic, inclusive, and just" (Porter, 2007: 34; Porter 2015: 8).

This definition is deliberately extensive. As Gerard Powers puts it, "peacebuilding can be defined quite broadly as everything implied by a robust, positive understanding of a just peace" (2010: 323). From another perspective, Carolina, a combatant in the guerrilla movement in El Salvador, explains after being demobilized in July 1992: "Building it, making it, and not allowing it to collapse is very difficult to do. Peace is like something made of glass: if you drop it, it breaks" (in Bennett et al. 1995: 196-197). Making sure that fragile peace doesn't collapse is a long-term, ongoing process.

Chapter Outline

In the next chapter, I discuss the global trends that are affecting the impact of religion on international politics. I also look specifically at the relationship between religion and gender to show how religious texts are often used to justify patriarchal constraints on women's equality, freedom, rights, and opportunities to demonstrate leadership – and to show how some women are consciously reinterpreting these texts within their own traditions in ways that could be liberating.

Chapter three presents evidence of women-of-faith as agents of transformative change, especially concerning issues of social justice. In Chapter four, the discussion turns to how women-of-faith are represented in both formal and informal peace processes. Chapter five explores the challenges, priorities, and achievements of women-of-faith who work across religious and faith differences to build peace. In Chapter six, I look at how women-of-faith deal practically with victims of sexual violence to try to heal physical and psychological wounds. The focus of Chapter seven is the unique contributions that women-of-faith make in their practices of just peace – that is, how they "do peacebuilding" differently. And in the Conclusion, I summarize what the WPS community can learn from women-of-faith peacebuilders, highlighting the specific contribution women-of-faith make to *building just peace* and arguing that a more deliberate inclusion of women-of-faith is needed within the WPS community.

2

Religion and Global Trends

Global trends on religion influence the relationships between conflict, gender, and peacebuilding. I highlight four main ways this occurs. First, while religious beliefs generally espouse peaceful values, throughout history, there are many examples where religion and conflict coincide, particularly where religion overlaps with ethnicity and national identity. History shows that violent abuses and suppression of women's rights often are justified in the name of religion.

Second, the influence of religion on global politics is growing, along with a high proportion of believers in the major world religions. I suggest that it is important to note this trend, because religious beliefs tend to be strong in most countries where civil war rages. This is why I stress that peacebuilding that relates to local customs, including faith traditions, is crucial to foster culturally appropriate changes to values and practices that are required to improve gender equality.

The third global tendency I discuss is how religion often undermines women's security through its patriarchal assumptions and practices. This occurs through using religious texts to justify men's authority and constrain women's equality, freedom, rights, and leadership, making the contribution of women-of-faith peacebuilders a truly significant feat.

Fourth, I argue that despite the frequent negativity of religion in seeming to cause conflict, or to justify violence and repress women's rights, all religions have a vision of peace and the capacity to empower women, and it is this vision and capacity that I choose to highlight.

My central argument in this chapter is that despite religion's terrible record in aligning with violence in certain conflicts, and using scriptures to rationalize restrictive views toward women, it is reasonable to talk of faith's capability to foster just peace. There is significant evidence to show that the objectives and practices of local women's faith-based peacebuilding has great potential to transform conflict in local communities and build women's esteem.

Religion and Conflict

This first section acknowledges the long historical association of religion with violent conflict in specific contexts. It examines the manifestation of this conflict in places where ethnicity, nationalism, and religious identity coincide. The distinctive gendered impact of this conflict is noted.

Ethnicity, Nationalism, and Religion

Religion and conflict have an uneasy, often contradictory relationship in that sometimes religion initiates or spurs conflict, other times it transforms conflict to encourage peace. Historically, "religions have contributed to social discord and to harmony, and they have inspired and legitimized violence and peacemaking" (Volf 2015: 21-22). The reasons for these contradictions are numerous. Most sacred texts have contrasting messages that exhort believers to fight evil, yet also push "a pacifist motive that prohibits harming others and prescribes a love for enemies that seems to challenge the very foundations of the warrior motif" (Kurtz 2012: 284).

In the post-Cold war era, the identity politics attached to ethnicity, nationalism, and religion drove some conflicts. This is because many people identified strongly with political projects that were intermeshed with subjective dimensions, of being for example, a Serbian Orthodox or a Bosnian Muslim. Herein again, paradoxes arise. Some people seek security in ethnic and religious identity that aligns with national identity, such as Protestants in Northern Ireland identifying as British, or Catholics as Irish. Others share a religious affinity that extends beyond nationality (Katano 2008: 351), such as being born into the Roman Catholic community. Ethno-religious identity features strongly in conflicts where kinship, religion, economic systems, and language are linked. In Nigeria for example, there about 520 languages marking each different group. Where ethno-religious identity is a crucial marker, religious traditions may perpetuate negative enemy images of the other. This is of great concern because these conflicts occur in communities where people are living in proximity, and where combined histories are filled with hostilities, mistrust, and resentment toward the other side.

The risk of serious conflict is highest in places "where deep religious divisions coincide with strong political and social divisions" (Garrod and Jones 2009: 82). Examples of ethnic, tribal, or race divisions include warfare between Muslims in the Republic of Sudan and Christians in South Sudan, religious differences between Catholics, Orthodox, and Muslims in the former Yugoslavian nations, and hostility between Hindus and Muslims in India. Although the Myanmar government regards the Rohingyan community as ethnic outsiders, much of "the violence carried out against them has been led by nationalist Buddhist monks" against the religious affiliation of Rohingya as Muslims, complicating "Orientalist stereotypes of Buddhism as a religion of peace" (Shani and Saeed 2016: 65-66).

Given the strength of religious divisions, transforming these violent conflicts requires "tapping into religious, cultural, and national symbols, values, myths, and images that promote reconciliation, coexistence, and peace" (Kadayifci-Orellana 2013: 151). Locating values of reconciliation like accountability and forgiveness within the boundaries of sacred texts can provide acceptability of new behaviours. However, before reconciliation is possible, the tight intransigence of identity politics must be loosened, so that people can be open to an acceptance of others with different ethnicity, national identity, and religious beliefs. This is rarely an easy task.

Gendered Conflict

There is a gendered component to conflict in that men and boys often have different experiences of war compared with women and girls (Cockburn 1998; Meintjes, Pillay, and Turshen 2001; Pankhurst 2008). Galuh Wandita's ethnographic fieldwork highlights how violent conflict affects women. While her research is on women from Asia, the key patterns that emerge from her findings are relevant for women elsewhere. First, "women continue to experience systematic, conflict-related violence despite international efforts to prevent it" (Wandita 2015: 334). This violence includes sexual violence, as well as violations of economic, social, cultural, civil, and political rights. Second, when impunity, stigma, and discrimination are cultural norms, the absence of justice exacerbates gendered inequalities, and women lose confidence in articulating the injustices they experience because they cease to believe they will ever experience justice. For many women, their yearning for justice equates with a desire for truth, such as knowing the location of their disappeared family members, or the reason for illegal detention and torture, or why perpetrators of violence are not punished. Third, from the 140 women who participated in Wandita's research, none were involved in formal peace processes, despite active work at the local, informal level. Fourth, women victims who are still struggling for economic survival, because their father, husband, or son has disappeared, been killed, detained, or the family was displaced, or the property was destroyed, rarely achieve justice. Incredible stories of survival, tenacity, resilience, creativity, and strength in the face of violent adversity doesn't negate everyday practical difficulties of women's survival. Fifth, Wandita concluded that "widows, single mothers, and women left alone due to conflict are particularly vulnerable and need special assistance" (2015: 346).

In recognizing the extent of violence women suffer in war, not all of it is attributable to religious conflict; however, much of it is, particularly when religious beliefs intertwine with ethnic identity, and antagonistic notions of the "other." Religious symbolism often deems women as the inferior, subordinate "other." I suggest that responses to the gendered nature of conflict must be fully aware of how violence typically affects women and girls differently to men and boys. Addressing this concern is integral to the realization of UNSCR 1325 and to understanding the priorities of women-of-faith peacebuilders in strengthening women's security.

Religion and Global Trends

There is a resurgence of religion on the global political landscape. This correlates with high numbers of people for whom religion is meaningful. Global trends include the rise in religious fundamentalisms and violent extremism, as well as the growth of Pentecostalism. This discussion is necessary because it forms the backdrop from whence an analysis of the work of women-of-faith in peacebuilding can begin in subsequent chapters.

Resurgence of Religion and Politics

Prior to the development of the modern secular international state, religion was dominant. Forces of secularization pushed religion into the private sphere. In the twenty-first century, there is a resurgence of religion influencing political decisions. Observers mark the reappearance of religion on the global stage to the Iranian revolution of 1978-9 because Iran, with its Sunni Muslim majority, "had adopted a Western-derived, secular development" (Haynes 2008: 1). The religious resurgence isn't confined to a region or religion. Indeed, even despite their Marxist pasts, Christianity is growing in China and Russia. In developing countries, this revitalization of religion has political consequences given the booming populations. One reason for this boom is that: "More devout families – Jews, Muslims, and Christians – believe children are a blessing from God" (Thomas 2010: 508). Further, religiosity is often evident among vulnerable, poor populations where people "routinely face threats to their survival," but it has declined among the prosperous populations in "secure post-industrial nations" (Bellin 2008: 332).

From the 1970s on, evangelical Protestantism and Pentecostalism grew swiftly in North and South America, Africa, and parts of East Asia. Evangelical Protestants are fundamentalists in their literal interpretations of the Bible. They believe in conversion, a personal experience after a calling from God. Pentecostals stress the workings of the Holy Spirit. The 1970s saw the rise of the Christian right, particularly in the United States, with their massive influence on the national political scene. The Christian right identify with socially conservative policies on abortion, same-sex relationships, strict gender norms, and stem cell research. Typically, they promote the value of free market capitalism, minimal government intervention into economic policy, and propose that faith-based charities should deal with poverty, unemployment, and drug and alcohol addiction, rather than government funded organizations. In Europe, opposition movements to Communist regimes in Eastern Europe and increased migration accompanied the growth of the Islamic population in Europe.

The World Values Survey shows that worldwide, 83 percent of people believe in God (in Philpott 2009: 191). Practically, this resurgence of religion and politics has many consequences, one positive aspect includes stimulating religious organizations to respond to the need for economic and social justice, as well as for conflict transformation.

The Pew Research Centre (2016) explored the question: "How important is religion in your life?" Its research shows that for more than 80 percent of people in Afghanistan, Bangladesh, Indonesia, Iraq, Jordan, Pakistan, Palestine, and Thailand, religion is "very important." In Africa, "African religious ideas and practices often coexist, complement, or overlap" with Islam or Christianity and permeate the whole of life (Mwaura 2012: 257). In some African states, there is an extremely high percent of Christians and Muslims who find religion to be significant. According to this Pew Research, for Christians, in highest order, more than 90 percent see religion as "very important" in Tanzania, Liberia, Cameroon, and Zambia; and more than 80 percent in Chad, Ghana, Guinea Bissau, Kenya, Democratic Republic of Congo (DRC), Mozambique, and Uganda. For Muslims, in highest numbers, more than 90 percent see religion as "very important" in Ghana, Cameroon, Guinea Bissau, Kenya, Tanzania, Mali, Mozambique, Nigeria, Uganda, Chad, DRC, and Liberia; and more than 87 percent in Morocco and Ethiopia. Many of these countries have experienced or continue to experience intense violence and insecurities.

The Pew Research (2016) show some key changes in the global religious landscape. First, Muslims are the fastest-growing major religious group, primarily because of their fertility rates. Second, the share of the world's population who are Christian is expected to remain steady at about 31 percent, but the regional distribution is forecast to change with 38 percent projected to live in sub-Saharan Africa by 2050. "After the USA, the countries with most practising Protestants are now Brazil, China, and Nigeria" (Freston 2008: 26). Third, numbers of religiously unaffiliated people are increasing in the Global North but decreasing as a share of the world's population. On 2 April 2015, the world figures show 31.4 percent are Christian, 29.7 percent Muslim, 14.9 percent Hindu, 13.2 percent unaffiliated, 5.2 percent Buddhist, 4.8 percent folk religions, 0.7 percent other religions, and 0.2 percent Jews.

We can conclude that *religion is meaningful* to the greatest proportion of people. This conclusion has deep political consequences for people's aspirations and practises. My central aim in the book is to build on this conclusion to show how specific women practice *gender-sensitive peacebuilding* that understands the significance of local beliefs that are embedded in politics.

Major World Religions

In terms of the major world religions, there are examples of Christianity's support for brutal acts. Many Christians supported Fascists in Italy, Nazis in Germany, Franco in Spain, Pinochet in Chile, Videla in Argentina, Marcos in Philippines, Suharto in Indonesia, and "almost all Western implants and despots in Africa" (Vltchek 2014: np). Further, as Andre Vltchek (2014: np) points out, Christianity was allied with oppressive forces of big business, slavery, feudalism, and capitalism, as well as Western imperialism, racism, sexism, and colonialism. Additionally, it is "one of the major ideologies of Othering" (Žarkov 2015: 5).

However, during the 1950s and 1960s civil rights campaigns, black clergy in the USA "provided leadership and churches furnished networks and an ethos for non-violent mobilization," but from the 1980s onwards, the religious right embodies a "form of politicization which appeals essentially to the evangelical community alone" (Freston 2008: 37). The growth of the religious right was conspicuous in the former US President Bush administration, where the invasion of Iraq occurred with the blessing of many respected evangelical voices, seeing it as a chance to evangelize Muslims. Chris Shannahan (2016) warns against formulating quick stereotypes, because while the Christian right strongly supported the election of US former President Trump, black evangelicals, who aren't necessarily right-wing in their political beliefs, largely supported Hillary Clinton.

As I demonstrate in the next chapter, these voices of Christianity don't speak for many from the Global South, the less developed countries where wealth is seen broadly in terms of human development, or for feminists within the richer, economically developed countries of the Global North. Nevertheless, Christianity's association with Western imperialism, political domination of conquered continents, and economic exploitation of the "other," is indisputable. This association "gave rise to a duality between 'civilization' and 'barbarism'," perpetuated by the Western assertion of cultural superiority (Martín-Muñoz 2010: 24). The histories of many conflict countries are grounded in colonialism and missionary paternalism. The colonizers seek to convert and order the world towards the colonizer's identity and faith.

Understandably, in a post-colonial world that contests these processes of economic, cultural, and political conquest, "the West is being challenged by peoples who have been marginalized, colonized, and exploited to recognize diverse forms of humanity" (Welch 2012: 35). The post-colonial movement helps to identify power relations between the oppressor and the oppressed, calling into question "the boundaries between identity and difference, between cultures, nationalities, and subjects" (Keller, Nausner, and Rivera 2004: 3). In these borderlands, the *spaces in-between* rigid dualisms like them and us, or male leaders and female servers, present an opportunity to resist subjection, permitting the person previously marked as "other" to self-define as a historical subject. I show in following chapters how in such spaces of resistance, women-of-faith defy religiously justified gendered stereotypes to fight against oppression in support of freedom, rights, and equality.

A significant legacy of colonialism is the growth of "Islamism, or political activity and popular mobilization in the name of Islam," which emerges in response to the Muslim world's encounters with the West, particularly in the form of the "war on terrorism" (Ayoob 2011: 6). Out of the colonial experience emerges "the equation of the Islamic concept of jihad with 'striving' and 'struggle' for freedom and independence," providing a motive and justification for anti-colonial wars (2011: 8), from British India to Anglo-Egyptian Sudan, and Italian Libya to French Algeria. Now jihad is extensive, reaching to the international order dominated by the US and its allies, cementing a reductionist image of us and them. The rise in Islamophobia, with "global perceptions of Islam in negative and pejorative terms" results in "discrimination against Muslims for reasons of racial hatred and prejudices" (Martín-Muñoz 2010: 22). This hostility towards Muslims fosters antagonistic relationships. We turn now to explore some consequences of religious extremism. This background provides the context from which to understand the enormity of women's struggle to counter such extremism, whilst building peace.

Fundamentalism, Pentecostalism, and Violent Extremism

While analytically different, fundamentalism of both the Christian right and radical Islam often is associated with violent extremism. The violence is not always perpetuated by the individuals in question, but the acts may be justified by them. The growth of Pentecostalism is linked with branches of Christian fundamentalism, but not usually with violence. The effects of these intermeshing aspects of modern religion have some disturbing consequences for women's struggle against gender injustice.

Fundamentalist movements believe that true salvation requires strict, literal adherence to the original scriptures. They are hierarchical structures of religious authority, with beliefs in absolute truth, leading to one right religious path. These movements are present in fundamentalist Buddhism, conservative Catholicism, evangelical Protestantism, nationalist Hinduism, extremist Islam, and Orthodox Judaism. However, the largest growth of fundamentalist movements lies with the Christian political right and Islamic extremists. A reason for this growth is that in a fast-changing world, where people feel anxious by the loss of familiar certainties, fundamentalism may fill the gap in that it "provides a set of clear, unchallengeable beliefs, practices, and moral guidelines" (Garrod and Jones 2009: 157). In fundamentalist groups, women's voices usually are silent, suppressed, or devalued. There is some passive resistance, for example, evangelical women might defend male headship and female submission in home and church life, whilst living an egalitarian work lifestyle where they hold senior positions. These women tend not to identify as feminist.

Pentecostalism fits into this picture of global trends because it is "the fastest growing Christian denomination in the world…globally it is estimated to attract 120 million believers" (Garrod and Jones 2009: 168). Communist "China (along with United States, Brazil, Nigeria, and the Philippines) has one of the largest numbers of Pentecostal and evangelical Christian populations in the world" (Thomas 2010: 508), signalling a dramatic religious explosion. The intense community of the Pentecostal, charismatic movement, with emotionally binding personal relationships with other believers and with God, provides support for people living uneasily in a fast-paced, post-modern world.

Fundamentalism and Pentecostalism frequently coincide. In Africa, Christian fundamentalism is partially a response to the failures of modernization, particularly poverty, marginalization, and insecurity, or in places like Nigeria, it coincides with the perception that local Muslims are belligerent. "The poorer and more uneducated people are, the more they flock into the new Protestant Pentecostal churches, where the 'Prosperity Gospel' is quickly becoming the most preached one" (Vltchek 2004: np). Michael Kafero explains that the Ugandan church's congregations are mainly poor and desperate but believe that their contributions to the church "are planting seeds for their own future prosperity" (in Vltchek 2014: np). Uganda is suffering from its civil war, as is the neighbouring DRC, where millions of lives are lost in the brutal plunder of the DRC's natural resources by Rwanda and Uganda, on behalf of the West. The militia commanders in the DRC claim to be religious Christian leaders "serving God faithfully," while the Church manipulates poor neighbourhoods across West, East, and Southern Africa, "keeping people as ignorant as possible, pillaging their meagre resources, and blocking birth-control wherever it can" (in Vltchek 2014: np). Across the world, religious fundamentalism, market fundamentalism, and right-wing individualism merge, influenced largely by American and Australian churches.

Yet in another geographic context, there is resistance to these trends. Nancy Bedford (2012) describes the "gender paradox" of indigenous Pentecostal women and other women-of-faith in Latin America who are caught in a bind. They seek to reinterpret their sacred texts and traditions, "while at the same time they are instructed not to overstep certain implicit boundaries, which are constantly negotiated and shift across time, but which almost invariably have to do with gender, class, and race" (Bedford 2012: 186). I explore the impact of this struggle in the next and subsequent chapters.

All religions have the potential to enact fundamentalist, violent extremism, but not all fundamentalists inflict violence on others. Ideological and religious extremists will do anything to keep their identities or push forward their religious ideologies. Cultural, economic, and political factors act as triggers to this violent extremism. For example, in Nigeria, sharia law is used in some northern parts of the state and Muslim women are condemned to death by stoning for adultery. The growth in extremism isn't limited to one religion, despite the extreme actions of ISIS, the shortened version of Islamic State of Iraq and the Levant, sometimes called the Islamic State of Iraq and Syria, also abbreviated to Islamic State (IS) or its Arabic name *Daesh*, or to terrorist groups like Boko Haram and Al Qaida, who commit acts done in the name of Islam. In the Middle East, there are acts of violence against Palestinians committed in defence of Judaism in orthodox Jewish settler communities, or elsewhere in the West by Christian militia defending white supremacy, as cases in Norway and the US show. In Uganda, there are attacks on gay people. In Asia, violations are committed in the name of Hinduism or Buddhism. Buddhist extremists have targeted Islamic and Christian places of worship, with Buddhist fundamentalist nationalist groups on the rise in Myanmar and Sri Lanka (AWID 2016: 10). An understanding of these religious trends is necessary to counter the violence, and to comprehend the enormity of women-of-faith peacebuilder's resistance to it.

Religion and Gender

Patriarchy and Religion

Some feminists assert that all religions are inherently patriarchal if men hold power in all positions of authority, leaving "little space in feminist discourses for women who find meaning and agency within their religion" (Brown 2015: 301). However, feminists resist being boxed in, *pushing boundaries to find the spaces* where we can express ourselves. But men have written religious texts. Typically, within all the major religious traditions, those who interpret scriptures are men who hold positions of authority, many who use religious texts to rationalize women's subordination and sanctify men's domination.

When rationalization occurs, patriarchy is advanced as a religious principle, the idea that women should be in submission to male leadership and not to submit is a sin, a grave misdemeanor, and a rejection of faith. Wherever there is divinely sanctioned male dominance, there are oppressive restraints on women's leadership, and an emphasis on motherhood and domesticity as women's prime fulfilment, as well as the notion that female bodies are impure, but seductive. I contend, with others, that the patriarchal subordination of women "is a form of structural violence. It creates a trajectory of violent conflict from interpersonal relations through to communal, state, and international relations" (McGrory 2008: 20). Each of the major world religions "have consistently legitimated patriarchal culture and male domination" (Kurtz 2012: 267).

Patriarchy is embedded with fundamentalisms. Sacred texts are invoked to control women, "as God's will" with "a divinely commanded male leadership both inside and outside the home" (Mwaura 2012: 268). Patriarchal fundamentalist forms of religion hold women back from realizing their full leadership potential and capacity for self-fulfillment, although leadership sometimes is encouraged in women-only gatherings. This is the context in which women-of-faith peacebuilders operate, in continually struggling against religiously sanctioned cultural constraints.

Religious, Cultural Constraints on Women

Many violent practices used against women are cultural norms that are defended by use of certain interpretations of old scriptural texts. Challenges to these interpretations don't come easily. In keeping international protocols such as the 1979 Convention on the Elimination of all Forms of Discrimination Against Women (CEDAW) in mind, where state parties agree to modify customary practices that discriminate against women, there are many reservations to the convention that limit women's rights.

Martha Nussbaum (1999) explains some of the background to such reservations when she suggests that there are eleven problem areas for women's human rights in which religious discourse is a major influence.

- here religious discourse denigrates the value of women's life, and deprives women of basic sustenance, women suffer life and health issues of hunger, malnutrition, and unequal access to health care.
- Second, many religious norms don't speak out when women's right to bodily integrity is destroyed through "rape, marital rape, other sexual abuse, domestic violence, and genital mutilation" (Nussbaum 1999: 90).
- Third, women's right to seek employment outside the home is frequently denied by notions of divine orders.
- Fourth, when religious leaders confine women to the home, they deprive women of mobility and assembly rights.
- Fifth, the rights of political participation and speech are often denied women when religious doctrines state that they are unsuited for public roles.

- Sixth, the right of free religious exercise rarely exists for individuals who are born into strict religious systems.
- Seventh, religious law frequently does not permit women to own property or exercise full civil capacity.
- Eighth, some nations that rely on Islamic law "require all women to obtain a guardian's permission before moving abroad" (1999: 98), depriving women of independent travel.
- Ninth, religious laws play a major role in family law that limit women's degree of choice within Islamic, Hindu, Jewish, and Christian systems.
- Tenth, religious discourse restricts women's education rights, prioritizing the literacy and numeracy skills for boy children.
- Eleventh, religion plays a dominating role in stating norms on reproductive rights, contraceptive issues, and abortion.

We can conclude that religious laws have a major impact on women's human rights. Consequently, in places where these laws prevail, the idea of women participating in political decision-making on peace and security is foreign.

Cultural images and negative stereotypes about women infuse religious traditions, informing wider cultural practices. Many of these images influence strong "social norms regarding motherhood, chastity, and marriage" (Brown 2015: 300). Alison Boden (2013), in examining the function of gendered norms, writes, "to my mind, the world's religious and spiritual traditions are the biggest challenge to the idea of human rights, especially for women, because what is fair in the religions is not always what is equal" (2013: 1). Religions justify what they see to be natural divisions between men and women, which Boden explains means that they are "treated differently in order to honour their divinely mandated differences" (2013: 2). For example, reservations from Middle East and North Africa (MENA) states to CEDAW are rooted in religious and cultural norms. Boden breaks the rationale for reservations down. "Women and men are different, people from different castes are different, people from different religious communities are different, people of different races are different, people with different sexual orientation are different, and rights laws must accommodate these differences" (2013: 2).

This reasoning behind reservations to the full acceptance of CEDAW insists that freedom of religion must take priority over other rights norms. Consequently, despite the Arab Spring's hope for liberation, for most women living in MENA, the problem isn't that people have strong religious beliefs, but that religious laws are selectively interpreted in ways that usually deny the rights of women. Hania Sholkamy explains how religiosity in the Arab world shapes "bodies, dress, moral codes, and political choices" (2010: 255), where cultural and religious codes "have privileged the norms of patriarchy over those of human justice and equity" (2010: 255). Islamic feminists are trying to remove Western underpinnings around gender, fostering a nuanced understanding of power dynamics that can lead to empowerment for Arab women.

Women make many attempts to counter the dominance of religio-cultural constraints. Dubravka Žarkov, in criticizing the secular approach of mainstream Western feminism to marginalize women whose faith is important, suggests that when religion is "seen as a symbol of traditionalism and backwardness, an obstacle to emancipation," its inspirational motivation in the struggle for justice and women's rights is lost (2015: 5). Similarly, Jasmin Zine, who identifies as "a Muslim feminist and anti-racist scholar-activist," (2006: 1) maintains that while secular feminists have built transnational alliances to global anti-racist movements, they "remain ideologically at odds with faith-centred Muslim women who root their resistance within the space of religious reform" (2006: 2). The hijab represents one example often viewed by secular feminists as an instance of patriarchal oppression. Zine argues that notable Muslim feminists, such as Leila Ahmed, Asma Barlas, Amina Wadud, and Azzizah Al Hibri, while not seeing the hijab as a religious requirement, defend the civil liberty to wear it "as an assertion of women's agency over the representation of their bodies" (2006: 10). Zine's "struggles for faith-based feminism" are located within "new understandings of gender justice in Islam" (2006: 15). She proposes a "critical faith-centred" framework that understands the intersecting sites of oppression of class, colonialism, ethnicity, gender, race, sexuality, and the ways that religion has been complicit in perpetuating these oppressions.

This framework offers spaces to resist injustices and acknowledges that critically contesting received views takes courage. Examples of *faith-centred resistance to patriarchal restrictions* are outlined in the next chapter. Now, I am setting the foundations of the argument that this deliberate resistance to patriarchal, cultural norms is imperative as the basis for political engagement, and in countering the surge of violent fundamentalist extremism.

Countering Effects of Violent Extremism on Women

The Association for Women's Rights in Development (AWID) conducted a study of 1400 respondents, where more than 76 percent of women's rights activists surveyed confirmed the growing strength of religious fundamentalisms, and in the experience of 80 percent of these activists, religious fundamentalisms have a negative impact on women's rights (Balchin 2011: x). The survey respondents were from sub-Saharan Africa, East Asia, the Pacific, Latin America and the Caribbean, MENA, Western Europe, North America, Australia, and New Zealand. The characteristics these activists identify as being common to all religious fundamentalisms in every region, include "they are absolutist and intolerant; anti-women, patriarchal and anti-human rights; about politics and power; literalist and outmoded; and violent" (Balchin 2011: x). Reasons for the rise in religious fundamentalisms differ regionally.

For example, women's rights activists from sub-Saharan Africa note that economic factors such as poverty and inequality are significant. Sometimes joining fundamentalist movements is a survival strategy that promises material benefits of food and shelter. In Pakistan, inequalities give rise to a sense of injustice that seeks outlets. As Farida Shaheed notes, "some of what religious fundamentalists say resonates with people's feelings of injustice" (in Balchin 2011: 3). Additionally, women's rights activists in MENA, sub-Saharan Africa, and Southeast Asia frequently mention the failure of state institutions and services as a common factor for the presence of local religious fundamentalist groups, in that they fulfil some essential services, and thus are welcomed by the community. Where there is diminishing involvement of the states in community education, a vacuum is filled in places such as Pakistan with well-funded private religious madrasas, or in sub-Saharan Africa where states don't have the capacity to cope with HIV/AIDS pandemics, and well-resourced fundamentalist groups fill the gap in required services. As Pragna Patel notes, privatization that accompanies neoliberal global capitalism "is giving religion a space because the state then wants to offload its functions onto religious institutions" (in Balchin 2011: 4).

Other political factors give rise to religious fundamentalisms. Shaheed states that fundamentalist projects thrive where there is a denial of democracy, human rights, the right to participate in decision-making, and to decide about matters relating to personal choices (in Balchin 2011: 5). Women's rights activists in Central and Eastern Europe, Central Asia, and MENA note the impact of authoritarianism and the lack of civil liberties as major factors in the rise of fundamentalist movements that crush progressive political alternatives. Azza Soliman from Egypt suggests that even if states are battling religious groups, they may encourage fundamentalisms as a distraction from the corruption of the state (in Balchin 2011: 6).

AWID's survey found that globally, women's rights activists see discussions around the family, gender roles, and morality as tools "used by religious fundamentalists to secure and increase their power" (Balchin 2011: 16). AWID found that women's rights activists are actively resisting and challenging religious fundamentalisms in local struggles for human rights, pluralism, and democracy. As Zainah Anwar from Malaysia explains, "women's groups are in the forefront because it is women's lives that are at stake" (in Balchin 2011: 59). The point is not that men's lives aren't at stake, but rather that women's groups are addressing the way that violence affects their lives.

Many activists find that the most effective strategies lie in promoting and protecting pluralism and diversity, because they target the heart of fundamentalist intolerance and absolutism. In 2006, in a highly polarized context, Yanar Mohammed recounts an example from the Organization of Women's Freedom in Iraq. The organization brought together Sunni and Shiite poets, and in this freedom, created a novel space for improvised popular poetry to flow back and forth from one team to the other, creating an atmosphere "where there were no differences: men, women, Sunni, Shiite, age, nothing was a barrier anymore between people" (Mohammed in Balchin 2011: 67). I claim that respect for diversity, a principle to be developed further in Chapter five, stands as a solid foundation for building strong feminist solidarity within social categories of age, class, ethnicity, and religious belief. This respect is an essential aspect of peacebuilding.

In 2015, the United Nations adopted the Sustainable Development Goals (SDGs), including goal five, to: "Achieve gender equality and empower all women and girls." A significant impediment to achieving this goal lies in the growing strength of religious fundamentalisms to rollback women's rights, degrade human rights standards, and entrench discrimination. As noted, a hallmark of fundamentalist ideology that crosses religious boundaries lies in the control of women's bodily autonomy, limiting sexual rights, reproductive rights, and full expressions of equality. Women are taught what is correct, disciplined, behaviour to prevent sin. Hence to counter the effects of fundamentalist extremism on women, Shawna Wakefield, working for Oxfam International, agreed that: "We need to think more about which religious leaders to work with, when, why, and how" (in AWID 2016: 8).

Ozonnia Ojielo, working on issues of governance and peacebuilding for United Nations Development Program, Centre for Africa, urges examination of the conditions and processes which strengthen "othering," and pressure people to comply (in AWID 2016: 8). Ramona

Vijeyarasa, ActionAid International, explains the challenge of knowing "how to work with religious authorities in local communities, often elders, and traditional male leaders," but also critically reflects on whether in working through the existing structures, "local patriarchies" are reinforced (in AWID 2016: 8). The AWID report offers six main recommendations, namely, "addressing the structural conditions which facilitate religious fundamentalisms; acting on the warning signs of fundamentalism; promoting pluralism and diversity; avoiding homogenous notions of identity; working with partners; and supporting those already resisting fundamentalisms" (in AWID 2016: 9).

Resisting fundamentalism is necessary given its close association with terrorism. But Fionnuala Ní Aoláin (2016) suggests that despite women's roles in preventing radicalization, there is little evidence that these roles "extend to making any supra-national decision-making processes on countering extremism more gender-representative" (2016: 286). Azza Karam, who says "I could not be all that I am without my faith" (in Bordeau et al. 2008: 55), is critical of over-simplifications, and explains how caricatures often go: "religious fundamentalism is anti-democratic and anti-women → religious fundamentalists are enemies of democracy and women's rights → anyone arguing about/for religion is against democracy and women's rights. So, the solution is to not engage with religion at all" (in Bordeau et al. 2008: 53). This book shows why engagement is crucial.

While some women identify with fundamentalisms, join extremist movements, choose to become a suicide bomber, or defend their sons, male relatives, or spouse in extremist activities, other women are *actively resisting* the repressive dogma of their faith, in working to counter extremist violence. Radhika Coomaraswamy was Special Representative of the Secretary-General on Children and Armed Conflict and a former Special Rapporteur on Violence Against Women. The *Global Study* report under Coomaraswamy's guidance is a high-level global study on the good practices, implementation gaps, and priorities for action with UNSCR 1325. In line with Ní Aoláin's point above, the report argues that "increasing recognition of women's participation and empowerment should not be part of counter-terrorism strategies, but a part of the civilian peace agenda" (Coomaraswamy 2015: 227). There is a suggestion in the report that because mothers are in a distinctive position to recognize early signs of violent behaviour, their role can be utilized in preventing violent extremism, and deradicalizing children. In many danger zones, older women are the only ones who are trusted. In Syrian situations where international and national humanitarian workers are banned, older women "do the negotiating for the humanitarian needs of the community" (Coomaraswamy 2015: 226). Initiatives have been established in India, Ireland, Nigeria, Pakistan, and Yemen to provide spaces to mobilize mothers to discuss common concerns regarding violent extremism.

I think that attempts to counter any limiting stereotypical view of women as carers alone need to include an *empowerment* component for women to enable them to access education, income-generating skills, or decision-making around detection of early warning signs of violence. My case defending the roles of mothers in peacebuilding and qualifying the necessity for conversations on mothering to be linked with gender equality, are explored further in Chapters four and five.

After consultations in Africa and Asia, the study led by Coomaraswamy found that to counter violent extremism, rather than a top-down nation-building approach that supplements a military process, such as occurred in Iraq and Afghanistan, a distinct civilian process is necessary in "respecting the autonomy of local women peacebuilders and civil society organizations" (2015: 230). For example, possibilities include training women religious leaders to preach tolerance and to work as mentors, or women police officers engaging with local communities to prevent extremism. From 2005, Morocco certified women preachers (imams) "charged with promoting religious moderation and tolerance with the objective of curbing violent extremism" (2015: 230). These women work in mosques, communities, and prisons, talking with women and youth. In the consultations that led to this *Global Study*, one conclusion is:

Although research shows that societies that respect women's rights are less prone to extremism, women felt strongly that women's rights should not be securitized and should not be seen as an instrumental tool for countering extremism. Rather, women's rights are an end in and of themselves. (Coomaraswamy 2015: 222)

Local women-of-faith peacebuilders are well situated to communicate this message.

Religion and Peace

So far, this chapter has concentrated on the potential negative impact of religion in contributing to conflict, extremist violence, and the suppression of women's rights. But religion is also deeply connected with peace. The Global Peace Index, a measurement of peace indicators conducted by the Institute for Economics and Peace (IEP 2015) shows a steady deterioration of global peace. Their findings maintain that a significant reason for this global decline is related to "increased terrorist activity, which has been driven by high profile Islamic terrorist organizations such as the Islamic State, Boko-Haram, and Al Qaeda" (IEP 2015: 1). However, the institute suggests that a focus solely on these extremes doesn't provide a clear view of the role that religion plays in peace and conflict. In surveying the state of thirty-five armed conflicts during 2013-2015, "religious elements did not play a role" in 40 percent (2015: 2), and 86 percent "had more than one cause" (2015: 6). The conflicts that involved religion in 2015 include Afghanistan, Algeria, Central Africa, Central African Republic, Iraq, Israel-Palestine, Mali, Nigeria, Pakistan (two), Philippines, Russia (four), Syria, Thailand, Turkey, and Yemen (two). Regardless of religious tensions, factors such as lower state corruption, a well-functioning government, gender and economic equality, and good relations with neighbours, contribute to stability.

Religious freedom and the absence of social hostilities towards religion are related to "tolerance between different ethnic, linguistic, religious, and social economic groups within a country. A commitment to basic human rights and freedom are key characteristics of peaceful countries" (IEP 2015: 17). Peace is facilitated through inter-faith dialogue for trust-building, tolerance toward other views, and conflict transformation, "the replacement of violent with nonviolent means of settling disputes" (Little and Appleby 2004: 5). Despite the precariousness of violent conflicts, faith-based actors commit themselves to seeking the change that is necessary to build peace. All religions espouse a vision of peace.

Religious Visions of Peace

The major religions all have forms of nonviolence and peace as part of their religious traditions. All religions associate peace with equity and justice. Ursula King (2011: np) highlights these visions in the major world religions. Hindu prayers include "the invocation '*om, shanti, shanti, shanti,*' the thrice-repeated prayer for peace which invokes tranquillity, quiet, calmness of mind" (King 2011). The Buddhist tradition teaches a meditation on loving-kindness (*metta*) which starts with being kind to one's self, "followed by developing loving-kindness first towards a friend," then towards a person one is indifferent to, someone one feels an antipathy against, and ultimately, to include all persons (King 2011). For the ancient Hebrews, peace was a social concept that applied to harmonious relationships within the family, society, and between nations. The greeting *shalom,* "stands for truth, justice, and peace" (King 2011). The Arabic greeting *salaam* says, "peace be with you" – it is a salutation and blessing among Muslims, and connotes "contentment, good health, prosperity, security, and fullness of life" (King 2011).

Contrary to Western rhetoric which often associates Islam with extremist violence, most Muslims understand Islam as a religion of peace. Christians, despite their episodes of violent history, have a strong tradition of peace grounded in the Sermon on the Mount, with the message: "Blessed are the peacemakers" (New King James Version, Matthew 5: 9). Jesus' parting message to his disciple John, was "Peace I leave with you, my peace I give to you" (New King James Version, John 14: 27). Christian pacifists are inspired by Jesus' bias toward peace. The Christian liturgy repeats the phrase: "The peace of the Lord be always with you," to which the congregation replies, "and also with you." This ideal of peace is shared by all religions, at least in principle if not in practice.

Just Peace

"'Peace with justice' has become a trademark of many faith-based initiatives fearful that mere pacification would result if justice were not seen as a prerequisite" (Steele 2008: 5). David Steele (2008) supplies cases of faith-based just peace activism, including: at the pre-violence stage in the civil rights movement in the US, protests against apartheid in South Africa, economic development in Mozambique as preparation for mediation of an end to civil war; during violent conflict with famine relief in Nigeria, contesting illegal land seizures in Guatemala, developing early warning systems in Kenya; and post-violence efforts. A broad understanding of peace akin to "positive peace" that addresses root causes of violence (Galtung 1964) overlaps with the drive toward justice.

There are multiple ways to create stable, just, and peaceful societies. I suggest that considering all measures to do so is more likely to include the activities that women are engaged in. This broad understanding means that women are working for peace in providing essential social services, assisting the needy, healing individuals in local communities, promoting economic justice, caring for orphans and widows, working to stop domestic violence, and building women's rights. Joyce

Dubensky, Director of the Tanenbaum Centre for Interreligious Understanding, explains that broad understandings of peace help us to see that "women, are doing something everywhere, in the very small villages and towns, border crossings, in so many places" (in Marshall and Haywood 2011: 6).

One version of just peace is *restorative justice*, rooted in older traditions of community justice. Restorative justice is "inspired by the Sermon on the Mount, and by earlier biblical concepts like jubilee (a year of freedom, restoration, and forgiveness) and *shalom* (from Hebrew) or *salaam* (from Arabic), meaning 'peace with justice'" (Grey 2010: 88). In seeking breakthroughs in inter-group conflict, restorative justice is concerned with avoiding vengeance to seek right relationships between the remorseful perpetrator of abuse, the victim, and the community. Ideas of accountability, punishment, forgiveness, remembering, and truth-telling, are part of realizing just peace. Just peace is a normative orientation that informs peacebuilding as a "multidisciplinary, multiperspectival, and multi-dimensional engagement" between local and external actors (Omer 2015: 678).

Just peace is never straightforward. As an ideal to drive the processes of peacebuilding, it "is not secured simply by silencing the guns" (Evans 2012: 197). Transition from violence to sustainable peace must address root causes of conflict, including redressing war's injustices. Yet, tensions between the moral demands of justice and the political requirements of peace are always enormous, as examples like South Africa and Northern Ireland show. "All concepts of doing justice share the basic notion of putting right what is wrong" (Biggar 2003a: 12) to promote healthy well-being. Nigel Biggar argues further, "the ultimate goal of justice is also to make peace – by repairing damage, protecting victims, and reforming criminals" (2003a: 17). The arguments developed in this book demonstrate how realizing the goal of *just peace* drives women-of-faith peacebuilders' work.

Practices of Faith-based Peacebuilding

The field of religious peacebuilding with practices that target religious ideas, actors, and institutions has strengthened following the events in the USA of 11 September 2001. This emerging scholarly field argues that the religious dynamics of conflict must be understood and grappled with, and that the religious sectors within civil society "should be engaged effectively in comprehensive and strategic peace programming" (Hayward 2015: 307). Those involved in faith-based peacebuilding include lay and religious leaders working in religious institutions, faith-affiliated or faith-inspired service delivery organizations, international faith-based organizations with local offices, grassroots collectivities, and individuals. The actors are tightly interlinked within the communities, "inspired by the spiritual and religious traditions, principles, and values to undertake peace work" (Bercovitch and Kadayifci-Orellana 2009: 185).

Steele outlines four best practices that reoccur through faith-based peacebuilding. First, story-telling is a critical tool. "It can create empathetic bonds between people, clarify misunderstandings, help people explore their difficult experiences... and build the kind of relationships that can lead to joint implementation of any of the peacebuilding roles" (Steele 2008: 34). The place of story-telling in women-of-faith's work is explained in Chapter three. Second, joint activities bring people together in protests, statements of apology, advocacy for victims, worship services, or relief and development projects. Third, rituals form part of all faith-based groups and can assist trauma healing, whether through mourning, burial, praying, or singing. Fourth, "making peacebuilding part of a larger social endeavour" (2008: 35) helps to involve schools, media, and government. These practices recognize that religious values are part of the cultural substance of humanity. Faith-based peacebuilders are deeply rooted in the ordinary daily lives of people and can bring "credibility" to their engagement in peacebuilding (Powers 2010: 327).

We should never be uncritical of faith-based work because some is dangerous, attempting to change people's beliefs without sensitivity to cultural differences. But this is not my prime focus. I am examining the faith-based peacebuilding that differs from secular peacebuilding primarily in motivation only, where *building peace in local communities* is foremost, not religious conversion. I am looking at *faith-based actors who are inspired by values such as accountability, compassion, forgiveness, justice, love, mercy, patience, and truth*, seen in religious terms. However, practically, much of their work overlaps with secular peacebuilders: "on changing behaviours, attitudes and negative stereotypes;" educating all parties; healing trauma injuries; disseminating ideas on democracy and human rights; recruiting committed people to engage in peace work; "challenging traditional structures that perpetuate structural violence; mediating between conflicting parties;" reaching out to governments to incorporate peacebuilding into their policies; and encouraging the reintegration of former soldiers whilst also developing a sustained inter-faith dialogue (Bercovitch and Kadayifci-Orellana 2009: 176-177). Research carried out by Tsjeard Bouta, S. Ayse Kadayifci-Orellana, and Mohammed Abu-Nimer (2005) of twenty-seven Christian and forty-five Muslim organizations that are accredited to the UN Economic and Social Council sought to find out how religious peacebuilding differs from secular peacebuilding. While obvious weaknesses of religious peacebuilding include the risk of proselytization, they found that specific "strengths include strong faith-based motivation, long-term commitment, long-term presence on the ground, moral and spiritual authority, and a niche to mobilize others for peace" (Bouta et al. 2005: ix).

As mentioned, in analyzing women's role in faith-based peacebuilding, "the scholarship at the intersection of women, religion, and peacebuilding remains thin" (Hayward 2015: 308). Yet practically, women are actively involved in implementing projects at informal, grassroots levels. "Faith-based peacebuilding initiatives have implications for the implementation of UNSCR 1325" and other resolutions (Gueskens et al. 2010: 5). Indeed, UN Women "deems it essential to continue to foster partnerships with community and traditional leaders" (Karam 2014: 33). Further, I am maintaining that these partnerships must include women-of-faith. Evidence suggests that involvement of faith-based organizations is higher in contexts where there are active conflicts and humanitarian emergencies like in DRC, Sierra Leone, and Syria, where "almost 75 percent of basic care can end up being provided by faith-based organizations" (Karam 2014: x).

One of the chief recommendations of Coomaraswamy's report is that: "localization of peacebuilding programs must involve the participation of women at every level" (2015: 394). To make *localization* a major policy directive of international actors requires deep respect for the specificities of the provincial context. Where religion is an intrinsic part of cultural norms, I allege that drawing on faith-based leaders who are open to dialogue with all parties, is crucial in peacebuilding, because these leaders have a deep understanding of the local context and can access other levels of community and national power. Yet, reconciling the "universality" of UNSCR 1325 with the "particularity" of different conflict situations (Pratt and Richter-Devroe 2011: 491) can only occur through a bottom-up approach to building peace (Boutros Ghali 1992).

These ideas traverse new territory. Nicola Slee suggests that in studying the overlooked site of the faith lives of women and girls, "we are cartographers of neglected landscapes, charting maps that have not been made, until now" (2013: 17). Religion's influence on global politics is enormous. Religious traditions can promote chaotic violence or co-operative community. The practices of women-of-faith peacebuilders are a major factor in building just, peaceful communities.

***

This chapter explores the way that religion has a major impact on global politics and in individual lives. Initially, I outline historical reasons why religion is associated negatively with violent conflict, particularly where ethnicity and nationalism are closely tied to religious differences amongst neighbours. I then explain some of the features of religious fundamentalisms, Pentecostalism, and violent extremism, because their impact on women's lives often contributes to insecurity. Next, I show how patriarchal interpretations of certain religious beliefs cement cultural constraints on women's rights and bodily autonomy, foreshadowing examples to follow of how many women challenge these interpretations and defy these constraints. All religions have visions of just peace. Thus, it is reasonable to argue that faith-based peacebuilding can play a positive role in countering the negative tendencies of repressive religion. This positivity is likely to occur when there is an openness to dialogue with all parties to the conflict, and when peacebuilders work closely with local traditions to foster the constructive changes that lead to gender equality.

The central argument of this book is that for the women, peace, and security agenda of the UNSCR 1325 and its sister resolutions to be effectively implemented, the resources of local women-of-faith who are working to build gender equality and just peace should be more fully utilized. The next chapter explores the way that women-of-faith value ordinary experiences and the diversity of life narratives in demonstrating their transformative agency.

3

Women-of-faith as Transformative Agents

Women-of-faith peacebuilders are transformative agents of change. What does this mean? It means that they change the lives of individuals in communities. How? Through their daily way of life, they view *relationships* as integral to self-identities and to building secure communities, so these women prioritize working with all the complexities of people's relationships, emotions, feelings of safety, and connections to others, as the *primary foundations to their peacebuilding*. This relational basis to their work empowers individuals who go on to empower others. This understanding of the *primacy of relationships* stands as the theoretical underpinning to the ideas developed throughout the book. In this chapter, I make three main points.

First, I show how women-of-faith peacebuilders adopt a narrative understanding of themselves as living lives that are deeply intertwined with intricate networks of relationships. These women value differing life narratives that are shared in everyday stories and reveal deep meanings about individuals who live in culturally specific, complex, intersecting connections with others.

Given the importance of everyday ordinary experiences in women-of-faith peacebuilders' work, my second objective is to explore how faith is a chief motivator for the political activism needed to fight for just peace. I illustrate how for some women, their self-defined faith sits comfortably with feminism, while others resist Western ideas of gender equality.

My third point is that feminist women-of-faith peacebuilders are likely to understand the political tools that are needed for transformative activism, since they are motivated by their faith when fighting gendered injustices. Following on from this claim, I show why liberation theology is important to certain feminist peacebuilders. Their radical belief motives the fight to overcome the oppression that is experienced simply for being born a woman, and thus is liberatory.

The overall argument in this chapter is that a strong emphasis on *relationality* is a distinctive feature of women-of-faith peacebuilders' daily life philosophy and everyday practices as transformative agents of change. These women informally do much of the work required by the women, peace, and security (WPS) agenda.

Narrative Understanding of Agency

Women express agency differently. Sometimes women are victims of harms and feel powerless, deprived of agency, some women harm others in evil acts, or other times, women work as social agents to improve the life of others. UNSCR 1325 shifts the focus from women as always being victims of violent conflict, to women as capable actors in conflict transformation and peacebuilding. This shift does not minimize the tragedy of suffering in war, which is immense. However, as Felicity Hill points out, perpetually problematizing women, and always stressing their "absence" or "victimhood," fails to recognize "the problematic role of masculine identities in security discourse and actual wars" (in Cohn,

Kinsella, and Gibbings 2004: 137). It also understates the potential for women to be agents of change.

To understand the agency of women-of-faith peacebuilders, I now show how these women adopt a narrative understanding of the self which is profoundly *connected to others*. The connections are made in everyday life which increases the likelihood of being able to make a meaningful difference in people's material and spiritual lives.

Narrative Understanding of the Self-in-relation

There are two parts to my reasoning that a narrative understanding of the self-in-relation provides a distinctive basis to moral identity and to engagement in local experience: first, agency and choice define moral beings; and second, narrative agency requires others for human flourishing. Being able to express agency requires the opportunities to make self-chosen, deliberate choices and be responsible for their consequences. Agency is "always socially situated (relational), structurally embedded, and historically shaped" (Hudson 2016a: 202). War disrupts any sense of normality of being able to convey agency fully.

For example, Judy El-Bushra writes about women in Northern Uganda, Somalia and Somaliland, and Rwanda, who despite not having formal power, still demonstrate great resilience of their capabilities, and she describes their agency as "the strategies used by individuals to create a viable and satisfying life for themselves" in their very difficult contexts (2000: 67). This strength and expression of agency is never straight-forward. Agents must adapt to contexts, and in war and post-war, the adaptations are constant and harrowing.

Martha Nussbaum's "capabilities approach" helps us to see the difficulties with resilience in addressing questions like: "What are people able to do and to be? What real opportunities are available to them?" (2011: x). Nussbaum's ten central capabilities are life; bodily health; bodily integrity; sense, imagination, and thought; emotions; practical reason; affiliation; other species; play; and control over one's environment (2011: 33-34). War disrupts opportunities to enjoy these human capabilities. Victims of gross abuses and injustices do not cease to be moral agents. "The course of action that victims take to become survivors is a crucial part of their post-war narrative" (Porter 2015: 49). Women-of-faith peacebuilders assist communities of traumatized people in their journey to cope with deep pain and ongoing suffering, make courageous choices, or overcome the debilitating sense of loss that arises when there are terrible damages to lives, dignity, properties, and livelihoods.

My research convincingly shows that *women-of-faith peacebuilders adopt a narrative understanding of agency.* This is an appreciation that one's entire life story affects self-identity and how we relate to others. Obviously, we can withhold parts of our story and internalize them, or suppress painful parts, but in the background, they all influence our sense of self, to varying degrees. Narrative agency thus is "the capacity to develop a story about self in which one is the agent" (Cobb 2013: 159).

This capacity permits us to create a self-identity with which we can live. Narrative agency is enacted in everyday, ordinary, daily experiences of life. The analytic interest in this chapter lies in discerning what supports the processes and practices of women-of-faith peacebuilders as agents of change; is it faith, feminism, pragmatism, or a combination of factors that are needed to respond compassionately to victims' suffering? In exploring this agency, I explain the distinctive contribution women-of-faith make in building peace.

There are two important aspects to understanding narrative agency: a narrative understanding of the self, and the importance of the emotions. First, a narrative understanding of the self is grounded in a notion of being as "socially understood *individuals-in-relation*" (Gould 2004: 4). This view of moral agents accepts that the self exists in relation to others and develops through multiple enriching relationships. Certainly, within daily interactions with others, there are harmful relationships of power, exploitation, and abuse. These influence us in negative ways.

My point nevertheless is that human flourishing requires constructive relationships that encourage others, and where there is scope for mutual affirmation. For peacebuilders, the focus is a commitment to "doing security as though humans matter," something that can only be done when human security is "a critical project aimed at interrogating the sources of people's insecurity" (Hudson 2005: 164). This activity requires understanding the personal feelings of insecurity that arise through diverse experiences of injustices, human rights abuses, fear of violent attacks, drones, bombs, and the long-term effects of war.

Second, comprehending felt insecurities requires *sensitivity to the emotions*. Whereas traditional political science and international relations theory sees the emotions to distract from requisite objective responses, and thus to be of limited value in political analysis and practice, women's typical valuing of emotional attachment is a position that "analyzes emotions as containing cognition and then evaluates them positively, as having at least some value in the ethical life" (Nussbaum 1999: 73). Joy Meeker offers three reasons why the emotions are significant to a conflict practitioner who is aiming toward transformation: "emotions accompany conflict;" they "are crucial to social-justice efforts" in that they reveal what we care about and why; and "how we interpret the meaning of emotions impacts how we respond to conflict" (2016: 114). Often, this interpretation is absent in analyzing peacebuilding in transitional justice processes. Those suffering great insecurities experience feelings of anger, bewilderment, desperation, embodied pain, frustration, fear, helplessness, and shame.

I believe that adopting a narrative understanding of the self-in-relations allows greater sensitivity to the emotions and the reasons they arise. Sensitivity is needed because, as María Pilar Aquino maintains, experiences of people are "shaped by the suffering and the anxieties that come from poverty, social violence, fatal infirmities, and increasing human insecurity" (2007: 10). The struggle for human rights and gender justice emerges from the *lived experiences* of gendered discrimination, inequality, violence, and multiple forms of oppression.

Women's regular involvement in the local, community levels, lend itself to concentrating on life's ordinary concrete practices.

Everyday, Local Experiences

Research on transitional justice gives locally owned processes increased attention, to avoid elite-driven structures or abstract notions of justice (Mac Ginty and Richmond 2013; Richmond 2009). This local turn opens a space to rethink how agency takes place from below, in the margins, and grassroots. I make the case that for women-of-faith, as well as for most feminists, ordinary experiences of local people form the physical and psychological spaces for their work, influencing their perceptions of peace.

For example, Vjosa Dubruna, a Kosovar human rights activist says, "My understanding of peace is really based on my experience of it. Peace isn't just the absence of war, but a stable life. Freedom. And something that comes with freedom: true respect for diversity" (in Anderlini 2007: 75). Through experiences, knowledge is constructed, influenced by power relations, and cultural and religious beliefs, and emerges within relational, embodied understandings of persons. Ana Maria Tepedino from Brazil stresses how her feminist theology is the result of "concrete experience... The existential experience of searching for one's own identity" (1988: 165) in the context of webs of relationships. Consequently, "the theologies that arise out of such faith practices will necessarily be *works of friction*: theologies engaged in working out the implication of faith's involvement in the 'sticky materiality of practical encounters'" (Bedford 2012: 191). In war and post-war contexts, these encounters are fraught with massive tensions and constructions of otherness in the light of differences of religion, culture, ethnicity, and ideology.

In terms of the plurality of women's provincial positions, Christine Sylvester convincingly suggests that we need to recognize vastly different standpoints that reflect "the differing lived experiences and multiple fractured identities women have in the contemporary era, and the many political struggles to which these identities give rise" (2002: 216). The stark example she presents is that "there are western-middle-class-mother-feminist-peace activists and Zimbabwean-peasant-mothers-post-colonialist-trade-unionists-ex-guerrillas" (2002: 216). Recognition of such differences of socio-political positioning and daily life experiences leads to a feminist acceptance of dissonance, that there will usually be great disparity between individuals within groups that may contribute to tensions, but through engagement with the content and emotional impact of these tensions, these should not erupt into violent action. Rather, through dialogue and debate, an understanding of the nature of the differences can be acknowledged, partially understood, and respectfully appreciated.

Daily local experiences influence perceptions of peace and demonstrations of active agency. I now offer examples of the ways that experience and faith, are connected. During 2013, Fran Porter interviewed fifty-five Protestant and Catholic women who were aged between twenty-one and seventy-three and asked them to reflect on the 1990s peace process in Northern Ireland. In researching their Christian faith experiences, the impact of the troubles on women's lives was a prominent feature in the conversations. Porter defines faith as "a complex interweaving of life experience, personal commitment, belief and practice, and involvement with a community of believers" (2013: 97). She writes that the trauma of living in a violent and divided society renders faith open to critical questioning on, as a woman in her sixties expressed it, "where is God in the midst of all this?" (in Porter 2013: 97). A Catholic woman explained what it meant to her in feeling implicated:

> I would try and cross the divide and all that... try and break down barriers and let each other see that the horns the other person has aren't real horns at all, you know, it's just because of what we carry from our background and it's so silly carrying all this. (in Porter 2013: 98)

Porter found that for those women whose faith compelled them to become involved in countering the antagonistic negativity that abounds in a sectarian culture, "engagement with the difficulties of life in a conflicted society reveals an understanding of God as caught up in the trauma of human reality rather than detached from it" (2013: 98).

In a different context, Ela Bhatt, who founded the Self-Employed Women's Association in India, helping home-based, poor textile workers, is convinced that when coming together, women of all faiths have a great capacity for social change. She connects positive peace with commonplace actions. She too explains that peace "is about the ordinariness of life, how we understand each other, share meals, and share courtyards. And that is what women do. That very ordinariness...is what keeps communities together" (in Marshall and Hayward 2010: 6). Bhatt is motivated by broad Gandhian values of nonviolence and social justice, linking faith and peace.

The importance of *everyday, local experiences* extends to the inclusion of civil society organizations in the process of developing and implementing national action plans (NAPs) on UNSCR 1325. In doing so, the lived experiences of individuals are considered, as well as a "grounded understanding of community needs related to WPS provisions," and "recognition of forms of community knowledge in the development of the plans" (Kirby and Shepherd 2016: 384). Kirby and Shepherd (2016) outline regional action plans on WPS developed by the African Union (2009), the European Union (2008), the International Conference of the Great Lakes Region (2004), the NATO/Euro-Atlantic Partnership Council (2007), the Organization for Security and Cooperation in Europe (2004), the Pacific Region (2012), and the South African Development Community (2009).

In addition to NAPs, sometimes alternative regional action plans can offer meaningful opportunities for local women to show public leadership in peace and security governance. Localization programs as promoted by the Global Network of Women Peacebuilders, a coalition of women's groups and organizations from Africa, Asia and the Pacific, West Asia, Latin America, and Europe, advocating for effective implementation of UNSCR and the WPS agenda, decentralize the implementation of the WPS agenda to use the expertise from local authorities and traditional leaders. Localization programs in Colombia, Nepal, the Philippines, Sierra Leone, and Uganda are effective in supporting WPS principles. I contend that within civil society organizations, use can be made of local faith-based leaders in fostering these principles.

Situatedness of Lived Stories

Given a narrative understanding of the self that emerges in everyday life experiences, and the local turn in peacebuilding, contextualized narratives "are a primary way by which we make sense of the world around us, produce meanings, articulate intentions, and legitimize actions" (Wibben 2011: 2). The way we interpret these experiences change over time and in different company. But it is in the recounting of lived experiences that much of the meaning-making occurs. Theologians Stanley Hauerwas and Gregory Jones explain that of course there is an appeal with stories, but "what is significant is the recognition that rationality, methods of argument, and historical explanation have...a fundamentally narrative form" (1997: 4).

Practitioners who utilize a "narrative theology" start with the basis "that stories provide the context for understanding the meaning and purpose of our existence and therefore are, of themselves, a type of moral or theological argument" (Say 1990: 2). Part of the efficacy of stories lies in them being "a means of empowerment (for both storyteller and audience)" (Say 1990: 2). It is through stories that are told to us and to others that we individually and jointly examine our lives. Elizabeth Say maintains that: "If it is true that we are storied people, that we discover the meaning of our lives in our narratives, then for women's lives to become truly authentic they need to first create their own narrative history" in defiance of patriarchy (1990: 111). But finding one's voice is a crucial first step. This is no simple task for women whose voices are suppressed, silenced, or shamed. Say explains further that "women's narratives are... a quest to find the self to which patriarchy has denied existence" (1990: 131).

I am building a compelling case that "stories matter. They do things. They have political and material consequences. They function as windows into a particular time and place" (Wibben 2011: 106). Hence "the best way to understand how women-of-faith work for peace is through hearing their own stories" (McGrory 2008: 10). Story-telling enables people with complex backgrounds to make partial sense of their lives. Story-telling provides the space to be open about experiences, even horrific ones, but not everyone can do so, or wants to do so. *Hearing requires deep listening to the telling of stories,* with an open notion of interpretation, given that unexpected elements may crop up in story-telling. Certainly, "it is hearing individuals describe what displacement, death, and loss mean to them personally that really brings home the human cost of conflict" (Bennett et al 1995: 1).

Thus, gathering testimonies of experiences is a vital component of dealing with the past. Stories are crucial meaning-making tools in all cultures. For example, much African wisdom comes through shared memory, stories passed on to generations, producing collective, communal knowledge. Oral traditions are used to pass on myths, rites, and knowledge of ancestral practices. Indeed, "story-telling is one of the strengths of faith-based modalities of work" (Karam 2014: 39).

This first section explains a narrative understanding of the self-in-relation as an *agent of choice within networks of relationships.* It explains the importance of basing peacebuilding work in ordinary, everyday living where *story-telling is a channel to express the personal, emotional effects of war.* This provides the groundwork for the anecdotal stories told by women-of-faith peacebuilders throughout the book. Now I examine how faith and feminism combine or clash with the narrative agency exhibited by women-of-faith peacebuilders.

Faith and Feminism

Faith's Resistance to Feminism

Not all women-of-faith are feminists. Understanding why this is so, helps to grasp different motivations for peacebuilding work. Elisabeth Schüssler Fiorenza's definition of feminist work suggests that it:

> must challenge/destabilize/subvert the subordination of wo/men, rather than strengthen or reinforce it; must reflect appreciation of and respect for wo/men's experience by acknowledging wo/men's capacities and agency; must be sensitive to context – both the immediate and possibly the larger context as well; must be critical of the manner in which wo/men have both aided and resisted oppression, subjugation, and violence; must have as its consequence far-reaching changes in religion and society, as well as political and revolutionary significance. Hence, it must be practical, this-worldly, transformative, renewing, and transitional. (2014: 4)

Fiorenza maintains that the tasks associated with feminist work are *ethical-political imperatives*. Much of my analysis refers to the "work" done by women-of-faith peacebuilders, and I make frequent distinctions between the practical work done by these women, and the more politically motivated work done by *feminist* women-of-faith peacebuilders.

However, the relationship between faith and feminism is uneasy for at least four reasons: patriarchy's expectations; some young women's alienation from older women's feminist agenda; cultural danger in being labelled "feminist"; and visibility of social recognition. I elaborate on each reason.

First, women-of-faith peacebuilders often find themselves caught between deeply patriarchal religious institutions that prevent them from demonstrating leadership in key positions of authority; and a women's peacebuilding sector that typically, is shaped by Western feminism and individualized rights that challenges more communally oriented, faith-driven activities. The Western sector rarely considers religious actors to be intrinsic to achieving women's empowerment, the realization which is significant in cultures where patriarchal attitudes and behaviours are the norm. Despite these obstacles, sometimes women-of-faith leverage their position at the borders of religious traditions, increasingly challenging orthodox interpretations of scriptures, thereby confirming how their faith drives their activism to practise creative, dynamic forms of peacebuilding.

Second, particularly in Western nations or nations with a strong international influence, generations of young people grow up with the legacy of the women's movement, and its benefits of assuming the right to equality, but do not feel the need to identify as feminists. Shamillah Wilson, in a collection specifically looking at feminist voices from a new generation, stresses the diverse relationships young women have to the feminist movement. She suggests that despite young women being engaged in addressing oppressions and injustices, many "feel isolated and excluded from the feminist movement" (2005: 227). Some young women know that openly identifying as a feminist is not only problematic for those living in a context of militarization or fundamentalism, but worse, it may victimize them or threaten their activism. Young women aged between twenty-five and thirty-five attending a training institute in Bangalore in 2003, felt unsupported in their spirituality. Their reality is that they "do find themselves as part of 'organized religion' and feel that the disengagement of the feminist movement means that they are unsupported in their practice and in the challenge of dominant paradigms of religion, from within" (Wilson 2005: 231). For example, questions like: "Is it possible to be a Muslim and a feminist at the same time?" simply fuels "the fires of women who already have to defend such identities in their own communities" (2005: 231). Space must be created for young women to share their faith with secular feminists and feel comfortable identifying as young feminists of faith.

Third, in places where cultural, national, and political constraints play a key role in influencing gendered relationships, the danger of being labelled or identified as a feminist heightens. Zilka Spahić-Šiljak explains how in the former Yugoslavia, religious feminists faced a triple marginalization "by the state communist ideology, by secular feminists, and by their own faith communities" (2013: 177). When the war in the Balkans began in 1991, the socio-political climate changed, moving "quickly from socialism to ethnonationalism cloaked by ethnoreligious ideologies" (2013: 177). Diverse women's groups became involved in helping women and children survive the trauma. In 1993, the first women's NGO, Medica Zenica, an NGO which offers psycho-social and medical help to women and children who are victims of war and post-war violence was established in Bosnia and Herzegovina (BiH), and Muslim theologians were invited along with secular and atheist feminists to assist women to find refuge after imprisonment in war camps. Despite differing beliefs, the women shared the goal of building a peaceful security. Spahić-Šiljak contends that in BiH and the Balkans, feminist theology began "from the immediate and localized experiences of war, suffering, and pain. It erupted from the need to provide religious answers and comfort for the shame and guilt female survivors of sexual trauma felt" (2013: 184). I am demonstrating that in the face of massive cultural constraints, *many women-of-faith leaders adapt to contextualized experiences that prompt activism toward furthering gender justice and inclusive peace.* However, given ongoing strife, prudence, and the need for personal safety, prevail.

Fourth, and surprisingly, the marginalization within formal religious spaces that many women experience sometimes can free women from institutional constraints, allowing them to work creatively behind-the-scenes. This is positive and often path-breaking, but it does mean that women do not receive the public recognition that male religious leaders do. Women's invisibility blocks access to financial support that is needed for capacity-building and opportunities to influence policy-makers, often leaving women ostracized from involvement in formal peacebuilding projects. Yet curiously, some of these women "cite their very invisibility and marginality as useful, helping to ensure their safety, and the safety of those with whom they are working, or the effectiveness of their work" (Hayward and Marshall 2015: 15). Being on the side-lines and in the undefined borderlands, enables an identification with those who also are marginalized, and it provides flexibility to mobilize informal networks that exist outside of traditional power structures. Additionally, it means that permission from male authorities to proceed with activities is not needed. Action can occur speedily, avoiding red-tape obstacles.

Maryann Cusimano Love (2015) explains that for Catholic women peacebuilders, particularly nuns, this invisibility is often imposed, yet sometimes, it is self-chosen. While Catholic women are now more visible in public spaces, without ordination, their activities are sometimes overlooked, therefore "some women intentionally use this invisibility when they perceive that operating under the radar may make their work more effective" (Love 2015: 42). Love explains invisibility as a strategic purpose which varies by context, for example, "sometimes the word *peace* is avoided as too political, dangerous, and counter-productive" (2015: 47). For example, in the DRC, rather than branding programs as prevention of sexual and gender-based violence, or even as peacebuilding, labels that might attract the attention of armed actors, women working with the Jesuit Refugee Services International "brand the programs as education and vocational training" (2015: 46), thereby increasing the local acceptance of legitimacy.

Elsewhere, a respondent to an American study of 548 women-of-faith on this topic replied: "The intersection of feminism and faith, while it makes sense to me, scares many women and men who are devout in their spiritual practices" (The Sister Fund 2008: 23). Many women from various religious traditions deliberately slip outside of formal structures to operate with personal integrity, without always being labelled as feminist.

To summarize this section, I am not suggesting that faith is necessarily resistant to feminist beliefs and practices. However, for many women, there seems to be an uneasy relationship between their faith and received views of feminism. Patriarchal expectations within religions limit women's official leadership, but many women find creative ways to circumvent this limitation. Generations of young people who grew up with the legacy of the women's movement, take for granted that equal rights should be available, so do not always feel the need to call themselves feminist, because many feel alienated from the older generations' views. In some cultures, it is too dangerous to be called a feminist. For certain women-of-faith, there is a liberty in working behind official structures that an explicit announcement of a feminist allegiance might stultify. We can conclude that women in faith communities do the tasks required by feminist activism, sometimes realizing in retrospect that they have helped to achieve feminist goals of *equality, freedom, and justice.*

Self-identified Faith

For women-of-faith peacebuilders, the "faith" part of this identification is easy to explain. I operate with a broad-brush definition of who is a woman-of-faith, letting these women *self-define their faith.* I examine those faith actors who work to change harmful attitudes and behaviours to ones that lead to holistic, sustainable development of material, physical, psychological, and spiritual well-being.

Examples of this identification are diverse. Stephanie Dobson, responding to the limited scholarship conducted on personalized religious understandings in minority women's lives, and how faith dynamically interacts with localized contexts, interviewed twenty-six migrant Muslim women from nine different national backgrounds who were living in New Zealand from 2006 to 2009. She suggests that each woman's story demonstrates unique, "interactive, ways that faith creates new meanings and interpretive possibilities in local contexts, as well as providing emotional solace" in dealing with life stresses (Dobson 2012: 228). Dobson's conclusion is that faith constitutes a multi-layered feature in many women's narratives as "a source of ethical conduct and community-minded action, as well as a medium of resistive agency" (2012: 232).

This resistive agency has political implications in providing the means through which women can challenge unacceptable behaviour, including, but not limited to gender-based violence, and in seeing the radical potential of a feminist praxis, as I develop shortly. For example, Shireen, born to Fijian Indian and Dutch parents is active in the Islamic Women's Council of New Zealand which advocates for Muslim women. Her sense of self and faith provide support in being able to resist "othering" (2012: 234). In a different context of Judaism, Yael Israel-Cohen writes about the narratives of the women she interviewed who are working to change the status of women in Jewish synagogues, and she points "to cases in which active resistance becomes an important means to bring about change" (2012: 50).

Elsewhere, Jane McGrory writes of a workshop held in Timor-Leste in 2006 with women-of-faith from Papua, Timor-Leste, and Mindanao. In defining a woman-of-faith, she suggests that she "is someone who believes in a spiritual reality beyond the material. She is inspired and guided by her faith, which may be practised publicly or privately, individually or collectively" (2008: 6). She rightly concludes that while there is increasing literature on women in peacebuilding, there is scant reference to faith within it. In drawing on the discussions of the participants attending this regional workshop, the women reiterated that faith to them: "means justice, equality, and well-being for all... Peace requires justice in all aspects of life" (2008: 6). The message of *just peace* is retold. In drawing out some of the commonalities of experience among women-of-faith, McGrory shows that the contribution these women make "is both special and strategic to the transformation of injustice and building of peace" (2008: 8). McGrory explains that: "Challenging injustice and working for a better world are seen by many as the very essence of what it means to be a woman-of-faith" (2008:11). That is, "working for peace and justice is a way to live their faith in practice" (2008: 12), or as explained shortly, as praxis. Fredrika Korain from Papua refers to this activism as a "calling to promote social justice" (in McGrory 2008: 12). For these women, faith, everyday life, and activism are intrinsically connected to spur *just peace.*

At an International Fellowship of Reconciliation Women Peace-makers Program, organizers remark that in their experience, many women activists become involved in peacebuilding based on values that are present in religions such as "tolerance, love, and respect for human dignity," and activists "are sustained in the challenging work by their respective religious beliefs and spirituality" (Gueskens et al. 2010: 3). This book takes seriously self-identified faith as a key moti-vator in women's peacebuilding practices, maximizing usage of local knowledge, thereby increasing the chance of acceptance of change in communities.

To summarize this second section, I have shown how women-of-faith are inspired and motivated by their faith in their peacebuilding vocation. Most see the challenges of injustice and their striving for an *equal, free, just, and peaceful world,* to be a fulfilment of their agency. Some of these women identify with feminism, others do not.

Feminist Theological Praxis

Feminist Theology

Women-of-faith peacebuilders who are explicitly feminist strive for new ways of knowing and living out their faith, particularly taking an *experiential and narrative approach,* as outlined above. Nicola Slee suggests that in highlighting women's lives, "we do so because we want to hold up the holiness of ordinary women's and girls' lives, to say that their lives are sacred, worthy of painstaking study, that their lives are revelatory of God" (2013: 17), thus worthy of narration and visibility.

Feminist scholars of religion engage with contemporary complexities by interrogating received categories and definitions within diverse religious traditions, questioning the numerous twists and turns of conversations between stereotypes and revised ways of thinking (Peskowitz et al. 1995).

Feminist theology reflects on religion, faith, spirituality, and ideas about God, contextualized within the messy reality of the discrimination, subordination, and exclusion that many women suffer. At the heart of this activist endeavour "stands a shared commitment to creating a world where women (and all people) flourish" (Jones 2012: 24). Feminist theological research is based in the faith lives of women and girls, including experiences that are "deeply personal; they frequently invoke strong emotions and intimate relationships" (Berry 2013: 25). Feminist theology critically explores theological ideas that relate to religious beliefs and the nature of God, often adapting this exploration to different geographic contexts. It is explicitly committed to *changing gender inequality and injustice.*

Feminist theology is neither abstract nor esoteric. With a vision of women's flourishing central to its mission, feminist theologians reveal a powerful commitment to *practical activism.* Clearly what it means for women to blossom differs in varying geographical contexts, and to make this happen, "requires hard, pragmatically taxing, communal work" (Jones 2012: 25). Some of the conditions that are necessary for women to thrive, include "respect, safety, just compensation, access to education and healthcare, shelter, food, participation in decision-making, and the opportunity to pursue and enjoy desired forms of beauty and happiness" (Jones 2012: 28). This work to create the conditions in which this might be possible, includes lobbying, marching, fighting in the courts and in Church councils, organizing groups, building coalitions and alliances, working for social change in everyday ways, and determining how best to practice faith.

Struggles Against Injustices

For those who adopt feminist theology, faith drives them to an activism that is based on the struggle against injustices. This *activist struggle is crucial to the development of just peace.* "Faith teachings and understandings of justice and humanity provide a moral lens that help women to recognize injustice. Faith offers a frame of reference that assists women in identifying something as 'wrong'" (McGrory 2008: 10). This "spiritual activist" worldview prompts "further action and sustains the multiple ways we participate in social justice" (Lara and Facio 2014: 10). For example, Korain, a Catholic woman and human rights activist in Papua, states that: "if we take a critical perspective on what is happening around us, then we are certain to see that there is injustice, and that people's dignity is being trampled upon...this is not acceptable. To be active in our faith means that we...struggle to bring about change" (in McGrory 2008: 11). For these women, *faith spurs social activism.*

The injustices experienced are either personal and individualized, or a form of structural injustice, which exists when social processes place sizeable groups "under systematic threat of domination or deprivation of the means to develop and exercise their capacities" (Young 2011: 52). Iris Marion Young suggests that agents should think about their responsibilities in relation to structural injustice, in terms of a "social connection model of responsibility" (2011: 105). This model accepts that there is a moral obligation that derives from belonging to social networks of interdependence. This emphasis on *connection, cooperation, and responsibility* is consistent with feminist priorities to accept the shared responsibility to change institutions and processes to become more just.

Numerous examples show where this collective social action emerges for those who are sympathetic to feminist theology. Mexican theologian María Pilar Aquino maintains that given present-day realities typified by injustice, activity should be directed "to those currents of thoughts and emancipatory social movements that seek to fortify processes favouring a social justice paradigm" (2007: 13). She values feminist theologies that keep abreast of processes that promote "transformative visions and practices...of a new world of justice" and are "integrated into the frameworks of critical intercultural thought" (2007: 13).

However, American feminist theologian Carter Heyward, warns that spirituality is marketed in modern churches as a personal commodity, so public apathy to structures of injustice continue. Instead, Heyward makes a plea like Aquino, "to join in working for justice, peace, and compassion wherever we can" (2010: 16). She explains that in struggling against racism, war, sexism, and heterosexism, women "cross over – from a primarily private interest in God to a more public journey with others who are committed to particular justice goals" (2010: 16).

Typically, this is an alternative view of justice to standard liberal notions of a fair balance of interests. *It is a view of justice as restoring past harms and it is deeply imbedded in restoring damaged relationships.* Beverly Wildung Harrison writes that once injustice is acknowledged as a wrongful practice, justice "requires an ongoing commitment to finding fresh ways of 'undoing' past wrongs and initiating connections that enable life together" (2004: x). In places emerging from prolonged periods of conflict, the injuries are crippling, so dealing with the massive effects of genocide, killings, disappearances, and war-rapes, means dealing with the terrible unjust tragedies of war. But, in acknowledging that unjust acts include institutional, structural patterns of power and privilege, justice is linked also with meeting basic needs. It is also linked with *building good relationships* between individuals and groups within *decent communities* in forging *meaningful connections with others.*

Feminist theology makes this version of justice to be a central goal for developing personal and collective agency. These normative images of justice provide imaginative hints of what comprises a good society, a just polity, a transformed world, and for feminist theologians, the kingdom of God on earth. Personal accounts confirm this commitment to justice and faith. Marilyn McMorrow says: "I am called to work for 'justice, peace, and the integrity of creation.' In my religious order, we emphasize each one's call to become 'a woman of communion, compassion, and reconciliation' who 'seeks justice with the heart of an educator'" (in Marshall and Hayward 2011: 11). In other accounts where women who are anti-militarists, former fighters, or grassroots actors come together because of a commitment to social justice, but not necessarily to faith, Sanam Naraghi Anderlini explains their holistic notion of peace rooted in human security, where "peace is seen as freedom from violence; access to safe housing, employment, and education; equality in the eyes of law and society; the right to property ownership; a return to normalcy" (2007: 9). She says that the yearning for justice "is almost visceral in nature," where "the indictment of a war criminal" serves the legal demands of justice but doesn't "address the very practical and daily needs of his surviving victims. In such contexts, justice is needed, but it can and must take many forms" (Anderlini 2007: 154).

Some scholars and practitioners see religion as restricting the realization of justice. However, for the people of the Global South, "the struggle to 'live faithfully' amid the problems of world poverty, climate change, conflict, and development cannot be separated from the struggle for justice and emancipation" (Thomas 2010: 505). Nonetheless, the carnage of war and destructive violence continues, causing the devastation of communities and the suffering of humanity around the world as war and violence shatter individuals and communities. Yet under precarious circumstances, many women (and men) are motivated by faith and justice to work bravely to end the cycles of violent conflict.

One key area of injustice that women-of-faith work in, and is examined in depth in Chapter six, is that of sexual violence. I mention it here because in listening to the narratives of peoples' stories of experiences of injustices, Anna Höglund (2003: 346) argues that rape in war is a case not only of shameful indignity and violence, but of injustice. She develops a feminist ethics of justice that incorporates the importance of care in social practice. In terms of the cruelties of rape in war, Höglund maintains that a strong commitment to justice is required for women's human rights to be protected, because justice is "a relational concept," grounded in "respect for human rights and dignity" (2003: 360). Another way to express this is to say that one way to care for people is by respecting their rights, and every violation of women's integrity fails to do so. Concrete actions demonstrate being faithful to beliefs.

A reminder is warranted that gender justice, "the protection of human rights based on gender equality" (Valji 2010: 217), is influenced by a wide range of economic, cultural, social, and political needs. Thus, understanding the lived experience of women's lives is crucial if policies, strategies, and practices are to satisfy women's needs in culturally appropriate ways. Women's participation in all spheres of decision-making thus is fundamental to realizing justice. For women in the post-war period, restructuring their lives is focused on meeting everyday survival needs. What constitutes justice may take on different meanings to traditional Western notions of legal justice. For example, "given existing patterns of feminization of poverty, the aggravation of poverty when a state chooses to shift its spending from social services to military disproportionately affects women and women-headed households" (Valji 2010: 226). Injustice increases when spending is greater on military and defence budgets then on addressing gender inequality and meeting basic needs. Figures by Medie (2016) show that states "spend $1.6 trillion on arms, yet only 2 percent of their peace and security aid targets gender security."

Gender justice requires redressing all forms of gendered inequalities, and for most women, it is in providing resources for the provision of basic material survival needs of water, food, shelter, health, and education where justice prevails. Exploring this broad, practical view of justice is an important part of what this book shows – that the work of women-of-faith peacebuilders is significant in merging a faith-based activist approach to strengthening justice.

Transformative Praxis: Justice in Practice

I want to show now how feminist activism, driven by the need to counter insecurity and injustice, is a *transformative praxis*. Through active agency, women "negotiate ideas about 'whose justice' and 'justice for whom'" (Björkdahl and Mannergren Selimovic 2015: 166). *Praxis seeks radical change of structural injustices.* Praxis refers to the active engagement in strategies that lead to the fulfilment of ideals of human dignity, equality, and justice in practice. It is an active mode of being, with a deliberate strategy of action. Feminist women are dynamic participants in this faith-based conflict transformation, "even in instances when the root causes of conflict are not religious" (Oliver et al. 2004: 15). Their contextual praxis of intentional social activity speaks from local knowledge in specific situations, naming experiences, identifying suffering, and articulating possibilities for change, in response to calls for justice and compassion.

This is an *embodied praxis*. Its rationale of belief lies in its understanding of conceptual ideas of justice, and applying these to what is needed to eradicate unjust, systemic violent practices. One view of this praxis lies in drawing on the African concept of *ubuntu*, which confirms the *interconnectedness of humanity*, so that one grasps how the injustice of one person affects all their relationships. Thus, in translating "a praxis of belonging" into her conflict work, Joy Meeker seeks personal change "that is also fundamentally linked to social transformation" of networks (2016: 115). The practices of women-of-faith involved in community development work to further education, public health, and humanitarian relief, are down-to-earth examples of striving for socio-economic justice.

Some illustrations show the nature of justice in a transformative praxis. Asia Justice and Rights, an NGO based in Jakarta Indonesia, works to strengthen respect for human rights in the Asia-Pacific region. One of their projects examines the needs that women feel are required to obtain justice in post-conflict societies. Researchers for this project talked with 140 women from twelve geographical locations across Indonesia, Timor-Leste, and Myanmar. The research team included thirty-eight women and one man, all activists, researchers, or survivors. Stories tell the history of violence in Indonesia, constant fear in Papua, unsettled peace in Aceh, victims vanishing in Timor-Leste, decades of pain and loss on the island of Marabia, torture on the island of Baucau, grief in Bobonaro, and displacement of Karen women and others imprisoned for simply struggling for social justice. Mamik, a teacher in Yogyakarta was arrested, tortured as a political agitator, and sexually assaulted in an extremely humiliating fashion. Despite having her spirit broken, she said, "I couldn't do anything but beg the Lord for strength" (in Wandita 2015: 32). When asked to reflect on justice, she replied, "I cannot speak of justice because I never experienced justice in my life. All my rights were taken. How can I speak of justice?" (in Wandita 2015: 33).

Kadmiyati was imprisoned at Camp Bantul, Yogyakarta. She was too ashamed to describe what pain the women prisoners experienced, but said, "we could only pray...Oh God, why are they like that? Please forgive them" (in Wandita 2015: 34). She draws strength from her faith and for her, justice for the violence against the victims of 1965 would consist of finding out the truth of what happened, and why it occurred. On the Moluccas Islands, political prisoners of 1965 were held on Buru Island. In 1999, religious strife struck the province of Maluku, compelling Christian women to don a headscarf to protect their families. Hana Bano, a Papuan woman, was arrested, detained, and tortured by the military. The church is a source of strength for her, and as she participates in the congregation, her thoughts of "hate and revenge towards those who used me began to disappear" (in Wandita 2015: 92). Olandina da Silva Ximenes, a Timorese woman was ordered by the authorities to go to West Timor in 1999. She struggles to survive and living in West Timor she is regarded as an Indonesian citizen; hence refugee aid is not available. Despite her difficulties, she continues to pray for strength. "I just surrendered to the Lord" (in Wandita 2015: 142). This surrender is not necessarily an act of passive submission; it can be a conscious *strategy of resilience* in the face of massive injustices – a form of resistance to oppression.

Herminia da Costa was led to the forest when the Indonesians invaded Timor-Leste. A widow, she has seven children to support and while she owns land, she lives in the house her husband began to build before he died. She is filled with pain and says: "Justice is a word I often hear people using. Whether it is real or not I don't know, because I've never experienced it. We have suffered hunger and economic crisis, but no one cares about us. I don't know where the process of justice is" (in Wandita 2015: 198). Julieta, the coordinator of the Timorese Women's Populist Organization affiliated with Fretilin found strength through prayer, and still waits for justice. She says: "our suffering should be addressed. While I am not satisfied with the benefit I received, this is the reality faced by us women who struggled for independence. What is important is that there is no more violence" (in Wandita 2015: 199).

I am stressing that the praxis for *feminist* women-of-faith peacebuilders is intentional, social, and effective agency that occurs as a direct response to the suffering caused by injustices. It often bears the hallmarks of compassion, a quality that is examined in Chapter seven. This *praxis is always political and embodied.*

Feminist Liberation Theology

To conclude this chapter, it is worth looking briefly at how feminist liberation theology stretches the potential of women-of-faith to function as agents in a political sense. Feminist liberation theology is fundamentally geared toward liberating the oppressed. It "functions as a religious ethical political force of transformation for a new world" (Aquino 2012: 418), where justice, freedom, and peace prevail. It views socio-political struggles for justice as a way to "embody the presence and activity of God in the world" as a liberating presence (Aquino 2012: 420). A critical feminist theology of liberation believes that if women's subordination exists, this liberating purpose is unfulfilled.

The critical dimension comes into play when women challenge power relations, cultural norms and practices, and inequalities that suppress their rights (Björkdahl and Mannergren Selimovic 2015: 170). Driven by her faith, Aquino states that "a feminist religious vision of justice and deliberation for the marginalized humanity is what provides coherence and purpose to my existence" (2009: 205). What she calls "feminist intercultural theology" seeks to replace: domination with justice; subordination with emancipation; capital with human dignity; a predatory market with an inclusive community; domesticating religion with transformative religion; and absolutist faith with dialogical faith (2007: 23). Interculturality indicates a movement, a journey in-between spaces of present reality and a liberatory future. *These borderland spaces provide creative avenues for women-of-faith.*

Given cycles of destructive violence, a feminist theology of liberation enables faith-based peacebuilders to strive effectively to overcome the root causes of violence. Aquino calls on feminist theologians of liberation to work closely with peacebuilding scholars and practitioners to overcome simplistic approaches to conflict transformation, and instead, "to affirm, in religious and theological terms, the common humanity of people to recognition of wo/men's human dignity and human rights... in creating conditions of just peace" (2009: 207).

A praxis of liberation is always *contextual* because oppression and subordination emerge in social situations. For women-of-faith who practice a feminist theology of liberation, the transformation of cross-cutting forms of oppression and unjust structures and relations that occur from "the bedroom to the battlefield" (Marshall and Hayward 2015: 20), is integral to their practices and the real-world outliving of their faith.

Women-of-faith peacebuilders acknowledge all people's inherent dignity, whether victims, combatants, survivors, or agents of change. The point of acknowledging the dignity of aggressors is to recognize the essential humanness of combatants, even in committing inhuman acts. Moral agents can choose evil or good. Punishment for perpetrators of abuse thus should be appropriate, fair, and humane. Recognizing the humanity of former combatants is easier when remorse is shown. Those women who adopt a liberation theology strive for participatory and democratic processes, which means they are keenly aware of how power dynamics can subjugate, particularly between urban elite and rural poor, majority, and minority communities, or among antagonistic ethno-religious identity groups. Oppression has diverse faces, all stifling freedom. There are a variety of peacebuilders influenced by liberation theologies, "distinguished by Regions – such as Latin America, Africa, Asia – and by social groups – the poor, Hispanics, Dalits, women, indigenous peoples, and others" (Groody 2007: 202).

The Latin American Afro-feminist theology springs from the specific relational experiences of individual and community life of women of African origin in Latin America and the Caribbean. The theology that drives their peacebuilding is concerned "with the situations of racism, sexism, classism, colonialism, and anti-semitism which mark the life experiences of the oppressed in our societies" (López 2012: 160). Feminist liberation theologians, in addressing the need to overcome oppression, do not limit freedom to individual liberty, but couch the overcoming of oppression in communal terms, of *freedom in relationships within just societies*. I continue to show that this *relationality* is fundamental to the distinctive contribution of women-of-faith peacebuilders.

Regional variations show diverse cultural ways to overcome oppression. Namsoon Kang (2004: 107), a Korean, writes against any unitary classification of Western or Asian women. She explains that images of Asian women as always poor or suffering from starvation, rape, or battering, fail to "embrace the diversity of Asian women" (2004: 107). She warns against generalizing about Asian women's experiences of either oppression or liberation, because experiences occur in specific historical times that are shaped by a range of factors like class, culture, education, race, religion, and individual differences. As Kang expresses it, "Overgeneralization, oversimplification, and homogenization become a representation, and the diversity, complexity, historicity of the feminist theological discourse of those regions are suppressed" (2004: 110). Asia is vastly different in its cultural, economic, political, and religious diversity, and thus liberatory responses to these differences must be culturally and regionally specific for peacebuilding to be meaningful.

Elsewhere, African women's theologies are shaped by traditional African beliefs, as well as by versions of liberation theology. These theologies do not always explicitly identify as feminist, but more typically as African women's theologies. They seek "to unmask the cultural bias against women and the systems oppressing them, and to recover the basic, communal, liberative thrust of the Scriptures and African Religion," by encouraging people to be critically reflective and not simply accept oppressive, violent systems (Mwaura 2012: 271). The strengths of these theologies of praxis lie in their contextual responsiveness to African women's everyday lives where suffering and death dominate war-torn countries. Rosemary Edet from Nigeria and Bette Ekeya from Kenya write that regardless which religion people adopt, "no one escapes the African traditional religion of one's people. It is woven so tightly into the culture that none can claim to have moved completely out of the spirituality of Africa's own religion" (1988: 5). They suggest that in view of the damage done by missionaries and colonizers, to view the church as a positive factor in Africa is to struggle for equality and liberation in the interests of just peace. This struggle occurs in everyday experiences in the home, fields, or economic sphere.

To conclude, I suggest that a politics of liberation extends its goals of transformation of society in extensive, usually radical ways. Yet, the liberal peacebuilding agenda that is privileged by the UN and international gender advocates working through the UN, dominate post-war and transitional justice processes. I am demonstrating that women's groups who attempt to organize around UNSCR 1325, often do not adequately activate grassroots women. Yet all activist alliances can be utilized fruitfully in mobilizing women in conflict transformation and peacebuilding, "without romanticizing, homogenizing, and/

or essentializing their diverse experiences and forms of activism" (Pratt and Richter-Devroe 2010: 500).

The extent to which UNSCR 1325 can be used for radical socio-political transformation may depend on extending an understanding of the emphasis on prevention of violence in this resolution. Kirby and Shepherd remind us that this prevention refers to more than the prevention of gender-based violence; "there is also prevention in the sense of sustained social change to undo the conditions that produce violent conflict in the first place" (2016: 391). This goal to prevent violence requires substantial global transformation. The radical praxis of feminist liberation theologians contributes greatly to contributing to meet, even in a partial sense, this practical goal. The action plans developed by states to implement UNSCR 1325 need to consider ways in which localized civil society movements that are transforming societies by *practicing justice and building peace*, can be included in strategies in fruitful ways. Feminist women-of-faith peacebuilders often lead these struggles to prevent violence.

***

This chapter provides examples of women-of-faith as transformative agents of change. I began by explaining that a narrative construction of the self-in-relation views self-identity to emerge in relationships with others. Thus, narrative agency is demonstrated through the courageous acts of women-of-faith peacebuilders. I show that *story-telling* is one way to help traumatized women to understand themselves as agents, with meaningful, albeit painful narratives, and not simply as victims. I explain also that not all women-of-faith peacebuilders are feminist, and clarified that faith is self-defined. Many women who do not call themselves feminist, practice the principles and goals of feminism, particularly valuing *networks of relationships*, which I am arguing is the chief hallmark of women-of-faith peacebuilders. I explain also that feminist women-of-faith, and particularly those who identify with feminist liberation theology, gear their peacebuilding toward a feminist praxis, as a deliberate political attempt to bring just peace.

The chapter argues that women-of-faith peacebuilders play an immense role as transformative agents in fighting gendered oppression, in working to prevent violence, and building just peace. The next chapter explores the work of women-of-faith peacebuilders in actively participating in peace processes.

4

Women-of-faith Participating in Peace Processes

Few women-of-faith are represented in formal peace processes. So, why am I examining the topic? Because many of these women are greatly involved in informal processes or they are supporting others in informal activities. This chapter evaluates the contributions of those women who are present in formal and informal processes. It shows why more women of all political and faith persuasions are needed in these processes to increase the local acceptance of changes that enhance women's peace and security. The chapter has three main sections.

First, I explain what is involved in formal, multidimensional, peace processes where open dialogue is crucial. I remind readers of the obvious fact that women are scarce in formal negotiations, or as signatories to peace agreements.

Second, I build a case to show why it is significant for women-of-faith to be actively involved in all aspects of peace processes; for reasons of equality, fulfilling the UNSCR 1325 mandate, fair representation, because women's presence makes a difference to the topics brought to the negotiating table, and because their presence increases the likelihood of a peace agreement lasting. I use examples of informal activity in peace processes in some Latin American and African nations, and in the Pacific Islands.

In the third section, I critically scrutinize what is at stake when women draw on their social status as mothers to validate their peacemaking roles. Using examples from Bougainville, Palau, and Fiji, and Nicaragua, Nigeria, and Rwanda, I suggest that there are strengths in validating mothers' voices, but there are problems of an assumed feminine pacifism that confirms gender stereotypes.

The chapter argues that more women should be present in all stages of peace processes, and that the meaningful involvement of women-of-faith is vital to increase the local acceptance of the principles behind the WPS resolutions, particularly in countries where religious identity plays a major role in influencing community norms.

Formal Peace Processes

Given the broad definition of peacebuilding used in this book, peace processes also can be understood in a comprehensive way. Their purpose overlaps with the goal of conflict transformation, which is "the deeper long-term project of overcoming underlying structural violence and cultural violence and transforming identities and relations" (Ramsbotham 2010: 52). Oliver Ramsbotham suggests that peace processes involve a range of different measures to change conflict, including humanitarian relief for civilian casualties of complex emergencies; early warning devices that identify potential outbreaks of violence and advise on preventative or containment measures; preventive diplomacy with high profile diplomats, fact-finding missions and degrees of pressure placed on people; and peacekeeping operations that come with the agreement of concerned parties, to ensure or enforce the ceasing of violence.

A peace process involves more than statements of intent; it must engage the main antagonists in a conflict. All peace initiatives are fragile. John Darby and Roger Mac Ginty (2008: 3) suggest five essential criteria required to reach a successful peace accord: protagonists are willing to negotiate in good faith, they aren't just trying to gain information; key actors are included in the process, which of course is controversial because it includes those who have given orders to bomb, kill, destroy, and rape, and those who have carried out these acts; negotiations address the central issues in dispute; force is not used to achieve objectives; and negotiators are committed to a sustained process. When any of these break down, a lasting peace is jeopardized. Adrian Guelke (2008: 68) summarizes seven phases of the peace process, stressing that in practice these phases overlap: pre-talks phase; an era of secret talks; opening of multilateral talks; negotiating to a settlement; gaining endorsement; implementing its provisions; and the institutionalization of the new dispensation. As Charles Hauss reminds us, "there is no blueprint for conflict resolution... all conflicts are different, and those differences matter" (2010: 201).

Inclusive Dialogue

Peace processes involve intense negotiations between opponents. All sides of a conflict need to be able to place their interests on the bargaining table. However, negotiations are complicated by decisions about who will be present, whether it includes former rebels, warlords, and paramilitaries, and what the negotiations are about. Negotiations may be about ceasefires, disarmament, elections, political power, or amnesties. Alain Lempereur and Aurélien Colson stress the need to formalize the agreement before ending the talks, to check thoroughly the details agreed upon, including an action plan that outlines the responsibilities of each party, and the rights and obligations of all involved, "including making sure that the agreement falls within both parties' mandate" (2010: 9). Many conflicts have been transformed through these types of negotiations, including in Aceh, Bosnia, El Salvador, Guatemala, Mozambique, Northern Ireland, South Africa, and the border dispute between Peru and Ecuador.

Radical disagreements between opposing parties, are intense. "In the war of words, conflict parties cannot 'agree to disagree,' when, given the power to do so, they ride roughshod over the other's dearest interests" (Ramsbotham 2010: xi). With intractable conflicts, attempts at settlement and transformation continually fail. Part of the reason for the failure is the lack of *inclusive dialogue*, which I maintain is the key to *mutual understanding and peaceful conflict transformation*. Dialogue establishes the basis for building trust that strengthens relationships. Listening is as important as talking, and many women are good listeners. *With careful, deep listening, we begin to hear the voice of the other.* The stories told and hopefully heard are troubling – stories of hurt, pain, suffering, oppression, trauma, humiliation, and terrible loss. Outside parties can be of great help, as with the late Nelson Mandela's role in assisting productive dialogue in the 1999 Burundi peace talks.

It is increasingly recognized that explicit efforts to incorporate women in official dialogues on the peace process in the stages after termination of violence, improves the prospects for more durable peace agreements. Indeed, "women's participation increases the probability of peace agreements lasting at least two years by 20 percent. It also increases the probability of a peace agreement lasting fifteen years by 35 percent" (Coomaraswamy 2015: 41-42). These statistics are significant. So, why are women excluded, absent, silenced, or rare in formal peace processes? To answer this, I now explain that while women are marginalized in formal peace processes, many women are active in informal processes.

Formal Peace Processes

Multidimensional peace processes consist of Track one processes of official diplomacy, Track two processes of informal, unofficial, and citizen diplomacy, and Track three grassroots activities. If I was to concentrate solely on women's participation in Track one, the discussion would be brief, narrowed to a few examples with a few women.

In a 2010 study by the United Nations Development Fund for Women (UNIFEM), now absorbed into UN Women, women's participation in peace processes remains one of the most unfulfilled aspects of the WPS agenda. Curiously, many of the noteworthy examples of women's participation occurred before the passing of UNSCR 1325 on 31 October 2000. For example, in El Salvador in 1992, women constituted 12 percent of signatories and 13 percent of the negotiating teams; in Guatemala in 1996, women were 11 percent signatories and 10 percent of the negotiating teams; in Northern Ireland in 1998, they were 10 percent of the signatories and 10 percent of the teams; and in Sierra Leone 1999, women were 20 percent of the witnesses (Costillo Diaz 2010: 4). This study shows that since UNSCR 1325, there were no women present in peace agreements in Somalia 2002, Cote d'Ivoire 2003, Nepal, 2006, the Philippines 2007, and Central African Republic 2008.

An updated UN Women study (Castillo Diaz and Tordjman 2012: 4) shows that since UNSCR 1325, the only agreements where there were more than 10 percent of women included: 12 percent in negotiating teams in DRC 2003; 17 percent as witnesses in Liberia 2003; 20 percent of lead mediators in DRC 2008 in North Kivu, and also DRC 2008 in South Kivu; 20 percent of witnesses in Uganda 2008; 33 percent as lead mediators and 25 percent in negotiating teams in Kenya 2008 (but not as signatories); 33 percent signatories in Honduras 2009; and 33 percent signatories and 35 percent negotiators in the Philippines 2011. Overall, women constitute only "2.4 percent of chief mediators, 3.7 percent of witnesses, 4 percent of signatures, and 9 percent in the negotiating teams" (2012: 3).

These are disappointingly low findings. They provide strong reasons to continue urging the full implementation of UNSCR 1325 and related resolutions in all UN member states. I believe that women's presence in peace processes matters for at least three reasons.

First, women are affected by conflict and thus by the consequences of a peace agreement. Second, and related to the first point, women's inclusion in all stages of peace processes is crucial for inclusive social justice. Third, the presence of women makes a difference to the sorts of issues generally brought to formal peace processes. (Porter 2003: 249)

Women tend to bring different issues to the negotiating table. For example, on women's demands for security and protection, activists in Kinshasa, in the DRC, reminded participants in the 2009 peace processes that "activists are increasingly threatened, intimidated, attacked, and even killed because of their will to defend sexual violence victims" (in Costillo Diaz 2010: 13). The Uganda Women's Coalition for Peace, addressing the disarmament, demobilization, and reintegration (DDR) of female combatants, said in 2006, "Ensure that cantonment sites are women-friendly – that they are safe and provide healthcare, childcare, and training" and allow women combatants to report to women field workers (in Costillo Diaz 2010: 13). The Afghan Women for the National Peace Jirga, Kabul, in 2010, suggested that "families, rather than individual combatants, should be reintegrated in order to support community recovery and healing" (in Costillo Diaz 2010: 13). The All-Party Burundi Women's Peace Conference, Arusha, in 2000, reported: "It pains us very much that we and our daughters have suffered war crimes, such as rape, sexual violence, prostitution, and domestic violence that have gone unrecognized and unpunished. We ask that this agreement put an end to impunity" (in Costillo Diaz 2010: 13). The point stressed here is that there is sufficient evidence that unless women are represented at all levels of decision-making, as is mandated in UNSCR 1325, the issues that specifically concern women and girls go unaddressed.

Christine Bell and Catherine O'Rourke undertook substantial research using a data base of 585 peace agreements that were signed between January 1990 to May 2010. They coded references to women which included the following terms: gender, gender balance, gender sensitivity, gender-based violence, widows, girls, sexual violence, and rape. In summary, their research shows that:

Only 16 percent of peace agreements contain references to women, but that references to women have increased significantly since the passing of Resolution 1325, from 11 percent to 27 percent of agreements. This rise is more dramatic for agreements in which the UN had a third-party role (from 4 percent to 12 percent), than for agreements which did not have the UN in such a role (from 7 percent to 14 percent). (Bell and O'Rourke 2010: 954)

Bell and O'Rourke clarify that the terms of a peace agreement do not guarantee the implementation of its requirements, and the exclusion of an issue does not mean that it cannot be adopted in practice, but they maintain that issues not specifically included in the agreement can be tricky to prioritize post-agreement. If there is to be input such as donor funding from international sources, funding must be linked to the agreement's priorities. "In other words, although gender references may do little to further women's equality, without gender being mentioned the struggle for inclusion is even more difficult" (Bell and O'Rourke 2010: 947).

There is still much work needed to realize the mandate of UNSCR 1325 as the preamble says: "full participation in the peace process can significantly contribute to the maintenance and promotion of international peace and security" (UN Security Council 2000).

Informal Peace Processes

I now consider women's involvement in multidimensional peace processes in a range of places, seeking to find stories that demonstrate women-of-faith's activities. Multidimensional peace processes are concerned not only with establishing immediate security, but with facilitating the political process.

Informal peace processes include peace marches and protests, lobby-ing, secretive meetings, inter-cultural events to foster understanding of different groups, and local activism. These activities are conducted by a range of actors, such as UN entities, international, regional, national, and local organizations, grassroots organizations, peace groups, NGOs, women's groups, religious organizations, individuals, and women from all faiths. The activities may include former paramilitaries, ex-combatants, rebels, and fighters who have exchanged the gun, spear, machete, or bomb for engagement in political strategies within civil society and grassroots levels.

The nature of informal peace processes varies across cultures. Rita-mbhara Mehta (nd: 1) explains broad notions of peace across the South Asian region that reflect a rich multiculturalism, and an "intermingling of various religions and ethnicities" within the midst of many conflicts. She stresses how security in South Asia concerns not merely direct vio-lent conflicts, "but traditional security issues as well, such as individual dignity, water security, environmental security, food security, security from arms, ethnicity, and religion" (nd: 1). That is, insecurity affects far more than national and political security. It affects people's well-being. Mehta provides examples of the negative impact of religion on some women's insecurities. In Afghanistan, while Persian woman have been encouraged to participate in peace processes, Pashto-speaking women, typically from rural areas are marginalized, and "this discrim-ination is also seen as being linked to religious affiliation" (nd: 1). In India, the combination of fundamentalism with communalism and the inequalities of the rigid caste system contribute to human-rights viola-tions that target specific ethno-religious groups. In Nepal, "exclusion, discrimination, and marginalization based on ethnicity, gender, caste, class, religion, and geographic location underpin the conflict" (nd: 2). In Pakistan, religious fundamentalist parties have come to power with religiously motivated "honor" killings and a greater restriction on women's mobility. In Sri Lanka, the lack of participation of women in the peace process, custodial rape, and ethnic and religious conflicts reinforce discriminatory patriarchal practices.

Turning to a different geographic location, in 1996, the Northern Ireland Women's Coalition were voted into the top ten parties and earned two places at the negotiating table that led to the Good Friday Agreement. The two signatories were Monica McWilliams from the Catholic community and Pearl Sagar from the Protestant community, deliberately signalling inclusivity. This example strictly falls under formal peace processes but is included here because the work of the coalition extended beyond the formal sphere, in galvanizing urban and rural, cross-class, and diverse community groups on a wide range of contentious issues like policing, release of political prisoners, and jobs for youth rather than have them join paramilitary organizations. A British participant in the peace talks observed that when the parties became stalled by controversial issues about past offences, "the women would come and talk about their loved ones, their bereavement, the children and their hopes for the future" (in Hunt and Posa 2001: 46), reminding participants of the centrality of broad-based notions of human security. The coalition met around kitchen tables to do their preparation, with children playing on the floor, melding formal requirements with informal necessities.

In 2010, the International Fellowship of Reconciliation Women Peacemakers Program brought together thirty-five women from Azerbaijan, Bangladesh, Canada, Ghana, India, Indonesia, Israel, Kashmir, Kenya, Lebanon, Liberia, Macedonia, Madagascar, Malaysia, Nepal, the Netherlands, Nigeria, Palestine, the Philippines, Sweden, and the United States. These women included representatives from Buddhism, Christianity, Hinduism, Islam, and Judaism, as well as secular individuals. One participant concluded that there could not be a simplistic choice "between religion and women's rights. We need to claim our right to redefine religion, bring out its positive aspects in women's lives, and strategize against the negative practices that are being justified on the basis of religion" (Gueskens et al. 2010: 7). This need to strategize across a wide variety of concerns is expressed frequently, as the following examples demonstrate.

African Peace Processes

On the African continent, examples of women's involvement in peace processes are diverse. Examples are now provided from Kenya, Uganda, Nigeria, and Somalia, with attention given to inter-faith work in Liberia. Dekha Ibrahim, a devout Muslim woman, is a founder of the Kenyan Wajir Peace and Development Committee and Action for Conflict Transformation. This group draws on Islamic resources and local peacebuilding practices, including traditional ethnic and tribal networks and structures of leadership to deepen inter-religious relationships across diverse ethnic and cultural situations. The Committee formed in 1995 by local citizens who were affected by violent conflict, primarily between ethnic Somalis and national Kenyans, to bring local women, elders, youth, business people, and religious leaders together. Ibrahim "served as a broker in thorny Kenyan and international disputes" (Hayward and Marshall 2015: 1). She stresses the importance of plurality, diversity, and ownership of the participation, thereby including men and women, Muslims, Catholics, Anglicans, and Jews.

Another significant individual peacebuilder is Betty Bigome, a Christian Ugandan woman who was a principal mediator for the Ugandan government's direct negotiations with the Lord's Resistance Army for nearly two decades, and then was an independent mediator. Her work included talks with rebel leader Joseph Kony in 1992. The rebel leaders called her "mother Bigome," a concept to be analyzed later in the third section.

A regional women's organization that joins women in communities is the West African group, Women in Peacebuilding Network (WIPNET), launched in 2001 to build capacity of women to engage in peacebuilding activities across fifteen countries. The process of interaction is culturally important.

> Women meet in a safe place, sit in a circle, and place a large bowl of water with candles around it. They take turns sharing their stories and expressing their emotions. When everyone is

done speaking, they wash their own hands and the hands of the woman sitting next to them in the bowl to signify the washing away of their pain and the solidarity they have as a group. (Oliver et al. 2004: 25)

Part of the mission in the network is religious and political reconciliation. Bridget Usifo Osakwe, speaking as Program Manager at WIPNET Nigeria, acknowledges that women are still regarded as subordinate to men, an idea that is justified through religious teachings. She suggests that a crucial strategy of WIPNET "is to first engage these traditional institutions in a series of sensitization and advocacy programs, to deepen their understanding and generate interest on the necessity of the inclusion of women" (in Guesken et al. 2010: 13) within decision-making and political institutions. However, Osakwe cites a variety of groups such as the Christian Association of Nigeria, the Pentecostal Fellowship of Nigeria, the Justice Development and Peace Commission of the Catholics, and the Women's Wing of the Christian Association of Nigeria, as Christian groups providing a range of additional conciliatory and mediator roles. Osakwe says that particularly when governments are in disarray, these religious organizations: "may be the only institutions with some degree of popular credibility, trust, and moral authority" (in Gueskens et al. 2010: 21). This reminds us that much of the knowledge people have of the contributions that women make to religious peacebuilding are anecdotal stories, where "the challenge lies in framing 'success stories' at the grassroots and middle levels in ways that will impact policy analysis and reform" (Gueskens et al. 2010: 15). This reminder is important, because despite local successes, grassroots peacebuilding programs often stagnate when financial resources are exhausted, and the stories of success fade untold.

Somalian women played a constructive role in peacebuilding. John Paul Lederach explains that: "the women of Wajir didn't set out to stop a war. They just wanted to make sure they could get food for their families. The initial idea was simple enough: Make sure that the market is safe for anyone to buy and sell" (2005: 10), thereby making the market a zone of peace, typifying the drive for pragmatic solutions that were outlined in the previous chapter. The Wajir Women's Association for Peace formed. Given the women's ability to slide from clan of marriage to clan of origin, they were well-positioned to foster social change amongst strategic groups, creating the space for clan elders to meet. In May 2000, ninety-two Somali women stood outside the military tent in Arta, Djibouti waiting for the Somali National Peace Conference to begin. This was the fourteenth attempt since 1991 to find a peaceful solution to the civil war. These women were chosen to be part of delegations representing traditional clans, but their goal was to break out of clan-based allegiances. One delegate said, "we knew that peace in our country would come from cross-clan reconciliation, not official negotiations among war lords and faction leaders...so we cared for the wounded and build schools in communities regardless of clan, ethnic, and political affiliations" (in Rehn and Johnson Sirleaf 2002: 78).

The women were geared toward practical solutions, as explained in Chapter three. While the women came from four major clans and coalitions of minor ones, they presented themselves at the conference as a "sixth clan," thereby creatively reaching beyond the constructions of rigid ethnicity. Women lobbied for protection of the human rights of women, children, and minorities. Women-of-faith served as mediators with armed actors to create signs of security and protection. Asha Hagi Elmi, a Somalian, secured a place in negotiations by advocating for her participation from an Islamic framework. In 2004, she was the only woman to co-chair the Somali National Reconciliation Conference, and the first woman to sign the peace accord. She continues to encourage and mentor young women leaders.

The Liberian Women's Initiative (LWI) developed in 1994 from frustration and hope. Mary Brownell, an active member recalled: "Some of us weren't sure we'd make it because the warlords fight us with their guns, and we have nothing... So, I said let's go in faith" (in Marshall and Heywood 2011: 7). The initial efforts of the LWI paved the way for the Mano River Women's Peace Network (MARWOP-NET), formed in 2000, an original movement with links across Guinea,

Liberia, and Sierra Leone. MARWOPNET was a signatory to the 2004 Liberian peace accord, but first, there is a story to tell. The Liberian peace process provides a powerful example of the strength of women-of-faith. During the six-year civil war in Liberia, in April 1996, Charles Taylor's rebel fighters set fire to a Catholic church and its radio station in Monrovia. The church and its Justice and Peace Commission had been boldly opposing the war with its effects on civilians. The church was across from the home of Brownell who, in joining the crowd trying to extinguish the fire, sought to save the church, despite hearing a rebel faction call out that they were going to capture her. She was flown to Sierra Leone and four months later returned to Monrovia. In an interview in 2009 with Robert Press, she recalled: "we were guided by the hand of God" (in Press 2010: 23).

Elizabeth Mulbah, who in 1995 helped to conduct a training session in conflict resolution for the rival rebel leaders, said "it was all about faith" (in Press 2010: 23). The women weren't sure if the men would participate, but all four invited factions came, each bringing four members and formally dressed in European or African attire. To explain their careful dressing, Mulbah recounts that one leader told her "When your 'mother' calls, you have to be your best" (in Press 2010: 27). Both Christian and Muslim prayers opened the training sessions. Etweda Cooper, an organizer of the early peace efforts said: "we had literate women; we had illiterate women; we had women from every ethnic background; we had Muslims, we had Christians" (in Press 2010: 24). Cooper explained that part of the motivation for women-of-faith to come together was that as heads of households, women were carrying the burden of care of the family, and care was disrupted by watching children die, people starve to death, suffer from gunshot wounds, girls being raped, and husbands killed. As Cooper summarizes their stance, "we decided we are the survivors; we are also peacemakers... We make up the bulk of the population so why should we be ignored? So, we added our voices to the peace process" (in Press 2010: 24). This is a deliberate attempt to demonstrate the active agency that comes with a strong acceptance of the *responsibility to care for others*, a feature I argue is a unique aspect of women-of-faith's peacebuilding.

In 2002, as Charles Taylor declared a state of emergency in Monrovia, Leymah Gbowee and twenty other women met each Tuesday at noon to pray for peace. Christian and Muslim women joined together for a common cause. One powerful slogan, "Does the bullet know a Christian from a Muslim?" (in Marshall and Heywood 2011: 7) emphasizes commonalities, despite some refusing to pray with women who aren't of the same religion. The Liberian branch of WIPNET formed in 2003 as rival rebel factions intensified their attacks, uniting Muslim, and Christian women. Gbowee organized the Liberian Mass Action for Peace, a coalition of Christian and Muslim women who sat in public protest along the streets where Liberia's then President Taylor, drove past. They confronted rebel warlords. Gbowee led two hundred women into the negotiating hall, where they joined arms, and refused to let any man out until a peace agreement was signed. When warned with possible arrest, Gbowee threatened to strip naked, summoning a traditional African power. "In Africa, it's a terrible curse to see a married or elderly woman deliberately bare herself" (Gbowee 2011: 162). Gbowee's message was clear: "We will not allow them to come out until they give us peace" (2011: 162). Analysis of the drawing on maternal powers occurs below, for now, I sketch the picture of the active participation in informal peace processes by women for whom faith is a significant component to their search for peace and justice.

Pacific Island Peace Processes

In many countries in Oceania, Christianity and culture are tightly interwoven. In this section, I outline the way that women-of-faith in the Pacific Islands make an impact on peacebuilding, briefly examining Tonga, then Fiji and Bougainville in more detail. To preface this discussion, it is useful to reiterate, as Marie Ropeti, an ordained minister of the Presbyterian Church of Aotearoa New Zealand states, the mission of Pacific women theologians is to be a voice of social critique, exposing injustices, and encouraging "free and critical debate on whether progress towards a just and peaceful society is being advanced or inhibited" (2003: 138). This mission includes pointing out social injustices, including as Ropeti expresses it, "the enduring social evil of patriarchy" (2003: 138).

The Pacific Islands have experienced lawlessness in Papua and New Guinea, coups in Fiji, and ongoing risk of unrest in Bougainville and the Solomon Islands. However, minimal attention is given in scholarly work to how women's peacebuilding minimizes the frequency of regional conflict. Efforts to build security in the Pacific are ineffective if they are secularized, because faith is a crucial resource for local women peacebuilders. This argument has massive implications for accomplishing women's peace and security agenda in relation to the full realization of UNSCR 1325 and its sister resolutions. Nicole George shows how women have practised peace advocacy since decolonization, challenging geopolitical violence, including nuclear testing in the region, and showing strong evidence of political agency. She demonstrates "how women activists have drawn on faith values to motivate and legitimate their peacebuilding work" (George 2015: 120). Her stress is on the twofold strand that for Pacific women, faith is a reason to confront any normalization of violence, and faith legitimates their social and political activity.

Building on Karen Brison's (2007) notion of "communalism," George looks at the ways in which individual agents work within community obligations, weaving faith-based efforts into their peacebuilding. George is responding critically to typical feminist views on global security that identify cultural violence, diffused "within religion, ideology, language" as the primary cause of gendered inequities (Hudson et al. 2008: 21). To always adopt this view diminishes the role that religion can play in peacebuilding, and the contribution women-of-peacebuilders make in transforming insecurities that exacerbate state conflict. George maintains that it is imprudent to either minimize the links between faith and insecurity in the region, or "to imagine religion can only be a source of regional insecurity" because "across the Pacific

Islands, the relationship between gender, faith, and security is far more complex" than many who promote macro perspectives of security would have us believe (2015: 122). Let me show why.

Women in the Pacific have always been in the frontline of civil society work. In the Pacific, civil society covers religious and secular organizations that address humanitarian and sociocultural needs of the community. For Pacific women activists, feminism is a communal enterprise "in that when Pacific women become empowered and influential, whole communities can reap the benefits" (Griffen 2006: 14). Arlene Griffen explains the significance of the symbolic concept of "weaving" that is built into the imagery of many faith-based women's groups.

> While the women weave together, they share stories and ideas of family and community and the world and of a woman's place in it, so that a parallel kind of weaving together of a Pacific world-view and vision is also taking place, which informs their actions in everyday life. (2006: 17)

Some examples of weaving follow.

In Tonga, the churches have immense power and authority. Family, community, and national events acknowledge a spiritual aspect. "Individual's social, cultural, and economic roles, attitudes and actions are determined by the strength of his or her affiliation with the church" (Maka 2006: 27). Most community-oriented NGOs have some association with churches. The Catholic Women's League, set up in 1992 is the most active denominational organization in Tonga. It is affiliated with the World Union of Catholic Women's Organizations which has consultative status with UN bodies. From 1995 on, it moved beyond simply improving general welfare of families to a more political advocacy for women's rights, focusing on family violence and abuse. The League runs two main programs. First, a Legal Literacy Project aims to educate women about their rights in relation to property, sexual abuse, incest, divorce, and child support. Second, the establishment of the

Centre for Women and Children is crucial in a culture where women's subservience is considered as a sign of respect, where discussing sex is taboo, and bringing harms of sexual abuse into the public is considered shameful. The Centre offers knowledge, counselling, conflict management training, and referral services. The League's achievements foster more mutually respectful partnerships in the face of patriarchal social, cultural, and church structures, and seeks to increase the full participation of women in family, church, and social positions.

Fiji is a clear example of consistent involvement of women-of-faith in small community-based groups. From the late 1960s, Fiji's Young Women's Christian Association led campaigns of protest against the damaging impact of regional nuclear weapons testing programs. By the mid-1970s, women activists in this group described their organization as committed to the promotion of "peace and a just world order" (George 2015: 126). Within Oceanic theology, there are beliefs that undermine women's well-being, such as references to wifely submission, patriarchal privilege in marriage, the idea of the suffering servant, and an obsession with women's virtue that could be seen to encourage women to tolerate marital violence. "Since the early 1980s, women's organizations in Fiji have looked to challenge the pervasive nature of gendered violence and the insecurities experienced by women in the conjugal setting" (George 2015: 123). For example, women's groups have drawn public attention to gendered violence through media advocacy, training sessions for those in law or policing, and through general awareness-raising campaigns. The Fiji Women's Crisis Centre involves religious institutions in anti-violence work, "to counter the tendency for religious leaders to reinforce ideas about the sanctity of family and marriage in ways that encourage women's tolerance of violence" (2015: 123). Places of religious worship are often a first point of contact for women victims of violence. Yet Shamima Ali of the Crisis Centre, says that "very often women are told to forgive and forget" when they discuss their family violence with religious leaders (in George 2015: 123). To counter this unhelpful mantra, the Centre held an inter-faith workshop for pastors, priests, pundits, and imams in 2012 to address this issue.

In Fiji, faith is built continually into peacebuilding. When the 2000 coup occurred, women from faith communities came together for prayer at Suva's Holy Trinity Anglican Cathedral. The Fiji National Council of Women, a peak body representing smaller secular and religious women's groups coordinated the vigil. The women dressed in black to mourn the threat of violence hanging over the nation, and this church became a site for Christian resistance, resistance being a key aspect of feminist theological praxis, as explained in the previous chapter. As Nisha Buksh, coordinator of the Fiji Muslim Women's League and a founding member of Fiji's National Council of Women told George in 2002, "the prayer allowed women to meet in one place, to come together and pray for peace. It was about prayer and networking and creating a movement" (in 2015: 125). George explains that in talking with Buksh, a Muslim, her words echoed feminist Christian theologians about how faith provides "the basis of a common human experience that could be drawn upon to build security" (2015: 125). The multi-faith focus of this prayer vigil provides a foundation for incorporating a WPS perspective in an inclusive fashion.

Religion undoubtedly shapes the public space in which women activists work in the Pacific Islands, and the space is politically constraining. It takes courage to challenge patriarchal notions of acceptable womanhood, through faith-based resistive agency. In being "attentive to the nuances in the way the relationship between gender, faith, and security is configured," George defends "the possibility for faith-based transformative politics" that encourages efforts to challenge violence, insecurities, and injustices while impelling women to take critical action (2015: 129). This position builds on arguments made in the previous chapter of the potential for women-of-faith peacebuilders to be significant change agents. Despite ongoing unrest, violence, and persistent state weakness, the WPS agenda is advanced in numerous ways.

Since 2000, the Pacific Peace-Women Project, a trans-regional network of women's organizations from Fiji, Bougainville, Solomon

Islands, and Tonga works to spread awareness of and gain popular support for UNSCR 1325. Building on the regular peace vigils held in local churches, the networks develop political goals that resonate with the deeply held religious beliefs that are part of Pacific Islands culture, identity, and personhood. These peace activities allow "women to yoke religious norms of non-violence with the secularized WPS agenda" (George 2014: 318).

Prompted by a decade-long advocacy process by women peace activists in the region, in November 2012, the Pacific Islands Forum Secretariat launched a Regional Action Plan on WPS. The message of this plan is that for international conventions to be accepted and translated culturally as meaningful, the WPS policy framework should pay more attention to the ways in which faith is interwoven into cultural identity. The pursuits of activist women from Pacific Island countries, assisted by donor supporters within regional UN agencies and the Australian government's aid and development programs, means that UNSCR 1325 is well understood by many women from Pacific Islands Forum Member States. The Forum Secretariat understands how important it is to accommodate women's participation in conflict resolution and peacebuilding processes. Yet George (2014) argues that there are forms of "slow violence" such as climate change, rising sea levels, masculinized covenant structures, and militarism, that continue to heighten gendered insecurities, yet aren't identified as priority concerns within WPS policy documents. Human security is broad-based, affecting many dimensions of everyday life.

During 2009-2010, I conducted fieldwork research funded by the Commonwealth of Australia on "Women, Peace, and Security in Aus-AID Partner Countries: Analysis of the Impact of UN Resolution 1325." Anuradha Mundkur assisted this research (Porter and Mundkur 2012) and we met with the feminist women's theological group the Weavers, part of the South Pacific Association of Theological Schools, formed in 1989 to support women theologians and to advocate for the inclusion in male-dominated institutions. Weaving is a core cultural, communal activity in the Pacific Islands. Joan Taefono, a member of Weavers, explains the importance of reinterpreting certain religious doctrines within Oceanic Christianity, such as the theology of suffering which is used to encourage women's acceptance of "suffering in their daily lives" (in George 2015: 124). Another Fijian theologian, Ilisapeci Meo acknowledges that claims to equality require courage, but in her view, "faith should provide women with the motivation to respond to violence as agents who resist rather than victims who tolerate abuse and mistreatment" (in George 2015: 124). Courage is required to practice justice. I maintain that *resistance* is an active part of women's identities, often exhibited in peacebuilding practices.

Matt Tomlinson interviewed a female Methodist minister in Suva in 2009 and gives her the pseudonym of Tima. He concludes that Tima's identity as a female minister is a challenge in struggling with Fijian Methodism's patriarchal tendencies. She told him how mature senior pastors and workers have said to her "when we look at you, we see a woman, we see a female. But when you speak and when you do your work, it's like a man," a likeness that humbles yet shames her (in Tomlinson 2015: 87). Further, in Fiji, there is a rapidly growing Pentecostal ministry called Christian Mission Fellowship with a large membership (Morgain 2015: 108). The services in Suva take place in a mega-church auditorium called the Harvest Centre. Most of the ordained pastors are men. Even though many women are dedicated to full-time or part-time daily activities of this Centre, "to be an ordained pastor is seen as being in tension with women's desire for full involvement in family life" (2015: 111).

Building on women-of-faith's valuing of experience, Lydia Johnson writes about women's theologizing in the South Pacific context, explaining that their starting point "is the ownership of their own theological reflection" (2003: 11). She suggests that like other liberation theologians, these women do theology "from below," using their own experiences as the starting point. Such an ethnomethodology is rooted in a critical reflection on "'lived experience' in a particular cultural context," that insists on the "holistic interconnection of all forms of oppression" (2003: 11). Johnson stresses three additional characteristics of this contextual theology that highlight the difference women-of-faith peacebuilders make. First, they do so "experientially, giving free rein to intuition, imagination, emotion, and spirituality" (2003: 11). Thus, women highlight generative themes that they feel the strongest about, because this motivates them to take initiative in being moved to act against injustices, domination, inequalities, and all forms of cultural repression. Second, they practice theology "dialogically, as equal partners with all others who are engaged in a mutual search for meaning" (2003: 11). These practices involve a weaving of autobiographical narrative of personal, social, and global analysis into Biblical interpretation. Third, the theology is practised with deep awareness of women's situatedness in being on the margins of male-dominated institutions. Women quite literally "weave the mat" of their theological reflections, mulling on diverse experiences and building in their own personal narrative in relation to overlaps with others' narratives, just as one weaves strands of leaves or fibres together (2003:14). As transformative agents, women "weave their acts of liberating theology" (2003: 16).

Key individuals are inspirational change agents. After the civilian-led coup and insecurities spread across Fiji in May 2000, Sharon Bhagwan Rolls, a Fijian of Indian descent, and a women's rights activist, began to consider how women could challenge the discourses of insecurity. She brought women together to pray for peace at Suva's Holy Trinity Anglican Cathedral. These meetings continued daily for a two-month crisis period which brought together women from all of Fiji's faith groups. As a former journalist, in 2000 she developed a women's media communications organization called FemLINK Pacific, a media program raising women's awareness of UNSCR 1325. Its name indicates its ambitions: to build links across barriers of culture, faith, and age; and to connect the everyday challenges of women caught in conflict to the international WPS agenda. As part of its peace localization work, the group encourages women in the Pacific Islands region to translate the WPS provisions into local languages.

FemLINK Pacific links women's peace and security narratives from Bougainville, Fiji, Solomon Islands, and Tonga, building on the need for a holistic approach to security, in terms of what individuals in their communities need to feel safe and secure. This human security approach analyzes root causes of insecurities and maps local capacities that can redress these causes. This approach "is not only centred on people as objects of interventions, but also as providers of security in their own right, requiring their in-depth knowledge of the situation and context specific solutions" (FemLINK Pacific 2014: 5). This localization of peacebuilding facilitates community acceptance of necessary changes. FemLINK Pacific defines women's security in an all-encompassing manner to relate to all forms of violence that affect women's lives.

From 2006, Bhagwan Rolls was co-facilitator with the Pacific Islands Forum Secretariat, linking the Pacific PeaceWomen Project with women's organizations from Leitana Nehan Women's Development Agency of Bougainville, Ma'a Fafine mo e Famili of Tonga, Vois Blong Mere Solomon of Solomon Islands, and FemLINK Pacific of Fiji to promote regional awareness of UNSCR 1325. The networks enable women to develop links across faith boundaries and "challenge partisan actors' use of religion in ways that otherwise normalized racial tension and communal difference" (George and Doerksen 2016: 99). Faith plays a positive role in establishing these women's "'entitlement' to act as peacebuilders within communities afflicted by conflict" (George 2016: 380).

The Regional Action Plan on Women, Peace, and Security provides tangible strategies to enable effective participation of women leaders in the Pacific Forum Regional Security Committee. Bhagwan Rolls is Chair and Gender Liaison for the Global Partnership for the Prevention of Armed Conflict (GPPAC), a global civil society network of organizations working on conflict prevention and peacebuilding. The work within GPPAC "to articulate women's agency has not just claimed UNSCR 1325; it has transformed the resolution into a living document" (FemLINK Pacific 2014: 10). The policy for peace recommends that: "Building on the Pacific Conference of Churches' commitment to peacebuilding and conflict resolution, churches and faith-based leaders should explicitly support 1325 and include more women in decision-making positions, including through the development of curricula at theological colleges" (FemLINK Pacific 2014: 36). This is a powerful example of the argument being made throughout this book of the need for local women-of-faith to implement UNSCR 1325 through culturally acceptable strategies.

The Bougainville peace process provides an interesting comparison, with some overlaps with Fiji. The island of Bougainville off the coast of Papua New Guinea (PNG) was colonized under German control from 1899-1914 and then under control of the Australian government until 1975 when PNG gained independence. The first government school on Bougainville opened in 1960. Prior to this, the Catholic and Methodist churches provided all the education as well as health care and other services. The long-lasting influence of the missionaries to Bougainville from 1901 remains. The bulk of the population converted to Catholicism, the rest to mainly Methodism while continuing relationships with the local spirits. In Bougainville, Christianity is a cultural way of life for most people.

A struggle for independence erupted from 1989-1998 between the upper New Guinea security forces with the local militia and the Bougainville Revolutionary Army (BRA). Between 18,000-20,000 lives were lost (Saovana-Spriggs 2000: 58). In 1990, the PNG government withdrew services and imposed a blockade on the island, causing serious deficiencies of necessary services. During this political vacuum, particularly during 1990-1994, people turned to the churches for support and services. Each church had a women's group. The Arawa Peace Conference in 1994 saw women's groups, mainly church-based ones, come together with 25,000 attending (Tohiana 2006: 194). The Bougainville Inter-Church Women's Forum, led by Sister Lorraine Garasu, formed in 1995 to cater for the growing need for church women to meet. Women leaders Garasu, Ruby Miringka, Daphne Zale, Marilyn Havini, Helen Hakena and Agnes Titus, provided a spur for peace and reconciliation by forming prayer meetings and vigils, attending workshops, reconciliation ceremonies and peace marches, formulating peace action

plans, assisting people directly by dispensing basic provisions and leading bush health clinics, supporting NGOs involved in humanitarian
aid activities, conducting mediation training, and engaging in trauma
counselling (Tohiana 2006: 196). The Forum connected women from
the disparate groups across the island. Its contribution to broad-based
peacebuilding work is massive. Garusa states that women handled the
trauma of conflict better than the men because of their strong support
groups (in Howley 2002: 71).

Ruth Saovana-Spriggs cites the story of a woman who was educated
and trained by the Catholic mission and taught at the Catholic agri-
cultural centre before the civil war. She recounts how important it was
to "establish and nurture trust and honesty in the BRA, so that trust
and honesty would flow between us. One little move outside the rules
of the game could mean the end of our efforts, futile, and devastat-
ing outcome" (in Saovana-Spriggs 2000: 59). This woman, given the
pseudonym of Maria, talks of the complicated dynamics of building
trust, of trying to find the tiny opening that enables an opportunity for
negotiation. Maria says, "The young BRA men know we women are
important not only as landowners, but also as procreators and peacemakers. It finally dawned on them that the women are picking up the
bits and pieces from what they, the men, have destroyed" (in Saovana-
Spriggs 2000: 59). Brenda Tohiana writes of her own experience living
"life between two guns" (in 2006: 186) of the PNG Security Forces and
the BRA. Lives were constrained by curfews and blockades. In talking
with women, Dora told her that:

> Delegations of women, mothers, elder women, married women
> representing their districts went to talk to the authorities—they
> had to respect us—we explained that we wanted to deal with our
> own boys. We were committed to taking every opportunity to
> demand peace – to say -- you on the political side must talk. (in
> Tohiana 2006: 186)

Because of the civil war, the Leitana Nehan Women's Development Agency formed as an NGO in 1995, working in close consultation with groups like the Catholic Women's Association and Catholic Family Life, particularly in using non-violent approaches to combat violence. Their Strengthening Communities for Peace program seeks to build peace in communities by empowering women and youth as change agents. The women participated in political meetings, reminding the parties of the hardships suffered by ordinary people, and they appealed over the radio to BRA members to participate in the talks. Their role in mediating during the negotiations between the BRA and their allies was crucial to its eventual success. As Helen Hakena states, "when the boys came out of the bush they had to go and talk to the women, and the women would go and talk to the authorities" (in Tohiana 2006: 194). In June 2001, the province of Bougainville and the BRA signed an agreement with the Independent State of PNG for autonomy, officially ending a ten-year civil war over issues of culture, environment, land disputes, and the unjust distribution of wealth from the copper mine.

This section on informal peace processes shows how localized cultural and faith-based values influence women's peace advocacy and grant it acceptability and political credence. Women activists demonstrate resourcefulness in connecting indigenous, cultural, and religious knowledge about women's acceptable roles, to their activity in the broader processes of peacebuilding. There are implications for international players. Customary, faith-based institutions are strongly valued by local actors, and I suggest that this factor needs to be considered carefully when international actors are devising culturally relevant strategies to further women's peace and security, so that peacebuilding initiatives gain local acceptance and are sustainable.

Playing the Mother Card

In many of the examples of women-of-faith's activities in informal peace processes, women pull out of their pack the mother card, drawing explicitly on their socially esteemed role as mothers. How should this be understood? Can it be dismissed for simplistically assuming that all women are nurturing mothers? Clearly, they aren't. Not all women are biological mothers, but they may be nurturing women. Some men who aren't fathers are caring to others. Can one assume a feminine pacifism? Obviously not, because there are girls and women who choose to become combatants, or assert warlike aggression, behave in antagonistic cruel ways, or offer their body as a suicide bomber. How then can the mother card be understood, specifically within a feminist framework?

Sara Ruddick is a feminist theorist who explains that maternal thinking "is a discipline in attentive love" which emerges from the demands of a particular relationship of care, typically between a mother and her child (1989: 123). It can be argued also that this thinking emerges with all people engaged in attentive caring, so it includes nurturing mothers and fathers, or men and women in caring professions like health care, aid practitioners, educators, counsellors, or social welfare workers. Ruddick develops a politics of peace based around the moral orientation that emerges in "maternal thinking" and "preservative love" to reveal "a contradiction between mothering and war," in that mothering preserves life, whereas the military deliberately endangers "bodies, minds, and consciences in the name of victory and abstract causes" (1989: 123). What she shows are ways of thinking and cognitive capacities that emerge from the practices that are required in *attentive nurturance*, whether one is, or is not, a biological parent.

In determining whether women bring unique skills of attentive and preservative love to peacemaking, there is reliable evidence to show that women are more likely than men to be involved in grassroots movements, build coalitions across radical ethno-religious differences that are the cause of numerous conflicts, and be on the front lines of organizing humanitarian aid and practical assistance. Women seem to be more sensitive to *relational cues* than men, often have higher levels of empathy that they act on and have advanced nonverbal decoding skills. In dialogue with others, they are more likely to disclose firsthand experiences, which assists in developing meaningful relationships. Through this disclosure, they are more likely to deal with, rather than deny conflict, especially if the issues have emotional dimensions. Women are more likely to *develop and maintain networks that sustain communities.* These skills make women particularly helpful in the pre-negotiation and follow-up phases of building sustainable peace. This affirmation by no means justifies their exclusion in formal stages of negotiations. To the contrary, the preamble to UNSCR 1325 reaffirms the need for women's "equal participation and full involvement in all efforts for the maintenance and promotion of peace and security, and the need to increase their role in decision-making with regard to conflict prevention and resolution" (UNSC 2000). The contention I make is that women practice these *nurturing skills* irrespective of what stage of the peace process their skills develop. Telling and analyzing their stories is an important way to value women's contributions, made predominantly in Tracks two and three.

With these understandings in mind, it is prudent to examine some explicit examples where women draw on their mothering to claim special expertise in resolving conflict. The examples come from Bougainville, Palau, Solomon Islands, Nicaragua, Nigeria, Liberia, and Rwanda. The Bougainvillean women appealed directly for peace using protective language. The campaign they launched to bring home the young men who had taken up arms to fight for independence, called on the women's mothering instinct to nurture and protect human life, merging the pain they felt for the land with birthing pains. Helen Ikilai, a deputy headmistress in a community school tells how when the crisis started in 1990, the women gathered in a church to discuss the emergency and what to do. They met regularly for prayer, meditation, and discussion. Ikilai was abducted by the local BRA. In speaking to the young men in the army and the resistance, she told them that "we are your mothers," and when this was refuted, she replied, "we are all the mothers of all the people of Siwai. So, we are your mother too," to which there was no obvious answer, so the fighters were compelled to listen (in Howley 2002: 7). Reflecting on her experience, Ikilai acknowledges how much women did for peace and working with the chiefs on reconciliation, but sadly concludes that "now that we have peace, the voice of the women is not being heard" (in Howley 2002: 8).

Pat Howley, a Catholic priest who spent the times of 1975-1990 seeking to democratize schools in PNG, recounts a story told by Gloria Terikien, a social welfare officer, who when faced with a BRA soldier pointing a gun at her, asked him to imagine he was doing so to his mother, sister, or daughter, and said: "if you want to shoot me then go ahead. You cannot shoot a mother, or you would die of shame. We are all your mothers" (in Howley 2002: 10). He walked away. During this conflict, there were many appeals to motherhood. In 2000, Lucy Tsivora, a primary school teacher narrated the story of going to a soldier who was shouting at her, and she said to him:

> Before you shout at me and the other mothers, you must think. You must understand that we are the mothers. Maybe you think we did not care when you fought against the BRA and some of you died. We are mothers and when somebody from the BRA dies, we cry for them because we know that they have a mother at home. I do not like war. I stand up for peace. Now. You must understand you cannot talk to us like you did just now because you are my son too. (in Howley 2002: 163)

Howley explains the significance of the culturally esteemed role of mothers in providing for their families, by working in the garden, preparing food, looking after family members when they are sick, finding the money for school fees and clothes to wear, and the shame soldiers should feel when they do something which their mother doesn't approve. Chris Baria, a project trainer for Oxfam talks of the extraordinarily powerful role women played when they went into the bush to talk to the young men and says that "the mother has a position in the life of the young man, which goes back to his childhood and carries respect and authority, which they cannot ignore" (in Howley 2002: 164).

Elsewhere in the Pacific, Debbie Remengesav, former First Lady, Republic of Palau confirms that:

> Our roles as wives, as mothers, as neighbours and nurturers are actually where we can all take action in the peacebuilding process. In fact, there can be no global peace unless we are successful in achieving peace in our hearts, in our homes, and communities. (Remengesav 2011, np)

She confirms that Palauan culture, like other Pacific Island indigenous cultures, has traditionally been embodied by strong extended family relationships, a deeply embodied spirituality, and a system of traditional leaders and chiefs which provides the social foundation for governance and systems of justice. Within such a culture, women's roles as nurturers include their responsibility to convey good values to their children. Hence, it is unsurprising that women play a vital role as peacemakers in the home and community when conflicts arise. Remengesav states: "When men fight women have the ability to compromise, forgive, and to reconnect. When male leaders begin to go astray, it is often their mothers, wives, or sisters who have the power of love and moral persuasion needed to bring them back on track" (2011: np). However, caution is needed with over-generalizations about mothers' roles, a concern I analyze shortly.

The emphasis on women as mothers comes to the fore also in a statement made by Josephine Teakeni, Executive Director of Vois Blong Mere Solomons, a Network of People Building Peace in the Solomon Islands. In Suva, 2014, to highlight UNSCR 1325, Teakeni says that women "as mothers and women of our nations" are nurturing, and "naturally and traditionally peacemakers at home" and in communities;

"We are not only victims when there is a conflict, we are also part of the solution because of how we are," and that justifies the participation of women in all matters affecting their communal lives (in FemLINK Pacific 2014: 11).

In Latin America, María, coordinator for the Committee of Mothers of Heroes and Maters of the Revolution, Nicaragua, lost two of her sons who died fighting. When her husband asked her to choose between the revolution or him, she chose the revolution. She reflects that: "One gives birth with pain and raises them with love. We are all mothers. As the Christians that we are, we cannot support this hatred for another mother" (in Bennett et al. 1995: 215). Her rationale is that the hatred must be released to live a dignified peace and move closer to reconciliation.

In Nigeria, Esther Ibanga reflects on the work of women-of-faith, again reiterating "the voices of mothers as a force for moderation in families" (2015: np). In the campaign to rescue the schoolgirls who were kidnapped by Boko Haram in Chibok in 2014, she was part of an interfaith march to the governor's office in Jos to demand action. Working in poor, volatile neighbourhoods that are the breeding grounds for soldiers and young people who are prone to violence, she says: "We say to them: 'Think of us as your mothers.' No one else takes the time to engage with them, so they are receptive and open to changing their ways. That is how the cycle of violence is disrupted – one soul at a time" (Ibanga 2011: np).

Allison Prasch (2015) analyzes how Gbowee and the Liberia Mass Action for Peace activists, discussed above, relied on the cultural power of African motherhood. First, they "drew on their traditional maternal powers and framed the demand for peace as one motivated by the need to help their children" (2015: 188), that the real victims of war were Liberia's mothers and children, not the rebel warring factions. Second, they chastised Liberian sons for the destruction caused, "and threaten to enact what they saw as the most powerful curse available to African mothers: deliberate public nakedness" (2015: 188). Third, they constituted their Liberian sisters as political agents, capable of instilling change and demonstrating leadership. Prasch utilizes Karlyn Kohrs Campbell's definition of "rhetorical agency" as "the capacity to act, that is, to have the competence to speak or write in a way that will be recognized or heeded by others in one's community" (in Prasch 2015: 189). Prasch draws on the work of Nigerian feminist Oyeronke Oyewumi who stresses that motherhood is the cherished self-identity for most African women, but that this is not limited to one's biological children, but symbolically, extends to being mothers of the nation. As Prasch expresses it, "the women of Liberia – ordinary mothers, sisters, daughters, and grandmothers – succeeded not because of their political prowess or military might but because of their shared commitment to the children" (2015: 199).

In many cultures, including in the Rwandan culture, "women are culturally considered and trained to be peacemakers while males are trained for warfare and to be aggressive" (Mukansengimana-Nyirimana and Draper 2013: 3). Rose Mukansengimana-Nyirimana and Jonathan Draper stress the way that in Rwandan culture, it is assumed that women "are endowed with the capacity to restore broken relationships and create long-lasting friendships," and thus serve as bridge-builders between families, clans, neighbours, and tribes (2013: 3). However, these authors are mindful that these cultural norms, when set in a patriarchal society, do not allow women to reveal such qualities at a wider political level. Rwanda is in a unique position in having the highest percent of women in elected positions in its national parliament. Statistics from the Inter-Parliamentary Union, as of 1 October 2018, show 61.3 percent in the lower house and 38.5 percent in the upper house. This is not to understate the significance of women's role in communities in building social cohesion. It is rather to be wary of arguments that use women's socialized expectations of being nurturers as the sole basis for extending this role into the public sphere.

Peaceful Natures

What sense can we make of these global examples that link women-of-faith peacebuilders with mothering, broadly construed, when we apply a critical feminist lens? Can we conclude that all women have peaceful natures, and it is acceptable for them to operate predominantly in the family and in informal circles, or only in persuading combatants to engage in a ceasefire, but not be present in formal peace negotiations? I don't believe so.

In reflecting on women's engagement in peace processes in Bougainville, Hilary Charlesworth argues that:

> Women became engaged in peace activities not because of the peaceful natures but as a response to a desperate situation – almost a decade of conflict and displacement. The idea that women are somehow predisposed to be peaceful and are naturally gifted as peacebuilders presents a one-dimensional view of their lives. (2008: 357)

Yet this association of women with peaceable natures leads to a conundrum outlined by Judy El Bushra when she writes: "The problem is that women's role as mothers provides them with a platform on which to approach and appeal to powerful men, but it simultaneously undermines the desire to be taken seriously as political players" (2007: 140). What often happens is that women's active involvement in informal levels does not translate to serious contributions at the formal institutionalized levels, including peace negotiations, then as elected representatives. The requirements of UNSCR 1325 are stated as ideal principles, but usually are unrealized at the practical level. Research by UN Women (2016b) show that when women are included in formal peace processes, there is a "20 percent increase in the probability of an agreement lasting at least two years," and a "35 percent increase in the probability of an agreement lasting at least fifteen years."

Certainly, in multidimensional peace processes, women assist in breaking the trauma cycle. Their emotional skills make it possible for women to process traumatic memories and to empathize with others, even sometimes with "the enemy." Their relationship skills make them effective healers, and their role as caretakers and mothers make them gatekeepers for the next generation. But not all types of women's groups appeal to mothering. Also, there are different types of feminists: "pacifist or maternalist feminists who see women as peaceable;" or liberal feminists who support women's equality with men; and anti-militarist feminists who reject the stereotypes of women being naturally peaceful, and join with men, to oppose militarization (Pettman 1996: 107). Maternal imagery which draws on the protective instincts of women toward children and the vulnerable, and ways to intervene in undoing the gendering of violent masculinist behaviours in men, has its place, but caution is needed in slipping into narrow gender stereotypes.

While valuing all nurturing, I concur with Hilary Charlesworth when she explains why an emphasis on "the idea of women as peaceable... is a troubling development" (2008: 349). She suggests that in such thinking, there tends to be two main lines of defence. If women's special contribution is seen to come from feminine, womanly instincts, women's participation as active agents can be limited to traditional feminized tasks of nurture and mothering. On the other hand, arguments based on women's equality with men do not limit agency in the same way, although there is a danger of stressing "women's utility to peace" (2008: 350). Charlesworth draws attention to these tensions emerging in UNSCR 1325 when its preamble reaffirms "the important role of women in the prevention and resolution of conflicts and in peacebuilding" and emphasizes the importance of their "equal participation and full involvement" in promoting peace and security (UN Security Council 2000). Charlesworth's idea is that: "This language seems to suggest that women have a special role in conflict resolution and that this particularity should lead to their equality of participation in peacebuilding and conflict prevention" (2008: 350).

Charlesworth suggests further that an analysis of UN documents reveals four factors in a developing convention with respect to the WPS agenda. First, there is "an assumption that women are better than men at developing and sustaining peace" (2008: 351). Undoubtedly, this is problematic in assuming a centralizing naturalized female peacefulness that perpetuates stereotypical notions of nurture that run counter to an understanding of socialized femininity, or the prevalence of women combatants, or mothers who endorse their sons' hyper-masculinity. It doesn't address the need for male champions of protectiveness, and men showing attentiveness to the other, as well as a gentle nurture of those who are vulnerable.

Second, Charlesworth suggests that there is "a tendency to assert that women are more vulnerable than men" (2008: 351), and thus women and girls have special needs to safeguard. Of course, given that conflicts tend to affect women and girls differently than men and boys, a gender-sensitive approach to peacebuilding must recognize gender-differentiated requirements, and that gender-based violence is prevalent, with more women and girl victims. However, an overemphasis on vulnerability tends to exacerbate the notion that women and girls are passive, fragile beings requiring men's protection, thereby understating women's active agency. Some men too are victims of war, trauma, and loss, and thus also require attentive care, often by women.

Third, the emphasis on "the need to include women in formal peace negotiations" that emerges in the Beijing Platform for Action and UNSCR 1325 does not clarify its basis for inclusion (2008: 351). Does this mean that women have special skills in creating peace and in negotiating? If so, why are they largely absent from negotiating tables? If the inclusion of women is based on a natural affinity with peace, this reinforces stereotypes. A defence of equality underlies the urgency for women's inclusion.

Fourth, the persistent emphasis in UNSCR 1325 and the UN Peacebuilding Commission to integrate a "gender perspective" in peace negotiations refers to a slippage between sex and gender, so the perspective is reduced to considerations of women and girls. The challenge to aggressive masculinity and male domination in peace processes is omitted. Also, men's responsibilities to engage fruitfully and inclusively with women in building peace must be incorporated into gender perspectives.

Charlesworth's suggestion is for a need to alter the debate about women, war, and peace. First, she suggests that given the historical and current exclusion of women from decision-making on peace and security issues, there is a need "to revive an equality framework as the basis of the claim that women should be involved in conflict resolution and formal peacebuilding and to be more cautious about invoking the 'affinity' (or related 'utility') argument" (2008: 359). This contention is strong. Her point is that arguments made based on gender equality are less likely to restrict women's peacebuilding agency to traditional "women's work" (2008: 360). Her second suggestion is for the need to resist associating gender simply with women, but rather to take the impact of gender seriously in relation to how systems of meaning, expectations, and cultural practices affect notions of domination, force, and leadership.

In a context of gender equality, women-of-faith's peacebuilding agency expressed in the language of mothering can be valued without being reduced to essentialist norms, however, this agency should not be diminished to essentialist expectations of feminine nurture, but full, equal participation with men in decision-making is encouraged.

※ ※ ※

This chapter examines the role of women-in-faith in peace processes, broadly construed. The first section reiterates the paucity of women's participation in Track one processes, reinforcing that a much greater involvement is needed to realize the mandate of UNSCR 1325. Regional examples of involvement in informal peace processes show the importance of integrating faith into culturally appropriate strategies for furthering women's peace and security in ways that gain local acceptance. I contend that it is possible to frame security concerns of safety

and justice in ways that are compatible with cultural and religious beliefs. Next comes a critical scrutiny of women's reliance on their social
esteem as mothers, an extremely valuable role, but one that is usually
bound by restrictive social stereotypes that may limit participation in
the full range of decision-making on peace and security matters. I
argue instead that women are needed in all stages of peace processes
as intrinsic to gender equality; incorporating deep understanding of
local cultural beliefs; and challenging persistent male domination that
is needed to advance meaningful gender equality.

5

Women-of-faith Building Coalitions

Chapter five explores the challenges, priorities, and achievements of women-of-faith who labour across religious and faith differences to build workable coalitions that encourage peace and security. This work is never easy because these differences can be the source of, or major contributor to, violent conflict. The chapter contains four sections.

First, I explore the massive challenges in working across religious and faith differences. In conflict zones, these differences provoke antagonistic emotions or violent actions toward those who hold different viewpoints. I explain that women working in complex, multi-faith arenas tend to favour pragmatic solutions to problems, rather than dogmatic responses to correct doctrine.

Second, I demonstrate the importance of personal relationships to women-of-faith peacebuilders in developing alliances across faiths. I show that women-of-faith peacebuilders focus on solving down-to-earth dilemmas because of the priority they give to relationships, where a responsibility to care for those in need or who are suffering is a key guiding principle. In my view, this responsibility is a sign of the distinctiveness women-of-faith bring to their peacebuilding.

Third, by offering some examples of regional coalitions formed by women-of-faith peacebuilders, I show how women-of-faith, in forming coalitions across different beliefs, demonstrate great courage in beginning small grassroots organizations that sometimes grow into civil society movements. In doing so, they achieve many positive outcomes, thereby fulfilling peacebuilding objectives.

Fourth, I show that a significant challenge for many women-of-faith peacebuilders who work in coalitions, lies in opposing the rise of violent extremism that emerges with religious fundamentalisms and creates a fear of terrorism. But examples of what is being done by women-of-faith to overcome or minimize radicalization of youth, demonstrate women's actions as agents of transformative change in fostering pluralism.

Overall, I argue that the priorities for women-of-faith peacebuilders in working across faith differences tend not to focus on squabbles about who owns correct religious beliefs, but rather on finding *practical solutions for what is workable* in meeting fundamental needs. Again, this priority confirms the importance to women-of-faith in building *webs of relationships of people who can work in coalitions to build just peace.* The achievements of these coalitions across differences are considerable.

Pluralist Respect for Differences

Inter-religious Challenges

The answer to the question of how societies can respond to the opportunities and challenges raised by cultural, ethnic, linguistic, and religious differences is complex, and how to respond in ways that promote democracy, social justice, peace, and stability even more so. The literature on multicultural pluralism reinforces the need for people who share a common geographical space to "develop some agreement on rules of engagement that permits coexistence and promote justice"

(Kurtz 2012: 202). Yet what underlies this agreement and what happens when there is no agreement is not clear. Given the complexities of global politics, there is no universal sacred philosophy, but a variety of competing, ethical worldviews. Hence within a multicultural society, religious traditions need to ask how they can interact with others of different faiths and retain the integrity of their own faith.

Diane Eck, Director of the Pluralism Project at Harvard University, a project that has been running since 1991, explains the significance of the plurality of religious and cultural traditions in four ways. First, Eck (nd) explains that religious diversity is prevalent, but without meaningful relationships and encounters with those holding different beliefs, tensions are inevitable. This is because "pluralism is not diversity alone, but *the energetic engagement with diversity.*" This diversity is with different faith traditions, differences within these traditions, and differences between individuals within the traditions (Beckford 2014). Second, Eck (nd) clarifies that "pluralism is not just tolerance, but *the active seeking of understanding across lines of difference,*" by which she means that tolerance is a thin virtue, it does not require religious believers to know much about each other's differences. Indeed, we can remain ignorant about others and believe in stereotypes, but still claim tolerance to difference. Third, she maintains that "pluralism is not relativism, but *the encounter of commitments....* It means holding our deepest differences, even our religious differences, not in isolation, but in relationship to one another." Pluralism is demanding. Fourth, "pluralism is *based on dialogue.* The language of pluralism is that of dialogue and encounter, give and take, criticism and self-criticism. Dialogue means both speaking and listening, and that process reveals both common understandings and real differences." Dialogue does not assume agreement, but that there is a commitment to engagement. Pluralism requires the nurturance of constructive dialogue where both common understandings and real differences are acknowledged.

Religious pluralism includes the everyday relational interactions between individuals and groups. Debates about religious pluralism are part of broader discussions around identity and difference. Respect for religious difference lies at the core of pluralism. Yet "even seeing differences is not a simple task. It is often difficult for people to grasp different ways of being religious, and much more difficult to grant the full dignity and integrity of those who are religiously 'Other'" (Welch 2012: 357).

This discussion of religious pluralism has presumed the tolerance for difference that ideally exists within the multicultural West. Within war contexts, or in the post-war period, particularly where ethno-religious differences dominate, there can be no presumption of tolerance of diversity, let alone acceptance of pluralism. Hence the discussion from now assumes the animosity to differences that exists in conflict zones and lingers in post-war societies.

Pragmatism Over Doctrine

Can women of different faiths who come together for practical reasons to solve a specific problem avoid squabbling over dogma and scriptural differences? Of course, this isn't always possible, particularly in highly traditional societies or where fundamentalism reigns. But, at grassroots levels, as examples demonstrate later, women labour together on practical issues, whatever beliefs they hold. I suggest that issue-based faith alliances are particularly workable because they arise through being motivated to mutually resolve a solution to immediate or long-term problems. In such a context, determining the exact interpretation of different scriptures is less immediately relevant than finding food, water, shelter, health care, or supporting victims of violence. Hence "for interfaith dialogue, it may be useful to take *practices* rather than *doctrines* as a starting point for our conversations" (Jones 2012: 42).

Such a pluralist respect for differences confirms a practical "theology of pluralism" directed toward major ethical questions on inequalities, injustices, hunger, and lack of respect for differences (López 2012: 174). This theology, aimed at "practices that heal, transform, and enliven," is utilized "in the interest of justice for all" (Welch 2012: 363). As Sharon Welch expresses it, "We need practices that can enable us to bear rage, pain, and loss, and that open our minds to that which is fitting, beautiful, and audacious" (2012: 366). For example, in the face of disasters, often local faith communities are the first to respond to humanitarian emergencies. In 2012, the United Nations High Commissioner for Refugees (UNHCR) held its first formal multi-faith dialogue on the common values underpinning refugee protection in the world's major religions. Interestingly, "faith-based organizations have consistently been among UNHCR's top ten implementing partners" (Türk et al. 2014: 8).

As examples demonstrate below, *women-of-faith reach across ethnic, political, and religious divides in conflict zones, engaging in cross-boundary work to build bridges across communities.* "Often motivated by their own experiences of gender-based marginalization and oppression, women in these initiatives struggle over what it means to be a 'good' Christian, Muslim, Tamil, Marxist, and so on" (Hayward 2015: 315). The relationships built in this work deepen interpersonal connections that can draw on a range of experiences and thus lead to transformative possibilities, including advocacy work that influences decision-making to advance peace.

Webs of Relationships

Sometimes women organize within their own ethnic and religious groups. Other times, diverse groups of women come together simply to meet a concrete material need, or the joint yearning for fighting to cease. The reason why this is possible is that there is substantial evidence of the priority many women give to developing and sustaining relationships regardless of different beliefs. On first meeting, talk of family and personal issues tends to come before talking about politics, ideology, or theology. This emphasis on the primacy of relationships helps women who interact with those from vastly different ethnic and faith backgrounds to overcome many of the challenges that stay visible when stark differences are perceived as necessarily antagonistic. The reality of the differences remains, and tensions may be evident, but they aren't permitted to remain a stumbling block, despite often proving to be a major obstacle in the initial stages of getting to know each other. I maintain that the shared experiences of family and community life tends to be the starting point for consolidating constructive relationships.

Fiona Robinson argues that this valued relationality goes beyond simply saying that we are social beings, to the claim that both dependency and interdependence are fundamental features of being human (2011: 4). A feminist relational view of agency sees the complexity of everyday situated lives within *webs of interdependent relationships* as the foundation for reflection. For example, a group in Chicago, called Fierce Women of Faith is an interfaith group of women and allies who are working to bring peace in families and communities. They grasp the opportunities to work for change in their experiences as mothers, daughters, sisters, wives, aunts, surrogate mothers, mentors, and mentees. Mary Grey explains the defining features of a relational theology as "the ideas of mutuality, connection, compassion, wisdom, relation, and relational justice" (2010: 87) that binds these women.

The remainder of this chapter assumes that the examples of women-of-faith peacebuilders who build coalitions across difference, particularly in interfaith work, incorporate (either consciously or unconsciously through patterns of learnt gender socialization) these *relational ideas and practices*. The application is in war or post-war contexts. To clarify, there are significant organizations in the West like the United Methodist Women which has peace-related programs across Africa, Asia/Pacific, Europe, Latin America and the Caribbean, and the Middle East, with a membership of twenty-five million women and girls. Their message is that peace and just development counter unjust development and violent conflict. Where possible, I discuss small, informal coalitions that form outside of the West and from grassroots activism.

The claim I make in this second section is that women's commitment and capacity to connect across religious, political, and ethnic divides in conflict zones depends largely on their ability to *build interpersonal relationships* that create broad-based movements and communities for peace. The relationships allow women to probe "the national, ethnic, religious, and political identities that fuel conflict, without ignoring – and perhaps by engaging – the legitimate underlying concerns of particular communities" (Hayward and Marshall 2015: 20). One example these authors use is Visaka Dharmadasa's movement in Sri Lanka, the Association for War Affected Women that brings together women from both sides of the conflict who lost husbands and sons during the Civil War, to work together to end the violence.

Women Developing Alliances

Scholarly work on understanding how women-of-faith develop alliances across differences is needed. I agree with María Pilar Aquino that "the mechanisms for globalizing a feminist religious vision of justice through an explicit coalitional politics have not yet been fully developed" (2012: 435). In Aquino's view, coalition-building on local, national, regional, and global levels allows relationships to be fostered within newly developed organizations that are committed to bringing about alternative societal models.

Understanding the process of *coalition-building* is useful. Cynthia Cockburn's (2004, 1998) writings on coalitions across difference remain influential in feminist analyses of peace and war. Cockburn maintains that "the making and maintaining of working alliances across differences depend more than anything else on the capacity to step into another person's shoes and see the world from her position" (2004: 186 –187). In conflict societies, sharing stories is a typical starting point for women to build trust between former antagonists as both sides begin to realize that there is common ground in mutual pain and suffering.

Cockburn's work (1998) provides useful examples of building trust across risky politics. She stayed with women in three organizations: the Women's Support Network in Belfast, which represents women's community centres from both Catholic and Protestant areas and focuses on poverty and peace; Bat Shalom, an alliance of Israeli Jewish and Palestinian Arab women which focuses on a peaceful settlement to the Middle East, including an end to the occupied Palestinian territories; and the Medica Women's Therapy Centre in Zenica, central Bosnia-Herzegovina (BiH), a project established by German and Muslim, Serb, and Croat women to respond to the needs of those traumatized by rape and bereavement. Cockburn identifies similarities in the three groups in being women-only, with a conscious blend of ethnicity, nationality, and religion: "alliances holding together differences whose negotiation is never complete and is not expected to be so" (1998: 14).

Cockburn identifies six identity processes that are common to each group. First, they affirm differences in a positive way. Second, rather than essentializing or supposing inevitabilities, they attempt towards a "non-closure of identity" (Cockburn 1998: 225) which allows for varieties of self-expression. Third, the groups found ways to reduce mainstream polarities by incorporating other differences, such as including Chinese youth in a Belfast program. Fourth, there is "an acknowledgement of injustices done in the name of differentiated identities" (1998: 226), that societies founded on shocking wounds must face up to the realities of layers of oppression. Fifth, care is taken to identify issues with which all felt mutually safe. Sixth, group processes gave equal weight to all voices and shared decision-making is important. Cockburn concludes that the crux of risky alliances is "*a creative structuring of a relational space between collectivities marked by problematic differences*" (1998: 211). The degrees of trust built over time fluctuate and come through continuing, meaningful dialogue across differences. I believe that this notion of a relational space is useful. It is creative, flexible, can be visualized and revisualized, and it rejects oppositional extremes.

During 1999 to 2000, Cockburn worked with seven women's organizations in BiH, and writes that "women saw women as the best hope for integrative working in these divided and embittered towns. ... The impulse to rethink enmity and recover friendships seemed to wake in women before men" (2002: 76). Cockburn also worked with women across the Green Line partitions throughout the Republic of Cyprus and the Turkish Republic of Northern Cyprus. The line was open for the first time for twenty-nine years on 21 April 2003. Cockburn uses the idea of the line as a symbol of the composition of difference and "otherness." She asks: "What is implied in the way we draw our lines, for inclusion and exclusion, closeness and distance, love and hate" (2004: 24)? Cockburn advises against the drawing of a line by dominant identity groups. Rather, she talks of the strengths of being able to traverse imaginatively into others' positions, encouraging groups "to forge alliances of differently-identified groups resisting racism, fundamentalism, nationalism, and war" (2004: 38). Cockburn witnessed a "Hands Across the Divide" project that demonstrates a successful dialogue across difficult differences where participants understand plurality of relational spaces.

In another context, Andrea Blanch and Elana Rozenman (2008), write about a workshop organized by the Center for Religious Tolerance, held in Amman, Jordan, with Jewish, Christian, and Muslim women from Egypt, Israel, Jordan, Palestine, and the US. Challenges are great in such ventures where participation is personally risky, with a third of the women asking to be de-identified. Blanch and Rozenman formulate eight principles for women's interfaith peacebuilding. First, building trust is crucial because many women feel vulnerable and anxious in a mixed group. Second, once trust has begun, exploring religious identity increases understanding between participants in noting similarities and differences. Third, the process of acknowledging how all religions contribute to both intolerance and to tolerance is challenging in confronting negativity, cultural restrictions, and misunderstandings, but it encourages shared learning. Fourth, an international mix of participants requires attention to different political situations, religions, and cultural dynamics. Fifth, "maintaining a balance of power between the religions" is critical (Blanch and Rozenman 2008: 6) to avoid domination and powerlessness. Sixth, deep work on personal and group identity takes time and commitment. Seventh, there is a lack of resources to support local action. Eighth, women's interfaith work needs to expand to reach women in business, education, government, industry, and the professions. Women at this workshop who held significant positions in government and civil society, claimed they "had never had the opportunity to engage in an interfaith experience before, and were struck by the power of this model to break down barriers" (2008: 6). These eight principles seem broadly applicable in different contexts.

Jacqueline Ogega and Katherine Marshall (2015: 283-284) map transnational organizations that support women who are involved in interfaith peacebuilding. They conclude that this work creates opportunities for women to sidestep denominational and traditional patterns of patriarchy to build networks of support. This can include prizes and scholarships, such as those given by the Tanenbaum organization which works to combat religious prejudice and presents awards to "Peacemakers in Action" who are driven by their religious beliefs to make a difference. The take-away message in this first section is that giving priority to *building relationships*, women-of-faith frequently accept the *responsibility to care* for victims and eliminate suffering, and this shared commitment binds women within coalitions across differences.

Coalitions Across Differences

I focus now on the emergence of grassroots coalitions of differing types of women-of-faith peacebuilders, but it is pertinent to begin this section by briefly outlining some of the key large inter-faith international organizations to set the global scene. Geuskens et al. (2010: 56-68) outline an international directory of organizations specifically working for faith-based peacebuilding and gender justice. For example, the World

Council of Churches is the broadest, most inclusive ecumenical organization, operating in more than 110 countries, representing over 500
million Christians. From 1953, their Women in Church and Society
program began by stating that after World War 11, a dignified life
was only possible if women were actively involved in every initiative
of justice and peace by churches in society. These organizations have
differing purposes to deepen relationships; improve understanding;
find common ground; promote common action; and encourage com-
plementary action (Gopin 2010: 339). For example, the Council for a
Parliament of the World's Religions (CPWR), was originally organized
in 1893 in Chicago and reconvened in 1988 as a major forum of
interreligious dialogue. A CPWR document "Towards a Global Ethic:
An Initial Declaration" speaks of the ethical common ground shared by
the world's religions, committed to nonviolence (Groody 2007). What
is interesting to note is that the largest women's organizations work
through smaller, interreligious, and interfaith collaborations.

Ecumenical Women is an international coalition of church denominations and ecumenical organizations. It has standing with the United
Nations Economic and Social Council. The coalition is grounded in
faith and a commitment to global justice, training, and empowering
women to advocate for gender equality at the UN. Their understanding
of advocacy is that whilst it is "rooted in faith and is people-centred,
it does not start in the corridors of power but with people at the local
level, and with their daily struggle for life, rights, equality, and justice"
(Bordeau et al. 2008: 38). As a contribution to the Beijing Platform for
Action, the message of Ecumenical Women spoke to "the positive and
negative role religion can play in women's lives" (Bordeau et al. 2008:
17). Keeping these dual roles in mind is important in comprehending
religious constraints, but not dismissing religion as entirely patriarchal
and repressive.

The need to bridge secular and faith-based concerns, keeps crop-
ping up in the literature. Women-of-faith often feel that the WPS
agenda is anti-religion, and that WPS activists have not reached out
enough to listen to voices of women fighting for women's rights from

a position of faith. I say that social justice movements need both voices. Fulata Lusungu Moyo, a national from Malawi, suggests that a crucial requirement in bridging secular and faith-based matters is to "challenge existing social, economic, and religious systems that encourage gender inequity" by using gender analysis to interrogate religious beliefs, and to "read sacred scripture with gender justice lenses using hermeneutics of suspicion" (in Bordeau et.al. 2008: 51). This is when someone does not take religious scriptures at face value as literal truth, but questions their accuracy and historical input, as women-of-faith do.

Through more than fifty Inter-Religious Councils spread across regions in Africa, Asia, Europe, Latin America and the Caribbean, Middle East, North America, and the Pacific in more than ninety countries, Religions for Peace, founded in 1970, is the largest international coalition of representatives from the world's religions. This organization mobilizes religious communities to work together to prevent violent conflict and to rebuild peaceful societies. The leadership of women-of-faith often emerges, as already noted, because women are viewed as nonthreatening and able to articulate the needs of vulnerable people. In a woman from Sierra Leone's voice:

> We women-of-faith were able to gain access to the rebel leaders because we were seen as "doing God's work" and untainted by the politics and posturing of the war. The soldiers told us that we reminded them of their mothers (and their families), whom they had not seen in a long while, due to the war. (in Oliver, et al. 2004: 8)

This woman was attached to a group that was able to negotiate the release of fifty-two child soldiers in 1997. Religions for Peace taps into local women's capacities for leadership and effective action in a range of peacebuilding areas, such as conflict transformation, disarmament, rights, peace education, and economic development. Their Women's Mobilization Program began in 1998 to promote the role of religious women in peacebuilding and post-conflict reconstruction.

In seeking to achieve two aims to mainstream women-of-faith into all their programs, and to ensure that women's perspectives are included into planning, implementation, and evaluation, the program realized it must systematically document and evaluate women's faith groups.

Hence, in 2001, the Women's Mobilization program launched the Global Women of Faith Network, advancing women-of-faith as agents of conflict transformation. It is drawn from Baha'i, Buddhist, Christian, Hindu, Indigenous, Jain, Jewish, Muslim, Sikh, Shinto, Taoist, and Zoroastrian groups, all with a shared vision to build just, peaceful societies. The network "increases the visibility of religious women as powerful agents of change" (Religions for Peace 2009: 5). In 2009, it has thirty national networks, with five regional networks in five continents with more than one-thousand religious women's organizations. In Africa, it works on transforming conflict in building peace, plus elimination of poverty, conflict, and HIV/AIDS. In Europe, its focus is on social justice, peace, and an inclusive Europe. In Latin America, the emphasis is on developing unity, solidarity, equity, and reciprocity. In Asia, multi-religious networking is the goal. In North America, it seeks to advance justice and build peace. Consistent with broad understandings of human security and peacebuilding, women-of-faith work on diverse issues from climate change to local trauma healing, poverty, trafficking, and HIV/AIDS.

Jacqueline Ogega, Director of the Women's Mobilization program, writes that these networks of women-of-faith "offer a unique space where women with a stillness of heart, reflect on their work and create linkages with other organizations" in demonstrating leadership to promote just societies (in Religions for Peace 2009: 2). Ogega expresses a question guiding the program, asking what engagement for peace, gender equality, and women's empowerment means for religious leadership, given that "women bear the disproportionate burden of poverty, violence, and disease" (in Religions for Peace 2009: 2). This question relates to the reconstruction pillar in UNSCR 1325. Note eight calls on member states to heed "the special needs of women and girls during repatriation and settlement and for rehabilitation, reintegration and post-conflict reconstruction" (UNSC 2000).

These large organizations show key interreligious challenges and collaborations women are engaged in across faith boundaries. I have explained that what helps the women face such encounters with radical difference is a commitment to relationships, and what follows, that is, the responsibilities assumed in caring for others. I believe that this *relationality* is a key factor in determining the uniqueness about women's involvement in interfaith, interreligious, or ecumenical collaborations. Examples that highlight this uniqueness now follows.

Regional Coalitions

Select examples of coalitions from different geographic regions show how in adopting a plural respect for differences, women-of-faith accept the responsibilities of care to seek pragmatic solutions to problems of insecurity. Rather than simply documenting what they do, my interest is in showing *what women do differently.* I give priority in my choices not simply to faith-based organizations, but to smaller groups that seek to break down antagonistic notions of the "other," and particularly those that work with different faiths. The Global Peace Initiative stress what they call "feminine values" of cooperation, inclusivity, and connection, and work in "receptive, responsive, and ever-evolving ways." While it is reasonable to question whether these values are intrinsically feminine and exclusively practised by women, or if they emerge through socialized patterns, they certainly are essential values for women-of-faith peacebuilders' practices of relationality. Men involved in peacebuilding can develop nurturant dispositions, but generally they are not as obvious or common.

The Global Peace Initiative for Women is an Asian organization founded to provide faith leaders with a forum to engage in causes for social transformation, and to provide women with strategic networks. Co-Chair, Buddhist nun Venerable Mae Chee Sansanee of Thailand, leads interfaith dialogue in conflict zones around the world, seeking to break cycles of violence. She directs a retreat centre that provides support to victims of domestic violence, unwed mothers, and prisoners. When conflict broke out in southern Thailand between Buddhists and Muslims, "Mae Chee led a peace walk in the south and reached out to Muslim women, bringing them to her retreat centre to build relationships with Buddhist women" (Hayward 2015: 313).

In Latin America, there are many examples of interfaith coalitions. In Honduras, Catholic nuns from the Sisters of Mercy order have been at the forefront of advocacy movements since the 2009 coup, using religious ritual and song as central components of their public protests. In Colombia, where 97 percent of the population identify as Christian, The Ecumenical Women's Peacebuilding Group (or as they are known in Spanish, GemPaz), engages in peacebuilding as women believers, by starting with the personal, that is, inner beliefs and faith practices. The impetus for the group is the call that they believe their faith makes: to live in harmony with one another and to work for the greater good. Virginia Bouvier, one of the founders of this group, reflects on the way that many "women have discovered a unique spirituality to be found with peacebuilding and also resignifying what it means to be a woman seeking peace" (in Vogt 2015), as distinct from a man's search for peace. The search often overlaps, but sometimes there are differences in how men and women typically proceed. As Bouvier remembers after initial exploratory meetings, "we realized that there was a certain resistance among the church hierarchies, who were all men. So, we decided to try something with the women" (in Vogt 2015). Monica Velásquez, an original member and leader, says that the "group is a healing and liberating space. For the women of GemPaz, this has been a transforming experience, in the area of faith but also politically and ethically" (in Vogt 2015). Women are daily seeking change, whether demanding the return of a captured child, or organizing with others to advocate for the participation of women in Colombia's truth commission, or advocating against corporate powers that profit from war.

Examples from the Balkans are enlightening. In 2003, the organization Religions for Peace, outlined above, facilitated training of women
from Islamic, Orthodox, Catholic, and Jewish communities of Kosovo
to come together for the first time since the end of the Balkan conflicts.
The women shared their stories of pain and loss. "The story-telling
broke down many of the barriers caused by the war, as women saw their
own experiences mirrored in those of former 'enemies,'" bringing the
women closer together, thereby strengthening their effective networks
(Oliver et al. 2004: 17). In a follow-up project, the Kosovo Women's
Working Group assembled a multi-religious delegation of women to
learn from each other's communities. The Islamic community hosted a
gathering for Bajram, the Islamic feast of Eid, the Catholic community
hosted a Christmas celebration in December, with the Orthodox community celebrating Christmas in January. There is nothing surprising
about these events. However, for most of the women, it "was the first
time they had been inside other religions' houses of worship since the
conflict ended. These gatherings broke down barriers of fear and mis-
understanding and engendered planning for joint projects" (Oliver et
al. 2004: 17).

Žene Ženama (Women to Women) BiH, develops women's capacities. This organization is led by Muslim women, "and advocates for integrating the good principles of all four religious' traditions of Bosnian
society (Orthodoxy, Catholicism, and Judaism, as well as Islam) into
its approach of peacebuilding as a factor for empowerment of people"
(Bouta, Kadayifci-Orellana, and Abu-Nimer 2005: 127). Their activities include capacity-building on themes of gender, peace, and security,
psychosocial assistance, and trust-building, in local communities and
across borders.

Carolyn Boyd Tomasovic, Managing Director of the Ecumenical
Women's Initiative, a Croatian-based NGO that is active in BiH,
Croatia, Kosovo, Macedonia, Montenegro, and Serbia, confirms that:
"Not enough bridges exist between faith-based and secular groups - a
separation that women find to be a significant obstacle in their work"
(in Gueskens et al. 2010: 25). This following quote exemplifies what

I am demonstrating. In working with women believers, Tomasovic states that:

> Without exception, all the women theologians with whom we have worked have had to fall on NGOs in order to create alternative spaces in which they are free to address issues that represent the core values of their faith: peace, nonviolence, justice, human rights, and equality. (in Gueskens et al. 2010: 25)

In many places, it is difficult for women's voices to be heard outside of grassroots spaces or established NGOs.

One story Tomasovic tells is a straightforward practical act where a Muslim woman called Muradija Sehu supported a Serb woman whose father had been murdered by Kosovo Albanians. This woman wanted to reclaim her life and walked to the Albanian part of the town where Muradija and other Kosovo Albanian women joined her to form a ring of protection, which tentatively began a process of healing through establishing trust and mutual understanding. In another instance, Amra Pandzo, a Muslim woman, felt that the children weren't being taught to discuss their faith and respect others' religious beliefs, which was reinforcing existing sectarianism. She worked with Christian and Muslim theologians to create a teaching manual that promotes religious tolerance. The head of the Islamic community gave her permission to use the manual, and by 2010, this was being used in "ninety-one schools in the city" of Sarajevo (in Gueskens et al. 2010: 26). In a similar story, a group of women teachers from schools in Bosnia worked in the segregated state schooling, where Muslim Bosnjaks and Catholic Bosnian Croats were educated separately in different shifts in the same school building. These teachers created a manual for secondary schools that allows the pupils to be informed about the different religions in the hope of eventually dismantling segregated schooling.

Zilka Spahić-Šiljak writes of how, despite the destructiveness of the war in BiH, the life stories of many "women disclose the power of humanity fuelled by faith in kindness, love, and God" (2014: xii).

By humanity, she refers to the ability to "heal, connect, and humanize others" (2014: xiv). These attributes define the uniqueness of women-of-faith's contribution. They prompt activities that give voice to the voiceless, help those in need, and provide safe spaces for women to tell their stories. Spahić-Šiljak is motivated to tell "a story of humaneness, heroism, compassion, friendship, respect, peace, and reconciliation" (2014: xv). She argues that narrating and listening to stories is "a political act" (2014: xx), given the choices people make. She had eleven in-depth interviews with women peacebuilders and clarifies that women's peace activism was not always motivated by religion, because for some women, socialist ethics of equality, or feminist ethics of justice and compassion were driving forces. However, the role of *relationships* is crucial for all the women Spahić-Šiljak interviewed, both in rebuilding broken relationships and in creating new ones, confirming my central claim on *relationality* as being intrinsic to the unique contribution that women-of-faith make. A summary of four of those stories follows.

Sabiha Husić, a traditional Bosniac Muslim, worked with Spahić-Šiljak in Medica Zenica on creating supporting networks for witnesses to wartime rape, and they used religion in the healing process. Spahić-Šiljak writes:

> My colleagues and I were deeply enmeshed in the pain, suffering, and trauma that these women brought to us. Their words were our words, and our deeply intimate, shared pain fuelled our desire to hasten the healing process. Out of these shared moments of suffering, feminist theology was born. (2014: 19)

For example, the organization were thoughtful when a child was born from rape, creating a loving ritual of a naming ceremony to connect the child with God, a practice which is outside of the Islamic tradition where men typically conduct the naming ritual. In Medica Zenica, the baby is passed around in this all-woman ceremony, which often changed the view of grandmothers who were loath to accept the child born from these circumstances. Husić says: "I live my faith in everything I do in my life. For me, that is what faith is" (in Spahić-Šiljak 2014: 28). Faith is demonstrated through practical acts of compassion and humanizing others.

Danka Zelić, a practising Catholic, formed the Women Citizens Association to assist returnees. She writes that "the notion of peace work to me represents a big bubble filled with many smaller bubbles. ... All the smaller bubbles consist of people who deserve the care of others. That, for me, is peace work" (in Spahić-Šiljak 2014: 40). Again, this emphasis confirms my central claim that *women-of-faith build relationships*, and then accept the *responsibility to care* for those in need, which logically follows. Zelić explains that to her, peacebuilding reinforces the practical message that it "means that I reconciled two neighbours who will continue living together and supporting each other, and their children will use the same bus to go to school. Peacebuilding means that for me" (in Spahić-Šiljak 2014: 42). Zelić works in a remote part of BiH on everyday concerns that returnees and displaced persons need, such as the provision of blankets and bedding, water installations, and pensions. Spahić-Šiljak writes that "Danka's sense of compassion came from the moral obligation she felt to stand for the justice and dignity of people outside her Croatian ethnic group" (2014: 53). Her understanding of faith is that it should be reflected in caring deeds.

Nada Golubović, a Catholic Croatian, began an NGO called United Women, Banja Luka, working on destroyed relationships and broken homes. Her peacebuilding orientation is influenced by "reconnecting people for the sake of reconciliation, fighting against domestic violence, and promoting women's political engagement" (Spahić-Šiljak 2014: 143). She works to politically empower women. Amra Pandžo was born into a secular Bosniac Muslim family and her marriage to a Serb was seen as outrageous. She uses religion as a platform for her peace work, building coalitions "through fostering confidence, opening dialogue between unreconciled viewpoints, and enabling different stories to be heard" (2014: 293).

All these stories reveal more of what is unique about women-of-faith peacebuilders. They include *forming networks that respond directly to people's experiences; compassionate responses to individual needs; and building positive relationships across differences.*

In the Middle East, Tawakkul Karman, sometimes called "the mother of the Yemeni revolution" and "the Queen of peace," is a journalist, human rights activist, and member of the Islamist party al-Islah. She founded Women Journalists Without Borders to defend the freedom of information and the role of the free press. During the 2011 uprising in Yemen, her leadership was recognized as she organized weekly sit-ins and lead rallies against unjust, policies. She was awarded the Nobel Prize in 2011. Asmaa Mahfouz played a similar role in Egypt's historic 2011 demonstrations in Egypt. Through employing social media, she helped to mobilize the movement that overthrew President Hosni Mubarak. Further examples of women's peace organizations in the Middle East are provided in section four below.

Exceptional individuals often spearhead the development of coalitions. Alaa Murabit moved from Canada as a fifteen-year-old to Libya and trained as physician. In her work to "amplify the voices of women," and to emphasize their experiences and participation in peace processes and conflict resolution, she recognizes "that the only way to ensure the full participation of women globally is by reclaiming religion" (2015a: np). As a young Muslim woman, proud of her faith, she discovered more of the religiously prohibited and culturally inappropriate aspects of her faith whist in Libya. When the Libyan revolution broke out in 2011, she began The Voice of Libyan Women organization that pushes for inclusive peace processes and conflict mediation. The organization redefines the role of women in society by using religious discourse to positively reinforce women's rights, roles, and participation, and to focus on challenging the socio-cultural values. Murabit uses the scriptures to call on verses that refer to healthy family relationships, encouraging the local community imams to promote the rights of women, including taboo topics like domestic violence (2015a: np). In providing an alternative narrative, she contends "that women's rights and religion are not mutually exclusive," but that women's presence at the table is essential. Murabit rightly reminds us of the contradiction of many conflicts that claim to be a fight for women's rights, and yet "fight extremism with bombs and warfare," thereby crippling local societies (2015a: np).

Murabit argues that religion and culture interconnect, thereby affecting the human rights of women and girls. Noting the argument that I repeatedly make, that religion's impact on culture is rarely considered in international efforts to achieve gender equality, Murabit reminds us that the undermining of gender equality is an early warning sign of extremism. She maintains that the purported religious basis of extremism should be challenged, because "the misinterpretation and misrepresentation of religion is used as a political instrument of hate and fear, propelling hostilities rather than diffusing them" (2015a: np), such as in the Indo-Pakistan war and the ongoing Palestinian-Israeli conflict. Murabit argues that it is possible to challenge the negativity of individuals and institutions that use religion as a method of oppression and fear, and instead, to support religion as a source of tolerance and understanding.

Initially, Murabit's organization promoted international human rights standards and conventions, then it shifted focus, seeking "to dispel dangerous cultural stereotypes and norms that have been misappropriated as religious law, and perpetuated by ignorance" (2015a: np). The organization does this through illustrating the historical role of Muslim women as economic, political, and social thought leaders. Thus, they use religion as a tool to fight for women's human rights in Libya. Murabit defends the idea that despite the terrible injustices that have occurred with religion's manipulation of history in the name of seizure of land and wealth, or the atrocities that occur in so-called religious wars, there are positive elements to claim. She believes that it is only through understanding ways in which religious extremists engineer beliefs that one can challenge them. Faith can then be a foundation for empowerment.

In Africa, there is vast variation between different regions in terms of the nature, impact, and effectiveness of women's movements. Not all movements champion gender equality. "Instead, they may have sought to protect women's roles of mothering and care-giving in traditional African societies. This may not always be empowering" (Gouws 2015). There are organizations that work within one faith, such as the Federation of Muslim Women Association of Ghana, working on reproductive health, capacity-building, and eliminating gender-based violence, but the focus of this chapter is on groups that are working across faiths.

Catholic Sister Marie-Bernard Alima of the DRC is the first woman to serve as the General Secretary of the DRC Episcopal Commission for Justice and Peace, in a country where half the population is Catholic (Hayward 2015: 313). In 2001, she created a civil society network called the Coordination of Women for Democracy and Peace. The group trains and supports women peace leaders. The network provides leadership in human rights, transitional justice, and increasing women's participation in the political sphere, as well as in combating sexual-based violence.

In Togo, the members of the National Commission of Justice and Peace recognize the need to collaborate with traditional authorities around the status of rural women which "deprive them of family heritage and inheritance by the traditional chiefs, in the case of the death of their spouses" (Rogers et al. 2008: 69). I have argued repeatedly, that gaining the trust of traditional leaders, including faith-based leaders, can open the way for consideration of how local communities can accept women's rights. About seventy rural women were chosen from the seven dioceses of Togo to be trained by an organization called Women's Group for Development and Democracy which specialize in the training of paralegal workers who foster women's awareness of their rights, and their role in promoting peace in grassroots communities. The women's roles include teaching "messages of forgiveness, acceptance of others, tolerance, and compassion" (Rogers et al. 2008: 67)

In Uganda, the Acholi Religious Leaders Peace Initiative (ARLPI) is an interfaith organization which brings together the religious leaders from Muslim, Anglican, Catholic, and Orthodox faiths, together with their constituencies, to participate effectively in transforming conflict. ARLPI works to engage interfaith communities to contribute proactively to bring peace in Acholiland. It acts as a springboard for mediation and advocacy regarding the situation in northern Uganda at national and international levels. The group uses an inclusive approach in its peace activities of dialogue, mediation, peace education, experience sharing during exchange visits, lobbying, and advocacy for dialogue to end the conflict. These activities have improved meaningful relationships of trust within the communities, which strengthens sustainable peace at local, district, and national levels. ARLPI believes that religious leaders play a key role in mentoring communities to create space for peace and live in harmony by reconciling with one another. The Women's Taskforce in the ARLPI initiated a Women's Empowerment Strategy which incorporates women's contributions in the peace process in Acholiland. An exchange visit in 2007 to the West Nile region enabled comparative learning about different conflicts and a sharing of experiences on coping with stresses of peacebuilding (Rogers et al. 2008:138). There is a strengthening of women's capacity in peace work due to ARLPI's purposeful involvement of women in its activities, training women in psychosocial support and conflict transformation which flows onto community sensitization on nonviolence and the importance of coexistence.

Currently, ARLPI is a partner in a pilot scheme to implement UNSCR 1325, empowering women in peace and security. Simiyu Wandibba cites examples of the Acholi Religious Leaders' Peace Initiative and the Inter-Religious Council of Sierra Leone as having contributed positively to "reducing violence and rehumanizing the 'other'" (in Ramadhan and Mang'eni 2010: 30). Additionally, the Uganda Women of Faith Network (UWOFNET) is an interfaith organization affiliated to the World Conference on Religion for Peace, Women's Mobilization Program, and the African Council of Religious Leaders, that partner with the Inter-Religious Council of Uganda. Sister Mary Goretti Kisakye, program coordinator for UWOFNET, stresses the need to make the role of women-of-faith visible in communities, "appreciating religious women's roles and the courage in facing challenges to building sustainable peace, justice, and reconciliation in families and communities" (Kisakye 2010: 3).

The Women of Faith Peacebuilding Network in Nigeria is a network of religious women who come from different religious communities across the country, uniting to raise understanding and engage in peace activities, chiefly in areas most affected by conflict. A core responsibility of this group is networking, which "has contributed to realization of mutual acceptance, tolerance, and trust among women, factors which have enabled them and their religious communities to expand and reach-out to those in need" (Ramadhan and Mang'eni 2010: 8). Esther Ibanga lives in Jos, Nigeria which has been beset by religious violence since 1994, because it lies at a flashpoint where the Islamic north meets the Christian south. She is the first woman to be a Christian pastor in her state. When more than five hundred Christians were massacred by Muslims in a nearby village, Ibanga lead a protest march with 100,000 women. After the march, she learnt that the massacre was a response to an attack by Christians against Muslims in another village. She met in secret with Khadija Hawaja who had led the Muslim women's march. They co-founded the Women Without Walls Initiative which "brings together women from the bitterly divided faiths to seek practical ways to curb the escalating violence that has claimed tens of thousands of lives" (Nickerson 2015).

In 1997, a group of women from different faiths in Sierra Leone formed the Inter-Religious Council of Sierra Leone. Fifteen women from this council met with the Revolutionary United Front (RUF) rebel group to negotiate the return of child soldiers. Haja Simatu explained what happened:

> I had never seen a rebel leader, only heard of the terror. Now, standing face-to-face with one, I just called on Allah to help us

negotiate peace. The rebel leader looked at me for a long time. Then he opened his mouth to speak, and his first words were "you look like my mother. I have not seen my mother for a long time. You also remind me of the way we prayed together. Shall we pray?" And this is how we began our first meeting with the RUF fighters. (in Ogega and Marshall 2015: 288)

These women drew on "their multiple identities as authoritative community leaders, mothers, and women of different faiths working together for the common good," so that instead of their actions being a threat to the rebel group, "they rehumanized the rebels, saying in effect that the rebels were like their children" (2015: 289). This rehumanizing is an aspect of *sensitive relationality* that I suggest recurs in women-of-faith's accounts of their peacebuilding.

Leymah Gbowee's story is told briefly in Chapter four, here different aspects are stressed. Gbowee says that in war stories, women are always in the background, or presented as marginalized victims. Her story is strong. When Charles Taylor's merciless rebels became brutal, she met with family and friends to pray for safety, but the war continued, and she felt her prayers were not being answered. Her anger increased. When President Doe's army began to target tribes, the Liberian Council of Churches offered asylum to people in danger, yet still people were "raped, slashed, shot, and hacked" (Gbowee 2011: 31). Her family escaped to Ghana, and they returned in 1991 when peacekeepers from the Economic Community of West African States Monitoring Group came. In 1992, Taylor's forces went on the offensive. By 1995, Taylor's party and the warring factions had signed the thirteenth peace treaty, yet by 1996, trouble was brewing. Taylor won the Presidency in 1997. In 1997, Gbowee begun work with the Lutheran World Federation Trauma Healing and Reconciliation Program and stayed for five years. The program started with story-telling so that people would know what they had been through and what they faced. Her definition of peacebuilding confirms a strong sense of relationality, what I claim is the distinctive characteristic of women-of-faith peacebuilders. For Gbowee, peacebuilding isn't simply ending a fight.

> It's healing those victimized by war, making them strong again, and bringing them back to the people they once were. It's helping victimizers rediscover their humanity so they can once again become productive members of their communities.... It's repairing societies in which the guns have been used, and not only making them whole, but better. (Gbowee 2011: 81)

In 1999, the West Africa Network for Peacebuilding was seeking to include women in its work. In late 1999, fighting broke out. Gbowee's work on trauma healing revolved not only around obvious emotional hurts, but the practical issues of care for child ex-combatants, jobs, and sanitation. She describes the excitement of the first meeting of the Women in Peacebuilding Network (WIPNET). The women began by sharing and unburdening themselves. She reflects on how unique this moment was in focusing on women building peace. She claims that in Africa, "No one else was organizing activist women across borders. The potential power of this movement was immense" (2011: 113). She recalled a story she had read about a group of Serbian Orthodox women and a group of Muslim women in Sarajevo during the Bosnian war. "They were on different sides of the besieged city, and one had electricity, the other access to water. And the women with water carried buckets to those who had power, so they could use their washing machines to get the laundry done" (2011: 113). These ordinary, everyday tasks keep one's humanity intact, and can be life-saving and soul-enriching during tough times. Gbowee summarizes the effects:

> WIPNET brought everything together for me: You can't cure trauma when violence is ongoing, so the primary effort must be working for peace. You can't negotiate a lasting peace without bringing women into the effort, but women can't become peacemakers without releasing the pain that keeps them from feeling

their own strength. Emotional release isn't enough in itself to create change, but WIPNET channelled that new energy into political action. (Gbowee 2011: 114)

The Liberian Women's Initiative and the Mano River Women Peace Network were already in operation. Gbowee's position as coordinator of WIPNET came as a surprise to many in the older organizations. In 2002, she gathered women to pray in the Christian Women's Peace Initiative. When she said: "You are asking, 'Who are these women?' I will say, they are ordinary mothers, grandmothers, aunts, sisters. For us, this is just the beginning" (Gbowee 2011: 124). Asatu, the one Muslim woman in the audience said she had gathered Muslim women to join in the movement. "Christian and Muslim women had never worked together, and certainly not for anything political. Asatu was proposing an alliance no one had imagined before" (2011: 125). The Peace Outreach Program began. For three days a week for six months, the women of WIPNET went out to meet with the women of Monrovia at the mosques on Friday at noon after prayers, the markets on Saturday morning, and to churches every Sunday. They went in pairs. "We gave all our sisters the same message: Liberian women, awake for peace!" (2011: 126). Gbowee explains that they worked in the world women inhabited, using women's networks to communicate. The Christian women continued to meet to pray, and Asatu continued to organize her Muslim sisters. The core of WIPNET devised a powerful slogan to show the importance of standing together: "Does the bullet know Christian from Muslim? Does the bullet pick and choose?" (2011: 129). The women agreed that Christian and Muslim women would retain their own leadership but work together. The women marched on the streets, demanding an unconditional ceasefire. More than two thousand women dressed in white met on a site where Taylor drove past. They called it the Liberian Mass Action for Peace.

When permitted to speak to the President, Gbowee said:

With this message: that the women of Liberia, including the IDPs, we are tired of war. We are tired of running. We are tired of begging for bulgur wheat. We are tired of our children being raped. We are now taking this stand, to secure the future of our children. Because we believe, as custodians of society, tomorrow our children will ask us, "Mama, what was your role during the crisis?" (Gbowee 2011: 141)

When the peace talks began, the women sat at the door and down the corridor, arms linked. While the war didn't end then, the women sent out strong signals of their anger at the destruction of war and their power to transform conflict. "Peace isn't a moment – it's a very long process" (2011: 168). The story is told often, but it is powerful.

At an all-Africa level, the Circle of Concerned African Women Theologians (the Circle), launched in Ghana in 1989, is a faith-based movement that creates networks and platforms to bring African women theologians from various religious traditions together. They meet for support and nurture, to research and publish, and to discuss the pertinent issues of poverty, violence, and HIV/AIDS. "Their theologies are set in post-colonial and post-independence settings, as well as the era of the multifaceted globalization process" (Amoah 2012: 241). The Circle has some roots in the Ecumenical Association of Third World Theologians. The majority are Christian. However, the group draws explicitly on varied narratives, given the challenges of the multi-religious dimension of Muslims, African indigenous religions, Jews, Hindus, and amongst Christians, there are evangelicals, Pentecostals, charismatics, conservatives, and liberals. Those involved "are contextual and liberation theologians" in the sense that they reflect on experiences that are set historic moments with their unrelenting struggles, that focus "on concrete and practical issues that call for action" (Amoah 2012: 241). Their theology is directed toward concrete projects that improve the lives of the marginalized and the voiceless, such as working with local governments to ensure that rural women gain access to a fair share of poverty relief grants. Members of the Circle are aware that the term "feminist" is controversial, and use of the term may cause communities to ignore them. Hence, while keeping the dialogue alive as to what it means to be called a feminist, many members call their work "African women's theologies."

This section highlights some global organizations that have been started by individuals and reach out across religious and faith boundaries to challenge stereotypes and gendered constraints. Many others could have been included. Work done in inter-faith coalitions of women's organizations shows the importance of affirming relationships in everyday, concrete contexts, as crucial to building the trust that is necessary in working with those who come from a different faith. The examples also demonstrate enormous courage of women in taking personal risks to enhance peace.

Opposing Violent Extremism and Fundamentalisms

After the 2001 terrorist attacks on the World Trade Centre New York, and the Pentagon Washington, many Western politicians and citizens demonized Muslims who became mis/identified with acts of violence, and as representing America's, if not the entire West's, new chief enemy. Hate crimes against Muslims escalated, even though mainstream Muslim groups condemn the terrorist attacks as being inconsistent with the Qur'an. Violent extremism can be defined "as the choice individuals make to use or support violence to advance a cause based on exclusionary group identities" (Slachmuijlder 2017). It is aimed toward eliminating the "other's group, culture, or religious identity. Understanding the contextually different drivers of support behind extremist movements is critical to peacebuilders. Search for Common Ground have programs in thirty-five countries across Africa, Asia, and the Middle East, with 80 percent of their global staff of six hundred coming from the countries in which they work (Slachmuijlder 2017: 5). Lena Slachmuijlder identifies frameworks to understand the drivers, including push and pull factors; individuals' vulnerability; and they identify prime risk factors as ideological values, psychological factors, political grievances, economic factors, and social motivators (2017: 8-11).

Extremist beliefs that fuel intolerance and violence are not found solely in Islam. Across the globe, extremist beliefs and movements appear to be rising. Buddhist narratives fueling hatred and violence against Muslims have escalated in recent years in Sri Lanka and Myanmar. In the latter, proposed legislation by Buddhist nationalist groups targets Muslim groups generally, and women specifically, calling for restrictions on women's freedom to marry whom they want, or to decide the number of children to have. In several African countries, such as the Central African Republic and Nigeria, Christian militia groups operate. Hate and extremist ideologies are on the rise in the US, promoted by those who claim to be Christians. To identify the Muslim community as the only religious group where extremist violence occurs is incorrect and counterproductive. It feeds the view in the Muslim world that the US and the rest of the West is targeting the religion of Islam, as well as Muslims living within Western borders, and states where violent Islamic extremist groups reign terror over moderate Muslims.

Terrorist threats have changed and grown in recent years. Different states designate different terrorist groups as a threat, with Al-Qaeda, Boko Haram, Hamas, Hezbollah, Islamic State of Iraq, and Syria (ISIS), and the Taliban, commonly appearing on state lists. The development of ISIS and its 2014 declaration of a caliphate, rule by a Muslim leader, intensely expanded the crisis of violent extremism, because in addition to controlling territory in Syria and Iraq, it embarked on a worldwide recruitment drive using social media, with thousands of people travelling from other countries to join ISIS. Militant discourses can inspire women on two fronts with "the tension between narratives of domesticity and *jihad*" (Seedat 2017: 6). Others become stay-at-home radicals, willing to commit terrorist acts in Western states, or support their male relatives in doing so.

Violent radicalization can be "defined as a process through which a person comes to embrace the use of violence to serve an ideology, religion, or political goal. Violent radicalization may lead to violent extremism and terrorism," with the rights and well-being of citizens threatened (Alderton 2016: 4). Factors leading to potential radicalization include political, socio-economic, identity, and religious issues. Chantal de Jonge Oudraat and Michael Brown argue strongly that "violent extremism and terrorism should be paramount concerns of the WPS community" and the counter-terrorist and WPS communities need to engage with each other "routinely and systematically" (2016: 1). They argue further that to link this counter-terrorist agenda to the work of women who are already on the frontlines of the fight against violent extremism, especially in Africa, Asia, and the Middle East, should "include strategic prevention and non-military measures" (2016: 2).

Within the call to implement UNSCR 1325, "prevention" typically refers to the prevention of sexual violence. However, I argue that women-of-faith peacebuilders demonstrate that prevention must extend to tackling root causes of conflict for there to be any chance of positive peace. Through relationship-building, community dialogue, and public engagement, prevention work extends to address grievances through nonviolent means; encourage marginalized groups to participate as equals in community life; debunk stereotypes; and express agency and leadership through nonviolent means (Slachmuijlder 2017: 17). In support of this argument, examples of this fight to prevent violent extremism are provided, first briefly in Asia, and then concentrating on examples from Middle Eastern countries.

Women Fighting to Overcome Violent Extremism

There are many empirical examples of women adopting effective nonviolent strategies that are embedded in the trust that develops through community involvement. I begin with some examples from Asia, drawn from the Asia-Pacific Women's Alliance for Peace and Security, which has seventy-seven loosely configured alliances across the range of Asian nations. In Pakistan, activist Mossarat Qadeem and her organization

PAIMAN Alumni Trust have "trained more than 655 mothers to de-radicalize 1,024 young men and boys, rehabilitating them and reinte-grating them into society" (O'Reilly 2015: 3). The trust engages with the youth and their mothers to provide livelihood alternatives. Nuns in the Philippines exposed the suffering caused by martial law in the 1970s and 1980s and use their moral power to serve as a pressure group to resist multiple forms of violence. "In Kurdistan, women are deployed to the Peshmorga, an elite unit of the Kurdish armed forces, to help face down the threat of terrorism in the region" (Wulun nd: 2). Groups challenging the rise against extremism in Asia include international solidarity networks such as Women Living Under Muslim Laws and the Association for Women's Rights in Development. The Malaysian NGO Musawah challenges extremist understandings of Islamic texts to disentangle religion from culturally condoned practices that accept violence and the subservience of women as the norm.

Indonesia has two main Muslim women's groups – Fatayat NU and Aisyiyah – both connected to Indonesia's two largest Muslim Organizations. Fatayat NU focuses on women's empowerment and has approximately six million cadres (Wulun nd: 6). Its mission is to eradicate all forms of violence, injustice, and poverty in communities by developing constructive, democratic strategies that promote gender equality. The group's counterterrorism activities respond to current issues rather than adopting a longer-term strategy on issues that affect gender equality. Aisyiyah focuses on the women's movement, social development, and the Islamic way of life. It runs education charities, health care, and economic programs, thus indirectly playing a role in the de-radicalization campaign.

One group that is specifically focused on deradicalization is Sisters Against Violent Extremism (SAVE). "SAVE is the world's first female counterterrorism platform launched in 2008, as a project of the Women without Borders organization," operating in Indonesia, and Yemen, India, Pakistan, Israel, Palestine, and Northern Ireland "to bring together terrorist attack victims" (Wulun nd: 7). The organiza-tion tries to connect victims with policy-makers and security experts to create mutual understanding among peoples within conflict areas. As with so many other women's organizations, there is a focus on the strategic role of mothers in families. "SAVE's Mothers for Change Campaign encourages and empowers women to take a firm stand against violent extremism ideologies in their homes and communities" (Wulun nd: 7). In Chapter four, I deal critically with the positive and limiting consequences of appealing to women's mothering roles as the prime basis for peacebuilding. To reiterate, I argue that *the social esteem that accompanies mothering must be tied to gender equality.*

Moving now to examples from the Middle East, in a UN Women commissioned 2016 a study carried out by the Al-Hayat Centre for Civil Society Development and Search for Common Ground, in Jordan with forty-seven interviewees, "85 percent of respondents (without a notable gender difference) believe that radicalization is occurring in Jordanian communities" (Alderton 2016: 7). The gendered analysis of this is interesting. Male respondents believe that the key threats posed by radicalization affect their personal freedoms, as well as the future of their families, and the quality of their work opportunities.

> Women's fears about the impact of radicalization relate directly to their daily activities – their day-to-day freedom of movement outside the home, their ability to find a job or an educational opportunity, increased violence within the home, and decreased opportunities for engagement and volunteering with their communities. (Alderton 2016: 7)

I continually stress the need to include faith leaders in the WPS broad-based agenda, however in this UN Women study, women's trust of religious leaders was mixed, and "46 per cent of respondents said they would refer to a religious leader if in doubt about radical religious ideas, while 21 per cent (all of them women) said they would not trust a religious leader in such cases" (Alderton 2016: 8). Of course, not all religious leaders support gender equality.

I note in earlier chapters that there are both positive elements of including women's role as mothers as part of their rationale for building peace, and harmful aspects that potentially traps women in stereotypical ways, minimizing public roles. However, it is significant that "the vast majority of respondents (95 per cent) perceive the importance of women's involvement in deradicalization efforts as stemming from their traditional social roles as mothers and their position within their families" (Alderton 2016: 9). Such a statistic cannot be dismissed lightly. To use motherhood "as an expression of women's agency in peace" is not necessarily essentialist "because motherhood is an undeniable aspect of most women's lived experience" (Hudson 2016b: 55). The UN Women study makes a range of recommendations, including increasing women's leadership as active agents in combatting radicalization, and supporting moderate female religious leaders, as well as finding male champions who collaborate with women as equal partners. "Most importantly, interventions should include structured programs for parents to encourage their children to be open to other cultures and religions" (Alderton 2016: 10). This openness is crucial, and I return to it shortly.

Sherizaan Minwalla lives in the Kurdish region of Iraq, working on human trafficking. In August 2014, about five-thousand women from the Yazadi community were captured from their villages by ISIS militants. Minwalla tells of a young woman whom she calls Ghazal who was captured and escaped and writes: "I realized that more important to Ghazal was how she challenged her captors than how they abused her" (2016: np). This is an example of the *resistive agency* outlined in Chapter three, and repeatedly recurring in accounts of women-of faith's peacebuilding. The young woman fought physically, and others tried to disfigure themselves, or cut their hair to pretend they were boys. Many survivors became stuck in displacement camps with limited access to health care and basic needs, hence when the Yazidi spiritual leader Baba Sheikh "issued a decision that said survivors should be welcomed home with honour" (Minwalla 2016: np), this has significant implications. Rather than always concentrating on women's victim nature, Minwalla suggests that "narrating their stories of strength, courage, and resistance helps to reframe their experience from narrowly constructed stories of rape toward a more balanced and realistic account of their experiences," presenting a more affirmative view of Yazidi women, despite their terrible experiences (2016: nd). Similarly, Manal Omar observes that women were willing to reach out across ethnic and religious divides in Iraq, stating: "They did it instinctively. And it wasn't the case that it was safe for them to do so – it increased their vulnerability...I think there is a natural desire for inclusiveness amongst women" (in Marshall and Hayward 2010: 11).

Within Israel and Palestine, the challenges of peacebuilding are great. Dena Merriam from the Global Peace Initiative of Women observes women's ability to build bridges, and argues that because women know how families suffer, and how differing layers of society are damaged, they are "more prepared to plunge in to try to solve the problem, more prepared to sacrifice for the solution" in searching for common ground (in Marshall and Hayward 2010: 11). This practical focus of women-of-faith underlies their distinctiveness. As an example, Elana Rozenman is an Orthodox Jew who, after her son was struck in a Palestinian suicide bomber attack, founded Trust-Emun, an organization which brings together Jewish, Muslim, and Christian women from Israel and Palestine to develop mutual understanding. In 2010, she talked about her motivations for working for peace through this organization: "I also wanted to work with religion, because I was a woman-of-faith. Religion is one area that can transcend, that can overcome divides" (in Kurtzer-Ellenbogen 2015: 117). She is also involved in an interfaith dialogue called Abrahamic Reunion but speaks of the difference it makes when women of different faiths meet in women-only groups. She suggests that on meeting, women immediately ask the personal questions about families, communities, domestic violence, and domination, "then immediately we move on from these personal topics and start work far more easily" (in Kurtzer-Ellenbogen 2015: 117; and Marshall and Hayward 2010: 11). I maintain that *relationality, everyday context, and emotional connectivity* are fundamental features of the distinctive way women-of-faith peacebuilders operate.

Women in Black is an interfaith grassroots women's movement with the motto: "for justice, against war." This movement began in January 1988 after the first Palestinian intifada broke out, and small groups of Israeli and Palestinian women met together at a major intersection in Israel/Palestine. Always dressed in black to signal mourning, they stood in silent vigils bearing witness to the atrocities of violence. The movement spread. In 1991, the movement began in Belgrade to oppose nationalist aggression and masculinist violence. In 1992, Women in Black began in India, responding to the mosque Babri Masjid being torn down by Hindu fundamentalists. The Organization's website lists Women of Black groups in Armenia, Argentina, Australia, Austria, Belgium, Canada, Colombia, Denmark, France, Germany, India, Israel, Italy, Netherlands, Serbia, Spain, South Africa, Uruguay, UK, and USA. These silent vigils are not passive, they are active, non-violent forms of resistance to militarism and extremist violence.

Frida Kerner Furman conducted participant observation in six interreligious dialogue sessions of the Interfaith Encounter Association in Jerusalem. Jews, Muslims, and Christians are invited to join neighbourhood groups to discuss religious commonalities and differences. The purpose of these meetings is to engage with the other. Interestingly, at the Jerusalem Women's Interfaith Encounter that Furman attends, the women speak about their problems and needs as being the same across the religious and political spectrum.

> Women's sharing of their experiences as women, often through the use of story-telling, situates this group within the definition of "dialogue," which expands the possibilities of interconnection across difference—in this case, across religion, but also cultural and gendered values and experiences. (Furman 2011: np)

The women bring enough food to the gatherings for a meal, symbolizing the welcoming of a stranger. Furman discusses the idea of a "personalized politics," and explains that the "term recognizes the importance of identifying, acknowledging, and providing support for perceived injustices experienced by fellow members" (2011: np). This *personalized politics* addresses the effect of power dynamics on people's everyday lives. Humanizing the assumed "enemy" is a crucial part of these encounter groups, legitimizing the other's narrative, reducing fear, and creating trust. These groups are one way of strategically deploying religious and peacebuilding organizations to offer the various actors in MENA with constructive, deeply grounded, normative *visions of collaboration* that challenge common understandings of the other.

Enabling Women as Agents of Peace

The question of what can be done to oppose violent extremism is a critical one, given the destruction, fear, and loss of lives that extremism causes. The Association for Women's Rights in Development (AWID) underwent a four-year strategic action-research initiative on resisting and challenging religious fundamentalisms. Their research is based on more than fifty in-depth interviews, eighteen case studies, and online surveys from 1,600 women's rights activists. "More than three-quarters of women's-rights activists surveyed by AWID felt that the strength of religious fundamentalisms has increased globally in the past ten years" (in Gueskens et al. 2010: 39). Such views have massive implications for the human rights of women because fundamentalist agendas typically have strong views on reproductive rights, sexual rights and freedoms, women's participation in the public sphere, family law, and the autonomy of women. *Enabling women as agents of peace* is a critical tool in countering extremist tendencies toward violence, because empowered women can educate youth against radicalization, and they can foster attitudes of openness and tolerance to challenge these dangerous tendencies. Garnering the support of influential men also is necessary to resist extremism.

Cassandra Balchin, consultant for this AWID research, suggests that most commonly, women's rights activists "characterize religious fundamentalisms as being 'absolutist and intolerant'" (in Gueskens et al. 2010: 36), manifest through aggressive imposition. A second frequently mentioned characteristic is that fundamentalisms are "anti-women and patriarchal" (in Gueskens et al. 2010: 36). As outlined in Chapter two, fundamentalists, in blaming social problems on the decline in the traditional family, usually promote rigid gender roles. Other common strategies of fundamentalists include violence or criticism toward anyone who dissents from truths presented as absolutes. Such intolerance leads to hate-speech, which translates to physical violence that occurred in Congo, Kenya, Lebanon, and the former Yugoslavia, and is on the increase in the West. *An intolerance of pluralism underlies fundamentalism.*

The United States Institute of Peace has also led projects on women preventing extremist violence in Nigeria and Kenya and their civil society partner, Women Without Borders has led a Sisters Against Violent Extremism project in India, Indonesia, Nigeria, Pakistan, and Tanzania. Women Without Borders has also begun a "Sensitizing Mothers to Recognize Signs of Radicalization" project, currently in India (Kashmir), Indonesia, Nigeria, Pakistan, Tajikistan, and Zanzibar. It adopts a "Mothers School Model," whereby trained local leaders conduct home-based meetings with groups of mothers in at-risk communities. Their aim is to "empower and enable mothers to become agents of peace and stability in their families and communities as cornerstones of an embedded security paradigm" to recognize and react to early warning signs of radicalization. Search for Common Ground also draw on mothers' powerful force. In Morocco, they organized "women-led dialogue caravans" with the idea of creating a space for dialogue among imans, youth, and men, to discuss the effect of violent extremism on family and community life (Slachmuijlder 2017: 19). Defying Extremism is a global network of rights activists, peacebuilders, and individuals from more than fifty countries and every faith tradition which is seeking to create alternatives to actions which dehumanize. Partners include Association for Women's Rights in Development (AWID), Women PeaceMakers

Program, The Gem Foundation, Joan B Kroc School of Peace Studies, University of San Diego, The Network for Religious and Traditional Peacemakers, NGO Working Group on Women, Peace and Security, Tanenbaum: Combatting Religious Prejudice, UN Women, Women Without Borders, and Women's Learning Partnership.

There is little doubt that an in-depth understanding of the processes of radicalization, whereby an individual becomes involved in violence that is somehow associated with their extremist beliefs, is crucial for peacebuilders, and requires recognizing the gender dynamics at play. Some women are involved as perpetrators of violence and terrorist attacks, and they provide active support and encouragement for violent extremists in their communities, both practically and in using social media. Yet there is an increased realization of how women can counter the spread of violent extremism because of their impact on family and communities in strengthening a "collective resilience against violent extremism" (USIP 2015: 9). There are pull factors that lure individuals into participation into extremist activities for those who are vulnerable and lack opportunities, resources, or support, and push factors include a lack of self-confidence, unhealed trauma, and exposure to generations of violence.

Sanam Naraghi-Anderlini suggests that regarding extremists, "the actors, ideology, and actions are deeply gendered" (in USIP 2015: 17) in that the young men who are the predominant actors often experience long-term corruption and repression, ineffective development policies, displacement, no access to school, and foreign military intervention so their aspirations may be to contribute to realizing their sense of justice. She explains that the ideology is closely tied with patriarchal understandings of religious texts that defines men's roles, and what it means to be a good wife, daughter, or mother, and where women's rights are viewed as Western and immoral. For example, "all-female Pakistani madrassas are rising in numbers where girls learn to be ideal mothers and transmit conservative beliefs to their offspring," which is interpreted as a sign of commitment to religion (Anderlini in USIP 2015: 17). Anderlini maintains that changes in the status of women is an early sign of conflict trends that might lead to violence. For example, an indication of the spread of less tolerant forms of Islam is a noticeable increase in Muslim women wearing headscarves in public and the decrease in their participation in public affairs (Anderlini 2007: 28). This intolerance happened in France, where the spread of extremist Islamism accompanied an increase in "honour killings" and violence against women in immigrant North African communities, and then the crisis looming in the Parisian suburbs ignited in riots in 2006. In Iraq, the US invasion helped let loose religious zeal, with a decline in the status of women, evidenced by the absence of girls from schools. Women's movements within civil society are vital to address the source of extremism by advancing rights, promoting tolerance to pluralism, and courageously speaking out against repression.

The West's generic negativity toward all aspects of Islam is counterproductive; it incites further violence. Ayse Kadayifci-Orellana (2015) summarizes some of the current Muslim women's contributions to peacebuilding. She suggests that because Muslim women are often marginalized from formal religious spaces, and their initiatives are frequently ad hoc at the grassroots level, they tend not to represent factions, so they aren't necessarily perceived as a threat. Working under the radar permits a flexibility to work with groups that official religious leaders may not be able to work with. Working in murky borders overlaps with Love's (2015) idea of strategic invisibility, discussed in Chapter three. Kadayifci-Orellana emphasizes the roles that women play in the family to integrate different points of views and encourage empathy. In nurturant roles, women are accustomed to *building relationships* and *bringing parties together*, and thus have a *good sense of the needs of victims* of war, such as orphans and widows. Most women are also comfortable with *working with intense emotions* that are required for a focus on healing and trauma. Ibtisam Mahameed notes the crucial role of coexistence and dialogue, and says, "there is no solution to extremism other than spreading the culture of coexistence and dialogue, skills that women master and possess" (in Kadayifci-Orellana 2015: 86).

When self-chosen, the wearing of Islamic dress and covering their hair helps activists to negotiate active roles in ways that gain community acceptance. Muslim women's peacebuilding roles include advocacy, education, interfaith dialogue, mediation, observer status, and roles in transitional justice. Locating their "initiatives within Islamic concepts, language, and terminology makes women's peace work more meaningful and acceptable to different segments of the Muslim community" (Kadayifci-Orellana 2015: 91). Women are credible voices reinforcing inclusive values and peaceful avenues for change.

I suggest that openness to pluralism, is a stronger idea and practice than merely tolerating differences. Nurturing a milieu of pluralism and diversity is imperative for resisting the growth of fundamentalisms.

> This means promoting positive inclusive identities to counteract the bounded, othering identities fostered by fundamentalists. It means encouraging intersectional feminist understandings of power and privilege and applying these ideas about culture and religion in order to see the latter as contested and power-laden... and refusing any justifications for discrimination based on religion, culture, or tradition. (AWID 2016: 34)

This holistic view of development activities is one in which multiple areas such as education, gender justice, health, human rights, governance, peace and security, and religious beliefs are considered as intrinsically interconnected. Dialogue between plural groups connects diverse coalitions who hold contrasting views. It aims at mutual understanding.

***

The building of coalitions across differences of religious belief, political ideology, or cultural and ethnic background by women-of-faith peacebuilders is a significant achievement. Rather than merely describing the achievements of these coalitions, the chapter highlights what is unique about them in terms of the special contributions that women-of-faith bring to peacebuilding. I argue that a profound respect for differences is needed for this work, a respect that goes beyond a mere tolerance of difference, to appreciating that *plural diversity* is a desirable aspect to living well. To this end, women-of-faith do not put their religious beliefs aside, but they seek not to let these beliefs be a stumbling block to the urgent requirement to *work together with others from a different faith on shared causes.* I show that it is the priority women-of-faith give to relationships in families and communities that leads to, and then cements, an accepted *responsibility to care for others.* This responsibility is embodied in the shared task of forming coalitions to work on fulfilling urgent, immediate needs as well as building sustainable peace and security. Examples of coalitions across many regions, highlight the unique contributions made by women-of-faith in various organizations. *Relationships, responsibility to care for the vulnerable, and emotive connectivity to others mark the distinctiveness of women-of-faith's peacebuilding.* Given the challenges of violent extremism, I argue that openness to differences, dialogue, and plural diversity is essential to counter extremism. Women play a key role in encouraging this openness.

6

Women-of-faith Empowering Violated Victims

Violence toward women and girls continues to be rampant in war zones. Sexual assault is used as part of war strategies to humiliate individuals and degrade communities. During this violence, bodies are violated, silenced, and shamed. Typically, it is assumed that violence toward women and girls is some type of sexual violence, and this assumption is understandable. Vast numbers of women and girls are brutally sexually violated, and they struggle enormously with the indignity of their victimhood. Yet cruelty extends into other post-war realms where structural violence contributes to widespread suffering of injustices. I begin the chapter by discussing sexual violence and end with considering structural violence. The content of this chapter bears directly on the "security" aspect of the women, peace, and security agenda, and the prevention of and protection from violence that is explicit in all the women, peace, and security resolutions.

Conceptual clarification of terminology is important. Some literature refers to sexual and gender-based violence (SGBV); others refer to conflict-related sexual violence (CRSV). The UN Women's framework refers to gender-based violence (GBV) which includes all violence that accrues because of one's gender. GBV includes rape, sexual assault, sexual exploitation, sexual abuse, physical assault, intimate partner violence, forced marriage, early marriage, emotional abuse, denial of resources, opportunities, or services, trafficking, harmful traditional practices like female genital mutilation or scarring, sex-selective abortions, female infanticide, and son preference. Some of these forms of violence occur to men and boys, as well as to women and girls. However, the largest proportion of these acts of violence are to female victims, and some abuses relate solely to women and girls. The violators are not always armed combatants, in conflict they include state forces, government security officers, the supposed protectors of UN peacekeepers, and civilians. The chapter contains four sections.

First, I explain the prevalence of war-related sexual violence against women and girls, to demonstrate the need for broad-based assistance for victims. I analyze what difference women-of-faith make in bringing *compassionate values* to their practical assistance of victims of violence. I show how many of the national action plans on UNSCR 1325 are geared toward including religious and faith-based leaders in educating perpetrators of abuse that all forms of violence toward women is wrong. These plans reinforce my argument that the more the WPS agenda can utilize local women leaders who are immersed in indigenous traditions, including local faiths, the more chance there should be of increasing the effectiveness of its implementation.

Second, I provide examples of what women-of-faith peacebuilders are doing to help heal traumatized victims. Selective examples show active engagement in constructively healing bodily and mental trauma of victims.

The third section briefly explores human trafficking of women and girls who are trafficked for sexual exploitation from conflict zones. I show that while the immediate individual rescue of each victim is massively liberating, longer-term strategies must challenge systemic layers of violence.

The fourth section extends notions of aggression beyond sexual violence to include the violence of structural injustices. I reiterate the position that is posited by feminist liberation theologians that asserts the need for global patterns of domination and oppression to be broken. I argue that a radical transformation of structural violence is needed, not merely rescue of individuals, even though each release is life-changing and thus of great personal significance.

This emphasis on the need for radical change reinforces the book's argument. Too often, the rhetoric of UNSCR 1325 remains as grandiloquence in not adequately translating to conflict transformation. To draw this argument out, the chapter tackles the controversial *protection of victims* versus *prevention of violence* arguments, and where priorities should lie for peacebuilders. My overall argument in this chapter is that both immediate protection of victims and enduring prevention of violence are necessary, and prevention of widespread, underlying violence is always preferable as a long-term strategy in preventing harm, and in tackling systemic violence.

Gender-based Violence Against Women and Girls

The normative connotations to root meanings of violence, are:

> denoted by the term *violare*, the basis of the word violation. Violence not only causes harm of various sorts; it causes *injury*. The distinction is vital. The Latin word *injuria* stems from the root *jur* or *jus*, which is the basis of ethical terms such as right and justice. Simply put, an injury is an injustice – a violation of that to which one has an ethically defensible claim. While many physical acts of force can cause harm, they do not all cause injury in this normative sense of the term. (Carlson 2011: 16)

To violate, or do violence can never be justified, whereas sometimes force might be needed, such as stopping a hostage-taker, or pain may be provoked when a surgeon cuts the skin.

Examples of violence against women and girls are alarmingly numerous. The World Health Organization (WHO) defines this violence as "any act of gender-based violence that results in physical, sexual, or psychological harm or suffering to women, including threats of such acts, coercion, or arbitrary deprivation of liberty, whether occurring in public or private life" (in Gerhardt 2014: 35). Elizabeth Gerhardt calls these acts "gendercide," or "the intentional effort to harm and injure millions of women and girls based on their gender" (2014: 20), and she suggests that "misogyny, domination, and patriarchy are the roots of gendercide" (2014: 148). This global, pervasive violence is rooted in cultural, social, and religious biases against women. Curiously, this violence is condemned by a broad church of groups from religious conservatives, through to evangelicals, mainline churches, and feminists. The recent exposure of institutional Church abuse, particularly in the Roman Catholic Church, but evident in most denominations and faiths, is much needed, but is not the focus in this chapter.

In terms of sexual-based violence, facts on the UN Women (2016a) website cite estimates "that 35 percent of women worldwide have experienced either physical and/or sexual intimate partner violence or sexual violence by a non-partner at some point in their lives." Sexual violence comes in diverse forms; forced sexual acts, vicious intimidating sexual harassment, trafficking, and rape. Conflict and post-conflict situations, often increase women's vulnerability to violence, because there is a culture of insecurity and uncertainty, heightened vulnerability, fear for personal safety, displacement, movement across borders, and the presence of aggressive, unruly combatants and ex-combatants. UN Action Against Sexual Violence in Conflict (UN Action) unites the work of thirteen UN entities with the goal of ending sexual violence in conflict. In support of UNSCR 1325, 1820, 1888, 1960, and 2106, they draw attention to the fact that rape in war is not inevitable, victims should not be stigmatized, perpetrators should be punished, and the constructive involvement of men in preventing violence is essential for much needed changes to occur.

In explaining war rape as a military tactic to humiliate, demoralize individuals, and destroy communities, UN Action statistics are alarming. They give examples like during the 2007 conflict in the DRC, an average of forty women were raped every day in South Kivu; between 20-50,000 women were raped in Bosnia and Herzegovina (BiH) in the early 1990s; 50-64,000 internally displaced women from Sierra Leone have experienced sexual violence from armed combatants; and hundreds of thousands of women were raped in the 1994 Rwandan genocide (UN Action nd: 2). WHO reports suggest that between 61-77 percent of Liberian women experienced sexual violence during the war (in Jones et al. 2014: 2). Numbers of rapes are always imprecise due to the shame of admitting to it, particularly when the abuser is known, and there are always difficulties in collecting accurate data whilst instability occurs during violent conflicts. Numbers are often verified when some security is restored, by documenting the timing of pregnancies that result, or the nature of physical ailments that arise during the abuse, or the depression that occurs if assistance is available to diagnose and then treat it.

Rape was used as a systematic weapon of war in Bangladesh, Bosnia, Indonesia, Kosovo, Liberia, Rwanda, and Uganda. Rape victims in armed conflict are subject to infections, including HIV/AIDs, terrible bodily injuries, pain, fistula, infertility, pregnancy, and intense psychological trauma, often resulting in long-term post-traumatic stress disorder, anxiety, depression, low esteem, and suicidal tendencies. Shame, stigma, and deterioration of family and societal structures result. Sexual assault affects physical and psychological health, as well as the way people relate to others. There are always "relationships between resilience, vulnerability, and contextual factors in the development of the traumatic response" (Reid-Cunningham 2008: 287). Assault is more likely to happen in places where individuals are socialized to devalue women.

In terms of the response to SGBV, in religious discourse, there is a "distinction between holiness and fallenness" which "intertwines with a distinction between purity and impurity" (Dikken and Lausten 2005: 118). Rape is viewed in many religions as a form of pollution. Shame often makes a victim feel guilty, thereby internalizing this sense of pollution, the feeling that one is dirty and damaged. The ongoing harm of deep, negative emotions is debilitating. Many women hide their feelings, and do not share them with others until support becomes available, and in war and post-war contexts, support can never be assumed to exist. "Whole villages can be displaced by the threat of mass rape, unravelling age-old social networks that have provided emotional and economic safety-nets" (Jones 2014: 5) within communities.

Considering systematic rapes, Nicola Jones et al. (2014) make six recommendations. First, there is the need to invest in community-level mental health services to support survivors and families to cope with trauma. Local women-of-faith who understand the culture can be of great assistance. Second, legal and community awareness-raising systems that support reporting of sexual violence, successful prosecution, and coping mechanisms should be developed. Third, the prevalence of aggressive practices of masculinity in post-war societies must be challenged. Fourth, economic opportunities should be strengthened to promote women's and girls' independence. Fifth, improved coordination systems that connect transitional justice initiatives to broader security sector reforms are needed. Sixth, sustainable funding is required to support the national implementation of UNSCR 1325.

Understanding the implications of rape on women is important to discern what support is needed. Research was conducted by Medica Zenica, an NGO mentioned in the previous chapter, that has been operating since April 1993 for survivors of war rape and sexual violence in BiH, and by Medica Mondiale, a German-based feminist women's rights organization supporting women and girls in war and conflict regions, with psychosocial and legal counselling, and trauma sensitive medical consultation. The research team interviewed fifty-one survivors who had used the services of Medica Zenica since 1993. This feminist research, committed to changing the status of women and following ethical principles of trauma-sensitivity, found that for seventy percent of the women, "the rape experience completely affects their life today" (Husić et al. 2014: 13). The researchers highlight the impact of religion on their research participants. For example, some Muslim leaders in Bosnia and Croatia "issued various statements intended to promote acceptance of rape survivors" in communities, and this had a positive flow-on effect because the leaders called on both husbands and future husbands to embrace these women, breaking the notion of them as "spoilt, damaged goods" (2014: 39). In many religious families in BiH, these statements "were in fact a strong entry point for survivors to open up to and be supported and accepted by their families" (2014: 40).

The research affirms religion as a coping strategy, and a form of consolation in the face of extreme hardship.

> For example, Elmana believes that God gives her strength, so she says: "Dear Allah gave me strength and mind to look at it this way." She said that she had bad dreams for a while and her grandmother told her "Take abdest before you go to bed and pray until you fall asleep," and it helped. (in Husić et al. 2014: 123)

In giving their life story in the interviews, most of the women said that "religion, their hope and faith in God, helped them to accept their experience, while others valued themselves through helping others to continue with their lives in various ways" (2014: 124). Elmana explains the importance of religious support in being able to join "with women who had special stories" (in 2014: 133), in going to the mosque. When asked about justice, most of the participants were pessimistic, hoping instead for God's justice. For example, Larisa said: "After all these years I am so deeply disappointed in justice, that for some time it had a great psychological impact. I found my justice. I found my justice in a spiritual way" (in Husić et al. 2014: 108). She describes this justice as her hope that all the perpetrators will be punished by God. She said: "The justice from social institutions, courts, I do not believe in it anymore.

It is not a justice for me anymore. For me that is ridiculing the victims. Nothing else. There is no justice there" (in 2014: 108).

Whilst sexual violence occurs everywhere, its manifestations have cultural differences. For example, Ritambhara Mehta (nd) highlights the issues which affect South Asian women, including trafficking, sexual violence, domestic violence, lack of justice for women, honour killings, women used as religious subjects, and religious fundamentalism. She suggests that: "During the time of conflict their bodies become markers of their religion/ethnicity/caste and gender, a battleground" (Mehta nd: 3).

Elsewhere, Felismina dos Santos da Conceição worked undercover assisting resistance fighters in Timor-Leste. Intelligence officers arrested her, and she was interrogated, beaten, and sexually abused. In 1997 she joined with other women survivors to found Fokupers, Timor-Leste's first women's organization working to counter violence against women. When asked to reflect on justice, she said it always made her cry, because, as she expresses it, "I can eat two or three times a day, but for many of my female friends, their life is still a struggle, and they are thirsty for justice" (in Wandita 2015: 183). Attributing justice to the ability to meet daily needs such as having enough to eat, is a different notion of justice to Western legal retributive concepts, one that peacebuilders should note. Felismina de Araújo who also hid in the Timorese forest in 1975 with her husband, working for the resistance and cooking for Falintil, was gang raped by soldiers and high-ranking officers whilst pregnant. She is still hoping "there will be justice. My husband's grave has never been found" (in Wandita 2015: 207). Jacinta de Araújo moved around the forests from 1975 cooking for the guerrillas. She was gang raped by married military men and a year later, she says: "My husband accepted me, and we offer our suffering to God" (in Wandita 2015: 231). This offering is not passive but is an active decision to move from victimhood to *survivor resilience*.

There is sufficient evidence that sexual violence against women tends to increase at the end of war (True 2012). Research shows that in the period deemed to be post-conflict, violence against women often "increases beyond pre-war levels and sometimes even beyond wartime levels," particularly when the partner is a former combatant (Pankhurst 2008: 293). Returning combatants, accustomed to acts of aggression, often bring this mentality into the bedroom and home. These connections between private and public acts of violence by combatants, former combatants, and generally other men, constitute an ongoing "web of harms" (O'Rourke 2013: 38), the unjust injury caused by violence. In both intimate partner violence and war-rape, the act of aggression by a spouse, soldier, paramilitary, or known person humiliates, degrades, and demoralizes. The nature of the harm ranges from shame and humiliation to pregnancy, especially when a child is born with mixed ethnic backgrounds. Other indignities can arise with HIV/AIDS, the onset of nightmares and fear, or ostracization from one's community. Yet even during a transitional period when a society is moving away from past violence, the violent masculinities that dominated during conflict continue (Ní Aoláin 2006b: 830), the very reason the term "post-conflict" can only be used with caution.

GBV can intensify during this transition, because where there are militarized identities, easy access to guns, and an acceptance of the normality of violence, the trauma of lingering insecurities remains. The actual suppression and inequality of women may be concealed behind the mask of newly developed, and seemingly progressive laws that are prompted by the international community, but often are not fully implemented when peacebuilding processes continue without ongoing international support. Yet rarely is intimate partner violence included in post-conflict assessments of political violence because it is not viewed as an intrinsic part of the accountability of a transitional justice process.

Educating Perpetrators Through UNSCR 1325

How do the UNSC resolutions on WPS deal with religion's influence in responding to SGBV? Of the eight WPS resolutions, only two mention religion, namely resolution 1888 (UN Security Council 2009a: note

15) calls on "religious leaders, to play a more active role in sensitizing communities on sexual violence," and resolution 2242 (UN Security Council 2015: note 13) urges member states "to address, including by the empowerment of women, youth, religious, and cultural leaders, the conditions conducive to the spread of terrorism and violent extremism." However, all the WPS resolutions address sexual violence.

UNSCR 1325 (UN Security Council 2000: note 10) calls for "special measures to protect women and girls from gender-based violence, particularly rape and other forms of sexual abuse, and all other forms of violence in situations of armed conflict," and asks for an end to impunity relating to sexual violence against women and girls.

UNSCR 1820 mentions "sexual violence" thirty-five times and calls on member states to ensure that victims of sexual violence "have equal protection under the law and equal access to justice, and *stresses* the importance of ending impunity...as part of a comprehensive approach to seeking sustainable peace, justice, truth, and national reconciliation" (UN Security Council 2008: notes 4, 10). It calls on UN agencies, in consultation with women-led organizations, to develop effective mechanisms to protect women and girls from SGBV in UN managed refugee and internally displaced person's (IDP) camps, disarmament, demobilization, and reintegration (DDR) processes, and in justice and security sector reform efforts. The need for multi-sectoral collaboration across disaster relief agencies, refugee and IDP camps, and peacekeepers is noted.

UNSCR 1888 mentions "sexual violence" forty-eight times. It refers to the urgency of states to bring perpetrators of sexual violence in conflicts to justice, to ensure that survivors have access to justice, are treated with dignity throughout the justice process, and are protected and receive reparation for their suffering, and it urges that justice concerns for victims of sexual violence should be central to UN-led peace negotiations. Of course, what exactly is required for justice differs depending on historical, and cultural needs. It recognizes that women and children "may feel more secure working with and reporting abuse to women in peacekeeping missions," and affirms "the important role of women in rebuilding society" (UN Security Council 2009a: preamble, notes 6, 18).

UNSCR 1889 states the need for "gender-responsive law enforcement and access to justice, as well as enhancing capacity to engage in public decision-making at all levels" (UN Security Council 2009b: note 10). Whilst this is not a direct reference to SGBV, the need for gender-sensitive legal frameworks to protect women and to prosecute perpetrators indirectly covers this. It continues to reiterate the requirement to appoint women to all levels of decision-making and to support women's organizations.

UNSCR 1960 recalls that few perpetrators of sexual violence have been brought to justice and draws attention "to the full range of justice and reconciliation mechanisms to be considered" (UN Security Council 2010: preamble). However, again, what is contained in this full range needs to be culturally appropriate. Including local women protection advisers in peacekeeping missions is one suggestion.

UNSCR 2106 recognizes the importance of investigating and documenting sexual violence in armed conflicts, to bring perpetrators to account, and extend justice for survivors. It outlines the need for a comprehensive approach to transitional justice that encompasses the full range of judicial and non-judicial measures. It urges concerns about SGBV to be included in all forms of transitional justice, justice sector reform initiatives, and strengthening the capacity of civilian and military justice systems in dealing with sexual violence. The resolution: "*Underlines* the important roles that civil society organizations, including women's organizations, and networks can play in enhancing community-level protection... supporting survivors in accessing justice" (UN Security Council 2013: notes 2, 4, 21).

UNSCR 2122 reaffirms "that sustainable peace requires an integrated approach based on coherence between political, security, development, human rights, including gender equality, and rule of law and justice activities." It reiterates "strong condemnation of all violations of international law committed against and/or directly affecting civilians, including women and girls in armed conflict and post-conflict situations, including those involving rape and other forms of sexual and gender-based violence, killing and maiming, obstructions to humanitarian aid, and mass forced displacement" (UN Security Council 2013: preamble, note 9). It seeks to encourage troop-contributing countries to engage with approved manuals on prevention of sexual violence.

UNSCR 2242 expresses "deep concern that acts of sexual and gender-based violence are known to be part of the strategic objectives and ideology of certain terrorist groups, used as a tactic of terrorism, and an instrument to increase their power through supporting financing, recruitment, and the destruction of communities" (UN Security Council 2015: preamble, note 14). Again, it urges prosecution and punishment for perpetrators of violence.

I now outline the responses of member states to these resolutions and the vexing issue of ongoing violence. UNSCR 1325 has four main pillars to address: prevention of violence; protection from violence; participation in peacebuilding and post-conflict reconstruction; and relief and recovery, with the normative pillar overlapping each pillar. In 2004, the UN called on member states to develop national action plans (NAPs) on the implementation of UNSCR 1325. In November 2018, seventy-seven nations (39 percent) had developed a NAP. The Women's International League for Peace and Freedom's PeaceWomen site show that at the end of 2023, one hundred and seven UN member states, 55 percent, have a NAP. Indeed, fifty-six states have one, twenty-seven have two, fifteen have three, six have four and two states are on their fifth plan. It should be noted that about 30 percent of these plans have expired and need updating.

It is beyond the book's scope to detail how these documents are formulated and what impact they make on the ground. From a straightforward search and find of the words "religion" and "faith" conducted in 2017, twenty-three mention religion and/or faith. The summary that follows is necessarily brief, but it shows those NAPs that call on religion or faith to eliminate SGBV. The summary provides context to the significance of my argument of the need to include faith-based organizations and local religious leaders who advocate gender equality, as crucial to the regional application of this resolution in addressing the broad WPS agenda. My purpose in providing the summary is to raise awareness that despite only two resolutions mentioning religion, many nations view it as *an imperative to incorporate religious leaders as part of implementation,* if there is to be any socio-cultural change to the elimination of violence against women, and to *increasing women's leadership in peace and security matters.*

For example, the first Australian NAP notes how "women from certain religious or cultural backgrounds" may be vulnerable to conflict (2012-2018: 6). This includes refugees to Australia and to women in the region. In its second plan it recognizes religion as a possible source of discrimination and reaffirms the need to incorporate faith-based organizations to realise the WPS agenda (2021-2031).

In Europe, the Croatian NAP encourages religious organizations to be involved in humanitarian work and "in the implementation of resolution 1325 and related resolutions" in conflict prevention, peace-building, and participation in peace negotiations. Italy (2010-2013: 7) recognizes the importance of respecting "local cultural and religious traditions" when interacting with Muslim women in Islamic countries, such as deploying women military physicians to Afghanistan and Iraq, and in having "female staff to conduct check-points and house searches." Given the need for continual support for women victims of violence in post-conflict and reconstruction phases, the Italian plan brought together Lebanese, Italian, and UN agencies for planning actions to benefit their home communities, signalling this as good practice in instances where there is weak established protection of human rights, or restrictions due to religious beliefs or traditions. The first Netherlands plan stresses the importance of the design of the legal system, particularly in places where justice is overseen by customary law, "elders, or religious and tribal courts" (2007: 8). Their revised plan gives examples of interreligious dialogue (2012-2015). Norway also pays heed in its NAP to faith-based organizations as critical to implementation, as well as engaging in religious dialogue at national and international levels

(2006: 9, 11; revised 2011-2013 and 2015-2018). In Serbia, religious equality is promoted in its NAP "as core values in the area of security" (2010-2015: 14), an important declaration given its historical record of ethno-religious conflict. To increase the participation of women, Slovenia organized a seminar on peacebuilding, interreligious dialogue, and gender equality (2010-2015: 25-26). To promote the inclusion of a gender perspective into peacebuilding activities, Spain's NAP underlines the need to consider religion, along with variables such as age and ethnicity (2007: 5).

In the Middle East, Afghanistan's NAP (2015-2022: 23), in seeking to prevent violence, emphasizes the need to involve young men and religious leaders in combating SGBV, and seeks to "establish provincial committees (young men and religious leaders) in Kabul and all the thirty-four provinces with the aim of involving them in combating violence against women." The Iraq plan stresses that human rights should be respected and applied equally, regardless of one's religion (2014-2018: 3), a claim built into the constitutional provision of Article 41, the right to freedom of worship.

In Asia, the Indonesian NAP recognizes that efforts to protect and empower women and children during conflict are never simple, but must involve religious leaders, along with a diversity of contributors. As part of its preventative strategy, it calls on "religious community forums of communication to give protection for women and children" (2014-2019: 19, 21). Japan stresses that their NAP should be implemented with consideration given to the unique needs for conflict prevention of ethnic, religious, or linguistic minorities (2015: 5, 12). In the Republic of Korea NAP (2014: 1), there is emphasis on strengthening pre-deployment training on human rights, gender equality, the necessity to eliminate sexual violence, and deepen understandings of local culture and religions. The Philippines NAP acknowledges that along with poor governance, injustice, and the activities of armed groups, "cultural and religious differences" are causes of armed conflicts that must be understood before being removed (2010-2016: 4).

In Africa, in the Democratic Republic of Congo (2010), representatives of religious groups sit on the National Steering Committee, the provincial 1325 Steering Committee, and in local implementation. The Ghana NAP (2012-2014: 20, 25, 27-28) acknowledges the input of faith-based organizations, and organizes gender-awareness seminars on SGBV, and holds training workshops on conflict prevention techniques for the national and regional houses of chiefs, traditional councils, and faith-based organizations, with the indicator of success being "increased acceptability of women as key partners in conflict and dispute resolution by traditional and faith-based leaders evidenced by the presence of women in these bodies." Kenya (2016-2018) includes religious and traditional leaders in consultations to progress their plan and incorporates faith-based personnel in health centres in refugee camps. Liberia's NAP (2009-2013: 27) acknowledges the role of faith-based organizations that were part of their consultation process. Practically, their prevention of violence strategy targets the education of "religious leaders, community elders and parents" who become sensitized to the problem. Senegal's NAP (2011) involves religious communities in alliances to fight against inequalities. Interfaith groups are part of a national task force to implement goals in Sierra Leone (2010-2014: 27), with an emphasis on faith-based organizations contributing to financing, and religious leaders assisting in preventing violence and assisting the vulnerable. Faith-based organizations are important to the implementation of Uganda's plan (2008-2014).

Having listed some of the specific NAPs that strive to include faith-based leaders, it is important to note the impact of regional context. For example, across Africa, the rise of Pentecostal and charismatic theology and practices outlined in Chapter two, is largely detrimental to women's well-being because of its attitude to women's rights and moral agency. If the devil is seen to be responsible for life's insecurities, there is frequently the belief that becoming "born again" will bless the new Christian with health and wealth, which rarely is forthcoming. Contradictions abound. "While the church's leadership teaches men to respect women and discourages gender-based violence, it at the same time places women in a subordinate place where they are the necks not the heads" (Mwaura and Parsitau 2016: 175-176). This encourages women's silence and submission, often exposing women to abuse.

Both the *protection* of those who have suffered sexual violence, and the *prevention* of violent extremism that spuriously uses religion to legitimize violence, are crucial. However, exclusively concentrating on these two goals fails to tap into the vast potential for women-of-faith to use their community networks to enhance more broadly all dimensions of peacebuilding, including attempts to prevent violence by increasing women's active participation in decision-making on peace and security matters. Given that within peacebuilding work, there is increased recognition of the importance of understanding regional realities, and for the localization of programs that reflect states' experience of conflict and emerging security, then localized knowledge of appropriate ways to prevent SGBV is imperative. Here, religious leaders can play a key role. However, often these leaders are exclusively men, which is why women-of-faith peacebuilders often work informally at grassroots and community levels.

For example, whilst not working within an explicit UNSCR 1325 perspective, Religions for Peace (2013), a large global network of different faiths mentioned in the previous chapter, document a wide range of ways that religious leaders and communities can work to overcome violence against women. Their message is that education and awareness are key to facilitating education for healing and leadership-building. An emphasis on prevention of violence is primary, encouraging the involvement of men, youth, and women in campaigns. Advocacy of policy change, public opinion, and new laws also are important. Support and care for survivors of GBV is paramount, especially because victims sometimes never reach survivor status because they are locked into the stranglehold of victimhood. "Survivors' voices must be heard, and in many contexts, religious leaders serve as one of the few safe listeners for survivors" (Religions for Peace 2013: 24). Stories told are full of rage, fear, shame, debasement, and accounts of terrible experiences. Addressing justice to end impunity is crucial.

Buddhist Grace Chung Lee says:

> For too long, religious leaders and individual people of faith have been silent before the facts of violence against women. It is time to break the silences and act. All people of faith are called to say NO to violence against women and girls. (in Religions for Peace 2013: 27)

Catholic Fabio Henao says: "I consider that this sensitivity for the suffering of women should become a hallmark of faith-based communities" (in Religions for Peace 2013: 27). Jewish Steve Gutow proclaims: "How dare we, who are the sons and daughter of prophets, not add our loudest voices to this debate and bring our texts and traditions into the fray of finding solutions to protecting women from violence and rape" (in Religions for Peace 2013: 27)? Muslim Johari Abdul Malik agrees that: "Somehow, men have not learned to treat women in the light of God's mercy" (in Religions for Peace 2013: 27). Anglican Desmond Tutu reiterates: "My humanity is bound up in yours, for we can only be human together" (in Religions for Peace 2013: 27). Pope Francis confirms: "Faith and violence are incompatible" (in Religions for Peace 2013: 27).

Both *protection of victims* and *prevention of further violence* are fundamental peacebuilding strategies, with prevention always being the long-term goal. Educating boys and men that all SGBV is wrong, often goes against cultural mores, which is why it is imperative that local, progressive, religious, and faith-based leaders are part of this gender transformative change strategy. Educating women and girls that they are agents of respect who do not need to accept any personal abuse involves massive changes in cultural assumptions that women are inferior, myths reinforced by traditional religious leaders.

This first section has highlighted the prevalence of violence against women, showing how women often link the violence they suffered to feelings of injustice. I showed how certain NAPs on UNSCR 1325 include the need for religious leaders to play key roles in working to protect victims and prevent further violence. However, caution is warranted. Helen Basini and Caitlin Ryan argue that despite sound attempts to situate national plans within local ownership, "they are driven by a bureaucratic approach to peacebuilding" that reflects an international agenda, which does a "disservice to the hard work and dedication of local women's organizations" (2016: 390). That local organizations frequently are doing the work of UNSCR 1325 without knowing about the resolution or their country's NAP is a massive bonus to local communities.

Healing Victims and Survivors

Trauma Healing

The central tension explored in this chapter is how to balance the immediate need of protecting women from violence and deeply felt harms, with the long-term goal of working to prevent violence from happening. In this second section, I address the urgency of providing meaningful trauma healing for victims. The Greek origin of the word trauma is wound, so psychologically, trauma is a "wound to the soul" (Kleck 2006: 344). As Jennifer Llewellyn and Daniel Philpott explain, "if wounds identify the harms to which the justice of reconciliation brings repair, practices are the concrete activities that bring about this repair," and they list socially just institutions, acknowledgement of suffering, reparations, accountability, apology, and forgiveness as relevant practices (2014: 27).

Many women-of-faith situate the full gamut of GBV to the forefront of their peacebuilding and justice-building priorities. Places of religious worship are often a first point of contact for victims of violence. Within this space, women-of-faith offer psycho-social and spiritual support that they hope will help to heal those who are victimized by war, through rediscovering their humanity. The violations can be so extreme that victims feel debased, their dignity quite destroyed. "The opportunity to tell one's story in one's own words…is not something other than justice; it is an essential component of justice" (Phelps 2004: 61), part of the rehumanizing process, of being made to feel whole again, initially, through having someone listen deeply to the story being told.

Hayward (2015: 317) offers examples of women-of-faith peacebuilders who assist victims. In northern Uganda, Catholic Sister Pauline Acayo, a member of the Acholi Religious Leaders Peace Initiative offers psychosocial trauma counselling and traditional indigenous ceremonies to more than two thousand former child combatants who were forced into sexual slavery from the Lord's Resistance Army (LRA) which is active in Uganda, the DRC, South Sudan, and the Central African Republic. Acayo had been abducted by the LRA, as were two of her brothers who she never heard from again. DDR programs tend to focus on capturing leaders and disarming them. Sister Pauline's work is with those who are vulnerable, leading rehabilitation and trauma healing programs, taking classes in nonviolent conflict resolution, and helping former child soldiers heal their trauma and shame. Some learn to become peacebuilders themselves.

This work is significant, because as Love suggests, "by lifting up vulnerable people so marginalized even among those displaced in war zones, and enabling them to make positive contributions to building peace in their communities," Sister Pauline's work "emphasizes the importance of participation, right relationship, and reconciliation as integral elements in peacebuilding" (2015: 53). This type of peacebuilding is transformative in changing old restrictive patterns that exclude the marginalized and vulnerable from community life. Sister Mary Tarcisia Loko also works in Uganda with child mothers, girls who had been abducted as sex slaves for the LRA. She was the first woman leader to serve as part of the Acholi Religious Leaders Peace Initiative, a group that negotiated among the armed groups. She said: "we are trying to give them a possibility to have them feel as though they are persons again" (in Love 2015: 54), something she could say, even though "the LRA killed her father, brothers, and many other family members and people in her religious community" (2015: 54). Her work as a trauma healer demonstrates that a commitment to community participation is not a mere buzz idea, but a powerful motivation to expand the range of people involved in participation.

Centre Olame, is a Catholic social assistance agency in South Kivu that provides practical and psychological assistance to victims of SGBV, empowers women to resist pervasive discrimination, and promotes local peacebuilding and reconciliation. Mathilde Muhindo Mwamini, director of Centre Olame has worked there since the mid-1980s, providing psychological and practical assistance to victims of SGBV. Sister Marie-Bernard Alima works in eastern DRC. In 2001, she created the Coordination of Women for Democracy and Peace. This is a civil society network that trains women leaders in human rights, lobbying against SGBV, and improving political knowledge as transitional justice leaders, "to encourage women's participation in politics and governance as both voters and elected leaders" (Love 2015: 24). The work is extensive, including medical assistance, psychosocial counselling, and trauma healing.

As part of prevention programs, Alima trains military, police, and security forces, and community and church leaders in programs to prevent SGBV, and to promote non-violent conflict resolution techniques. A surprising example she provides is "of a woman survivor of rape who, in six months, went through their programs, learned to read and write, and was elected head of her village, including by the men who had been her attackers" (Love 2015: 45). We cannot conclude from this that all women should be reintegrated back into communities where their abuser is present. Few women can do so, this is an exception, not the norm. Synergy of Women for Victims of Sexual Violence is a coalition of thirty-five women's organizations helping victims of SGBV in the DRC. Justine Masika Bihamba, the founder, continues to criticize the culture of impunity around sexual assault, a fact the UNSC resolutions reiterate.

These examples from Africa give a brief insight into the work being done to help trauma healing. What they show is not that women-of-faith peacebuilders necessarily provide more trauma-sensitive support than secular advisers. What they show is that for individual victims who find religion, faith, and a belief in God meaningful to their daily survival, sensitivity to their faith is an important part of their healing. For devastated women, trauma healing work is best done by local women who understand the cultural sensitivities of victims' harms, rather than the proselytizing and potential damage that sometimes is caused by outsiders who seek to do good, but unintentionally disregard cultural and religious sensitivities.

Human Trafficking

Human trafficking is a vast, global, organized crime. It is relevant in this chapter because many trafficked women and girls come from conflict countries. Of course, each victim who is "rescued" from a degrading life experiences a relief, a longed-for freedom, but I show that thorough ways of breaking long-term patterns of systemic violence also are needed if trafficking is to be slowed and eventually halted.

This argument is another slant on the protection of victims and prevention of violence priorities. UNSCR 2331 is a resolution on the "maintenance of international peace and security" which refers to trafficking in its preamble and expresses deep concern that acts of SGBV are associated to trafficking in persons as "part of the strategic objectives and ideology of certain terrorist groups" (UN Security Council 2016). This resolution emphasizes "the importance of engaging religious and traditional leaders, paying particular attention to amplifying the voices of women and girls alongside men and boys with the objective of countering terrorism and violent extremism which can be conducive to terrorism" (UN Security Council 2016). In its note eight, it speaks against any use of religious justification to "institutionalize sexual slavery."

Human trafficking is defined in the Palermo Protocol to Prevent, Suppress, and Punish Trafficking in Persons, Especially Women and Children (2000), supplementing the UN Convention Against

Transnational Organized Crime. Key concepts in the protocol include threat, use of force, or other forms of coercion, abduction, fraud, deception, abuse of power or position of vulnerability, and having control over another person for the purposes of exploitation. Indicators of trafficking for sexual exploitation include signs of deceptive recruitment about motivation for work; coercive recruitment, such as forced marriage, debt bondage, or violence on victims; recruitment by abuse of vulnerability such as abuse of illegal status, lack of education or information, or economic reasons; exploitation, such as excessive work hours, or low or no salary; coercion at destination, including confiscation of documents, forced tasks, or isolation; and abuse of vulnerability at destination, such as dependency on exploiters.

Beate Andrees (2014), writing from an International Labour Organization (ILO) perspective, a UN agency that brings together governments, employers, and workers' representatives to set labour standards, develop policies, and promote decent work, explains why definitions matter in developing reliable data to guide action on forced labor. She cautions that while naming all trafficking as "slavery" raises public attention to galvanize action, it does not necessarily help the world's poor or end their misery. "Ending slavery or forced labor requires targeted action to change laws, to bring offenders to justice, to protect victims, and to empower those at risk" (Andrees 2014). While preventative measures such as eliminating abusive recruitment, or aiding children to attend school, can tackle systemic problems of injustice, more is needed to safeguard decent work for all.

Modern slavery is defined as "situations of exploitation that a person cannot refuse or leave because of threats, violence, coercion, abuse of power, or deception" (Global Slavery Index 2016: 12). The creators of the Global Slavery Index estimate there are 45.8 million people who are subject to modern slavery (2016: 8). In top ranking order, countries that have at least one percent or more of slaves include North Korea, Uzbekistan, Cambodia, India, Qatar, Pakistan, DRC, Sudan, Iraq, Afghanistan, Yemen, Syria, South Sudan, Somalia, Libya, Central African Republic, and Mauritania (2016: 28), countries where violent conflict is rife or human rights are suppressed. I return to the equation of trafficking with slavery later.

The ILO website (2016) cites the following statistics on human trafficking "Almost twenty-one million people are victims of forced labor – 11.4 million women and girls and 9.5 million men and boys...forced labor in the private economy generates US$150 billion in illegal profits per year." According to the ILO, the numbers of victims of forced sexual exploitation represent twenty-two percent of all victims. This issue is important in a book on peacebuilding, because "traffickers often use routes through countries that have been engulfed by conflict, since border controls and normal policing are reduced" (Heyzer 2006: 108). Post-war situations worsen the vulnerability of women to trafficking because their everyday social and economic support networks are diminished; they are often displaced or moving away from known communities, and desperation for survival mounts.

UN Office on Drugs and Crime (UNODC) statistics differ from the ILO ones, and they state that the magnitude of the trafficking problem in terms of numbers of victims "is hotly debated as there is no methodologically sound available estimate" (2014: 34), given that much of this activity is undercover. Hence with caution, they estimate that for the 2010-2012 period: 49 percent of detected victims are adult women, and 21 percent are girls, meaning that women and girls constitute 70 percent of victims. When this is broken down, sexual exploitation accounts for 53 percent among all detected victims in Africa and the Middle East, 48 percent in the Americas, 26 percent in East Asia, South Asia, and the Pacific, and 66 percent in Europe and Central Asia (UNODC 2014: 9). Overall, in 2011, they suggest that 53 percent of detected trafficked victims were for sexual exploitation (UNODC 2014: 13), higher than ILO statistics. The gender breakdown of detected victims of trafficking for sexual exploitation 2010-2012 is 97 percent women and girls (UNODC 2014: 41). The ILO and UNODC statistics vary, but deeper analysis is beyond the scope of this book.

Churches' Responses to Trafficking

Religious institutions are often complicit in suppressing or hiding the sexual abuse of boys and young men, as well as girls and young women. Religious institutions rarely do enough to contest sexual violence that is initiated by clergy and lay workers. Yet, women-of-faith peacebuilders often prioritize dealing with abuse as intrinsic to their just practices. The theological spectrum that takes sex trafficking as a central justice focus is wide, from feminist groups through to Christian right organizations and not all link justice to building peace.

It is worth noting that human trafficking, particularly sex trafficking, is the cause chosen by some evangelical groups, as a focus on fighting injustices. Within the United States, evangelical Protestantism is growing as the largest religious group. Some reasons for the growth of these religious groups' focus on anti-trafficking concerns are political. Under the former Bush's administration, faith-based organizations were eligible to receive federal funding and the evangelical advocacy on human trafficking grew. For most evangelicals, the fight against slavery is linked to social purity and moral reform. Trying to stop sexual slavery is politically uncontentious, running parallel to the right-wing concerns of advocacy around family values and rescuing women from having to work outside the home, reinstating traditional gender roles as a mark of freedom. International Justice Mission is the largest Christian anti-trafficking organization in the US with eighty fulltime staff in fourteen countries. This mission adopts a "rescue-and-restore model of activism" (Bernstein 2010: 61). Brothels are raided by police and NGO workers, and trafficked women are "rescued" and placed in a rehabilitation centre, but sometimes these raids "exacerbate violence against sex workers" (Ahmed and Seshu 2015: 174) when corrupt police officers beat women or divert them to other forms of sex exploitation.

The group known as A21, which stands for "Abolishing Injustice in the Twenty-first Century" is an anti-human trafficking organization that fights slavery around the globe. This non-profit organization has paid staff members around the world and a vast team of volunteers. There is a focus on Europe, with Greece as a primary gateway for victims from eastern Europe, the Balkans, and Nigeria, and on Ukraine as one of the largest exporters of women to the European Union, Middle East, and Southeast Asia, and on Bulgaria as a source and destination country for ethnic Roma women.

While not having peacebuilding as a central goal, the organization has a four-pillar strategy, like the four pillars of UNSCR 1325. The first pillar is *prevention*, seeking "to stop individuals from becoming victims of human trafficking by providing awareness, education to the next generation, and interrupting the demand" (A21 2016). Education curriculum is aimed at potential victims of trafficking in schools, orphanages, and universities. Yet, Dian Haynes (2017) claims there is a lack of data to demonstrate evidence that awareness campaigns assist potential or actual trafficked victims. The second pillar is *protection of survivors*, by providing a safe environment, including restoration programs in aftercare facilities. There are two-prongs to this pillar: rescue offering support to local law enforcement and governmental agencies in training, investigations, and data collection; and restoration, supporting survivors physically and emotionally through education, vocational training, and repatriation assistance such as craft enterprises. Supply of resources by A21 of water, warm showers, and housing projects for refugees in Greece in 2016 is a constructive move as refugees are at risk of exploitation. The third pillar of *partnerships* works with fundraisers, governmental agencies, and community members to maximize support through training, sharing education materials, planning new prevention initiatives, collaborating, and sharing information with law enforcement, government agencies, and local service providers. The fourth pillar is *prosecution* of traffickers, including providing survivors with legal counsel, and strengthening the legal responses to human trafficking to reinforce accountability. Their ambitious claim is: "We believe that through this 4 P Model, we will see human trafficking end in our lifetime" (A21 2016). Supporters of A21 celebrate the rescue of

each new survivor by police, border officials, government social workers, or a neighbour as a "safe victory."

The organization's website claims that modern day slavery "can and
will be ended in our lifetime" (A21 2016). Their language is on becoming a rescuer of "real people with names, faces, hearts, feelings, and des-
tiny" (A21 2016). Every statistic represents the life of a human being.
Christine Caine, founder of A21, integrates justice into her statements
(A21 2016), such as: "Together, we will see the injustice of human trafficking abolished;" or "I love that what is consuming our conversations
are issues of justice and mercy;" or we're called "to move mountains of
injustice and allow rivers of mercy, compassion, truth, hope, and justice to flow." There are assumptions that: "together we are bringing an
end to slavery right now" (A21 2017: 10); the claim is that "we're stopping human trafficking before it starts" (A21 2017: 17); and "slavery is
abolished when we rally together" (A21 2017: 27). Undoubtedly, A21
achieves many positive outcomes. The rescue of everyone is liberating.
However, as expanded shortly, faith-based rescue initiatives must be
situated alongside of structural efforts to amend systemic injustices to
halt entrenched patterns.

Saving slaves while saving souls has a stark historical irony, given
that many Christians justified the slave trade. It is not Christianity alone
that adopts trafficking as a moral campaign. Sushma Joshi comes from
Nepal and a strongly conservative Brahmin family from Kathmandu.
In her culture, purity, chastity, and virginity are highly valued. She explains how Nepal experienced a growth of NGOs in the 1990s after de-
mocratization with many anti-trafficking measures aimed particularly
at "rehabilitation" and "rescue" (2015: 81). Joshi clarifies further that
many of these organizations were "dominated by urban, middle-class,
predominantly Brahmin-Chettri women, and fuelled by orthodox,
gendered moral ideologies" (2015: 81). Joshi explains that the need for
anti-trafficking organizations to "portray the girls as completely chaste
and innocent victims," perpetuates the custom of chastity, despite
knowing that some of the trafficked girls go to India with men with
whom they have had sexual relationships (2015: 82). In being critical

of the emphasis on rehabilitation and rescue, Joshi asks the challenging questions whether these programs stop trafficking, "or do they merely hinder women's mobility across states without providing them any other viable alternative to sources of income, employment, and livelihood" (2015: 88)? When trafficked girls and women return to Nepal, Joshi explains how "the focus is to make them into 'decent' women with bourgeois sensibilities. There is little effort put into making them independent and self-reliant" (2015: 89).

The role of global poverty in driving the dynamics of trafficking in conflict-affected countries often is ignored by contemporary abolitionists, who stress sexual integrity and rescue. While each liberation is of immense personal significance, I move now to posit as an alternative strategy, the empowering that comes to survivors when peacebuilders also address structural injustices.

Empowering Survivors

In concentrating on sexual slavery, abolitionists "neutralized" the political struggle around labour, migration, and sexual freedom (Carrington 2015: 37). Feminist peacebuilders agree that what is needed is less of an individualistic rescue and save approach, because it can be paternalistic, moralistic, and its long-term effectiveness is questionable. Rather, what is more helpful is a concerted effort on improving gender equality, through addressing systemic racism, socio-economic reforms, immigrant rights, mental health, employment, prison systems, and broad-based social justice realities where anti-trafficking strategies are rooted. These goals are part of broad-based understandings of peacebuilding.

Noeleen Heyzer, former Executive Director of UNIFEM (now UN Women), rightly points out that human trafficking includes "debt bondage, forced labor and enslavement of adults and children, but also child soldiering or sexual slavery" (2006: 101). As noted, the sheer numbers of people being trafficked are difficult to discern accurately given the secretive, illegal nature of the activity. The trafficking of women is discernible with the movement of people within and from conflict zones as refugees and internally-displaced persons. In contexts of insecurity, vulnerability increases. The rescue of each person who has been trafficked is a miracle of freedom, but this stress alone does little to instigate structural, expansive, long-term preventative change.

I support Heyzer's argument of the need for a *gender-responsive, human rights-based approach to trafficking*, given that "violations of human rights are both a cause and consequence of trafficking in persons" (2006: 112). She proposes a range of actions that address the factors generating both the demand for trafficking and the supply of persons. These include economic empowerment for women and girls; livelihood strategies; safe migration and citizenship rights; transforming gender-biased attitudes in countries of destination; and integrating human rights and development strategies (2006: 113-119). Similarly, Kerry Carrington also defends the need to address trafficking at its structural roots, tackling "migration intakes, ineffective labour protection for poor and unskilled workers, and endemic gender, race, and class discrimination that facilitated demand for exploited labour" (2015: 38). This comprehensive approach to trafficking is geared toward systematic, long-term strategies.

A range of organizations take this structural view of the changes that are needed. The Coalition Against Trafficking in Women (CATW) is an NGO that works to end human trafficking and the commercial sexual exploitation of women and children worldwide. CATW holds Special Status with the United Nations Economic and Social Council and was a key consultant at the UN Transnational Organized Crime Meeting, the outcome of which is the Palermo Protocol, the most recognized legal instrument on human trafficking. It is the world's first organization to fight trafficking internationally and is the world's leading abolitionist organization. It engages in advocacy, education, victim services, and prevention programs for victims in Asia, Africa, Latin America, Europe, and North America. The Global Alliance against Traffic in Women, founded in 1994 has more than one hundred organizational members. It applies a human-rights based approach to addressing trafficking and links trafficking with gender, migration, and labour frameworks. Caritas Europa, assist trafficked persons and address root causes of trafficking. Their counter-trafficking underlies the need to fight poverty and social exclusion, as well as responding to emergencies that arise from post-war needs, all tasks closely aligned with peacebuilding.

Protection versus Prevention

I return the discussion to a refinement of the protection of victims versus the prevention of further violence debates that are crucial to the politics of peacebuilding. I argue that both are needed, but *prevention should be the primary long-term strategy.*

Research by Sarah Edwards on behalf of the Anti-Trafficking Monitoring Group in the UK, found that protection and prosecution tend to frame anti-trafficking work, rather than prevention (2012: 3). Yet prevention tackles underlying causes with the intention of reducing the numbers of victims. The Council of Europe Convention on Action against Trafficking requires states: "to take a holistic approach to prevention by implementing measures to address the underlying and structural causes of trafficking (through social and economic initiatives)" (in Edwards 2012: 3). Such an approach includes education about trafficking, engaging transport operators and commercial carriers in anti-trafficking, assisting legal migration, and strengthening national coordination. Addressing the demand is difficult because it requires male champions to deconstruct traditional masculinity throughout all levels of society. A successful prevention strategy addresses empowerment of those who are exposed to trafficking, as well as the "political or economic relationships which create the social and economic conditions that fuel the problem" (Edwards 2012: 4). Prevention reduces potential victims' vulnerability, and increases the risks involved to potential traffickers. In post-conflict contexts, *prevention strategies of peacebuilders should be linked to international development, human rights protection, poverty reduction, and social inclusion strategies,* all aspects of post-conflict reconstruction within transitional justice.

Within the globalized capitalist economy, as well as in post-war contexts, certain women see sex work as their only option to survive or feed their family. All interventions that are introduced by women-of-faith peacebuilders that address poverty, hunger, disease, illiteracy, and economic independence help to reduce SGBV and the shame that comes with being trafficked or forced through circumstances to sell their bodies. Rescue-based anti-trafficking efforts free individuals, but the broader concerns of structural violence and economic determinants of exploitative globalized labour must also be addressed. A holistic anti-trafficking policy is centred on protection *and* prevention in the context of universal human rights, recognizing workers' access to, or lack of, justice. Only then, can opportunities for empowerment occur.

I conclude by returning to the idea that violence against women and girls includes not only sexual violence, but the gendered violence of injustices in everyday life. Through re-examining the emphasis on justice in the UNSCRs on WPS, I show the importance of addressing structural, systemic violence against women, as a way to prevent further victims from being harmed, and also to empower survivors.

Violent Injustice of Everyday Lives

The empowerment of violated victims is more likely to occur where there is an abundance of support. Many women-of-faith peacebuilders provide this support as healers and careful listeners. For feminist women-of-faith peacebuilders who witness violent injustices in everyday lives, a transformative praxis requires strategies to transform violence, understood broadly, and thereby overcome the crippling nature of insecurities and injustices. Religious understandings of peace, *shalom,* or *salaam,* all embrace interrelated interpretations of social justice and reconciliation. Whilst UNSCR 1325 does not refer to justice, all seven of the sister resolutions do. These resolutions are outlined above in section one as they relate to sexual violence, here I reiterate the points relating to addressing injustices, as background to the justice emphasis of praxis that follows.

UNSCR 1820, writes of "equal access to justice" (UN Security Council 2008: notes 4, 10). UNSCR 1888 refers to the urgency of states to bring perpetrators of sexual violence in conflicts to justice and to ensure that survivors have access to justice (UN Security Council 2009: notes 6, 7, 8a, 17). UNSCR 1889, again stresses the need for "gender-responsive law enforcement and access to justice" (UN Security Council 2009: note 10). In its preamble, UNSCR 1960 draws attention "to the full range of justice and reconciliation mechanisms to be considered" (UN Security Council 2010). UNSCR 2106 "*Underlines* the important roles that civil society organizations, including women's organizations, and networks can play in enhancing community-level protection… supporting survivors in accessing justice" (UN Security Council 2013: notes 4, 12, 16c, 18, 21). UNSCR 2122 reiterates the need for an integrated approach to building sustainable peace to include "political, security, development, human rights, including gender equality, and rule of law and justice activities" (UN Security Council 2013: notes 2e, 10). Its recommendations recognize the need to eliminate obstacles in women's access to justice. UNSCR 2242 urges "member states to strengthen access to justice for women in conflict and post-conflict situations" (2015: note 4).

Justice plays a significant role in these resolutions, with good reason. Without justice, peace remains fragile. To move past any oppositional politics of a "protection versus participation" pull, Paul Kirby and Laura Shepherd identify two approaches. The first approach links sexualized violence and participation, recognizing "that women are unlikely to be able to participate effectively in peace and security governance if their immediate security environment is compromised by the prevalence of sexualized and gender-based violence" (Kirby and Shepherd 2016: 381). Given repressive and patriarchal religious beliefs that are used to legitimize violence against women, increasing the participation of women in public decision-making settings requires extensive changes, not only to layers of structural and cultural violence, but to the religious beliefs and practices that normalize men's violence toward women in everyday life. Kirby and Shepherd's second approach propose "a deeper, cross-institutional and meshing of the parallel pillars of the WPS agenda...and connects protection from and prevention of violence to participation at multiple levels" in all processes of peacebuilding and post-conflict reconstruction (2016: 381). The WPS agenda can collaborate with religious peacebuilders to engage in constructive transformation of a world that currently is built around intersecting structures of domination, oppression, and submission. A holistic framework intersects with changes in economics, justice, security, and formal politics to realize this transformation. Of course, in corrupt, unjust contexts, this sounds remarkably idealistic.

Ending the spiral of violence is needed to free humanity from diverse forms of oppression. The active struggle for justice involves creating flourishing relationships at every level of society. *Justice creates the conditions in which dignity is affirmed and relationships can flourish.* The distinctive contribution of faith-based actors lies in the extent to which their peacebuilding practices back the eradication of injustice. This includes adopting a reverence for people's lives, respect of dignity, compassion toward those who suffer, and support of projects for sustainable communities. Women-of-faith peacebuilders make a massive contribution to preventing victim violence, and empowering violated victims to transition in their journey toward becoming survivors.

***

This chapter examines how women-of-faith peacebuilders empower victims of abuse. In acknowledging the terrible extent of sexual and gender-based violence, the chapter shows that whilst the UNSC resolutions on women, peace, and security all discuss sexual violence, only two mention religion. Yet, a sizeable number of national action plans on implementing UNSCR 1325 draw on religious or faith-based leaders to help curb the prevalence of conflict-related sexual violence. Examples, mainly from African nations, show women-of-faith peacebuilder's active involvement in helping women and girls move from trauma-tized victim of abuse to survivor status, someone with resilience, who can proceed through life without always being troubled by disturbing reminders of demeaning acts endured, and the negative consequences of being abused. I then suggest that while every life that is "rescued" from sexual slavery is valuable, individual release does not necessarily lead to long-term empowerment, and it does little to attack structural reasons why trafficking is growing.

For empowerment to be practised in cultures where gender equality is not the norm, strategies to further women's active agency, must be locally driven. Given that violence emerges in many forms of injustices that are inflicted on people's everyday lives, actively working toward the prevention of all forms of violence, the protection of all victims of violence, and the prosecution of perpetrators of abuse, requires transformative strategies to address root causes of violence at cultural, political, economic, personal, and religious levels. The work of women-of-faith peacebuilders to eliminate any acceptance of the inevitability of violence, and act to undo, or lessen victims' hurt, is essential, as too is the support of male champions.

7

Women-of-faith Practising Just Peace

Chapter seven explores further the unique contribution that women-of-faith make in their practices of building just peace. It brings together many of the themes already introduced in the previous chapters. The chapter has four main goals.

My first goal is to confirm the unique contribution that women-of-faith peacebuilders make in fostering just peace. I focus on the value that many women place on accepting that women from a multiplicity of faith backgrounds *can work together* to realize shared aims of improving gender equality and justice.

Second, I explore the role that *compassion* plays in women-of-faith's practices of just peace. I show how women-of-faith peacebuilders demonstrate compassion, and engage deliberately and diligently in empathy, attentive listening, and open respectful dialogue. I also demonstrate that for women-of-faith peacebuilders, compassion means a variety of ways to respond to the suffering caused by war injustices.

The third goal examines what is needed to foster *reconciliation* in societies recovering from antagonistic and distrustful relationships. Examples show that reconciling relationships requires the building or rebuilding of relationships anew, where acknowledgement of harm caused or suffered, apology, forgiveness, and trust, are observed. I argue that women-of-faith peacebuilders tend to bring their commitment to relationships, a responsibility to care, and compassion to their acts of reconciliation, signalling unique responses.

Fourth, I outline examples of individual women-of-faith who deliberately practice just peace. Selective instances of women-of-faith who *purposely integrate their faith into their pursuit of justice in peacebuilding activities* are provided to highlight their distinctive contribution to peacebuilding.

My overall argument is twofold. First, the women, peace, and security community of academics, concerned students, policy-makers, NGOs, development and aid practitioners, UN advisers, grassroots groups, and interfaith organizations, can learn from understanding more about the localized work of women-of-faith peacebuilders who build just peace. Second, a more concerted effort to include this faith-based work into international partnerships is of immense value in increasing women's participation in WPS matters in ways that are culturally acceptable, because these women include an understanding of deeply rooted religious, cultural, and faith beliefs.

Women Doing Peacebuilding Differently

This entire book is based on a hunch that *women-of-faith are doing peacebuilding differently* from men-of-faith, and their driving force for activism and political engagement differs to secular women working on the WPS agenda, even though they share common goals. This chapter proceeds with this inkling to demonstrate what their practices reveal. It is true that, as outlined in Chapter five, some women are engaged in violent extremism or acts of violence that they maintain have religious legitimacy. While not dismissing this, because it is an increasing concern, I focus rather on those examples of women-of-faith who are working for peace.

Hence this first section examines the way that women-of-faith include individuals from multiple faiths to understand and respect those differences that frequently are the reasons for violent conflict. For example, Mona Siddiqui, a British Muslim who works on Christian and Muslim relationships, maintains that "values such as justice, equality, empathy, religious freedoms, and human rights for all may seem to be distinct values of secular modernity, the Enlightenment heritage, and the preserve of liberal democracies. But they also resonate across diverse religious populations" (2016: 84). She agrees that these are all politically and theologically charged terms, but their concern is with establishing moral accountability and *principles that connect humanity*. Such an aspiration toward *shared values* and making *meaningful connections* guides the political activism of the women discussed in this chapter.

Inclusivity and Difference

Inclusivity matters. I return the reader to the active notion of agency – or why we deliberately do what we do. In earlier chapters, I argue that a feminist relational view sees agency as situated in everyday lives; interdependence as fundamental to being human; and differences as inevitable in life narratives. Being *inclusive to differences* is an integral part of this view of agency. It is, as argued in earlier chapters, a commitment to relationality, which Fiona Robinson (2011: 4) suggests goes further than merely saying we are social creatures, to the claim that both dependency and interdependency are fundamental aspects of being human. This narrative understanding of the self-in-relationships requires great sensitivity to what others need to live a decent life, and how others can be included in policies, practices, programs, and strategies in ways that genuinely are inclusive of cultural practices, including cherished beliefs. Questions of inclusivity should be asked continually, such as inclusion in what and inclusion of whom?

To say that feminists prioritize differences within narratives is to include the multiplicity of locations that constitute diverse women's lives, always paying attention to context. Clearly in peacebuilding work, the environment matters enormously, whether the stories emerge about living in and through war, escaping from bombed territories, life in internally displaced camps, hiding in the jungle, struggling in refugee camps, or looking for opportunities in those post-war, transitional justice moments where there are prospects for transformation.

When we begin to unpack what is really involved in multiplicity and pluralism, there is great variation in what is included and how significant it is. For example, in Ghana, the traditional Akan indigenous religious wisdom for living together in a community of men and women is encapsulated in one proverb – *Wonsom! Wonye nipa* (Come, let's hold it together). What this means is that:

> When there is a problem to be dealt with in a community, everybody, irrespective of their religion, race, class, or gender, is useful and needed for dealing with the emerging problem. To be human, in this saying, is to be the one who cares and is concerned with the needs of people despite their differences. (Amoah 2012: 247)

The application of this proverb of course throws up emotive and practical challenges of how faith-based communities can work together on issues that, in this instance, affect different African women.

Often, feminist debates around sameness and difference lead to an impasse, where it is understood that most women share similar social locations in relation to patriarchal gendered stereotypes, yet are vastly different in respect to how race, class, sexuality, ethnicity, presence or absence of children, level of dis/ability, geographic location, and religious beliefs intersect in complex ways. Christian theologian Jeannine Hill Fletcher suggests that we must go beyond this impasse, "for neither total sameness nor radical difference works in real encounters with people of other faiths" (in Pui-Lan, 2012: 57). There must be space for theories and practices on multiplicity and hybrid identities. Such a mixture of backgrounds allows women to identify, even partially, with aspects of identities that do overlap, and as examples demonstrate, this facilitates partnerships across boundaries of religious differences. This identification might simply begin with a group of mothers needing to find food for their families. Typically, this collaboration occurs in grassroots movements where women of different faiths sometimes work separately, but more frequently come together to work for justice and meet practical needs. I contend that *inclusivity* is valued by women-of-faith peacebuilders as *taking seriously the differences in life narratives*.

Equality and Justice

Intrinsic to the reason why inclusion is important to women-of-faith peacebuilders is a feminist *commitment to equality*, even when many of these women do not explicitly identify with feminism. In addition to equality, the theme of justice flows throughout this book, particularly as it relates to creating just peace. The *just peace* is more than combining justice and peace, it is an affirmation that one is not fully possible without the other, they are intricately intertwined. *Gender equality, justice, sustainable peace, and care for others are interrelated*, but working out how to bring them together is complex. Women-of-faith are significant in combining these interrelated goals and practices that help to build a caring, just peace.

Understanding the relationship between justice and care is important. Carol Gilligan, a moral psychologist, argues that justice and care are "two cross-cutting perspectives" that cut across egoism and altruism (1982: 25). Her view is that because we are all equally vulnerable to all sorts of suffering, "the moral injunction not to act unfairly toward others, and not to turn away from someone in need, capture these different concerns" of justice and care (1982: 20). Paying attention to care alone is insufficient, because the caring woman can lose her autonomy and rights when she is taken for granted, and her care is exploited. Hence to avoid seeing care as any form of paternalism, the practices of care such as *attentiveness, responsiveness to others' needs,* and *responsibility to care,* need to be integrated with virtues of justice, such as fairness, rights, and autonomy. As Anna Höglund expresses it, to care for others requires a respect for their rights (2003: 361). In going beyond an individual rights-based discussion, I suggest that the feminist ideal of equal inclusion is in the hope that through taking on the responsibility for care of others, a form of justice will be done. Expressed differently, *the failures of injustice reflect the failures to care for people.* These failures and responsibilities to redress them come to the fore, particularly during transitional justice processes when new laws and policies around equality and justice are formulated.

An example of bringing equality and justice together is pertinent. In the 1997-2004 reform era in Iran, women were at the forefront of prioritizing the need to rectify gender inequality in ways that challenge key interpretations of Islamic law. Women could do this by reconciling their "religious and political beliefs by widening the Islamic framework and finding legitimacy within it" (Anderlini 2007: 127). This way of framing women's rights within a modified form of Islamic discourse, is a useful safeguard for women against any traditional religious counter-attack. In 2006 in Iran, women reached cross the political, religious, and ideological divides to launch "a campaign to collect one million signatures in support of changing gender-based discriminatory laws," and framing this as a social issue that affects primarily women, regardless of class or religious learning, was instrumental in the movement gaining support (Anderlini 2007: 37). These Iranian women challenged the existing power base through a lens of social justice, confirming their religious faith. This approach enhances the likelihood of an acceptance of change and shows how women work for just peace in creative ways.

This first section maintains that including a range of different identities and beliefs in peacebuilding work broadens the likelihood of widespread transformative change. It also contends that considerations of religious differences are needed to realize the merging of gender equality and just peace in culturally relevant ways.

Demonstrating Compassion

What role does compassion play in practices of just peace? Is compassion essential for just peace? How is compassion possible if all humans have the capacity for cruelty and evil? Quite simply, I believe that all humans also have the capacity for good, thus also potentially for compassion. Circumstances, gendered socialization, and fear of the other, tend to suppress this human capacity.

In this second section, I argue that for women-of-faith peacebuilders, their faith drives their *acts of compassion to do justice* and *help the vulnerable*, particularly those who suffer injustices. Within religious traditions, charity, sympathy, empathy, and compassion take on different meanings. I place them initially under the heading of empathy and explain some of the differences.

Empathy

Before explaining empathy, it is useful to look at a related concept like charity. Religious beliefs have long been associated with a humanitarian charitable ethic. Michael Barnett and Thomas Weiss (2008: 20) state that in terms of international assistance to humanitarian needs, religion-inspired NGOs such as Catholic Relief Services, CARE, Oxfam, and World Vision are among the top contributors. Indeed, charity is a fundamental aspect of religions' mission, a cornerstone of practising faith.

> Christianity's notion of love and compassion includes the idea of charity and obligations to strangers. *Zakat*, which roughly

translates to voluntarism, is one of the five pillars of Islam and reflects Islamic identity, commands various forms of charity, and is intended to foster solidarity within the community. *Tzadakah* and the idea of repairing the world makes charity in good works part of the Jewish identity. (Barnett and Weiss 2008: 9)

Take for example the African continent, where religious groups play a significant role in the health sector, "delivering 25-75 percent of services and playing a key role in the provision of care and treatment in the wake of the HIV and AIDS pandemic" (AWID 2016: 29). However, we should be mindful that within many religious, charitable organizations, there can be moralizing of messages about sexuality, gender, prevention of disease, and stigmatization of those with HIV/ AIDS that undermine the right of women to insist on fidelity or safe sex. However, without the charity shown by religious organizations, massive gaps in health care would widen.

Western-based aid agencies increasingly work in countries with large Muslim populations and thus need to be sensitive to diverse religious beliefs. Islamic humanitarian organizations began to respond to the drought and famine in the greater Horn of Africa in the late 1970s and to the war in Afghanistan after the Soviet Union invasion of 1979. Laura Hammond writes that a central tenet of Islam is "the fusing of charitable work with spiritual duty... and those following this approach may be accorded more trust by Muslim communities because it is more familiar than the self-declared secular approach to humanitarianism that many international aid agencies espouse" (2008: 178).

Sympathetic humanitarian responses arise out of fellow feeling for others, trying to understand what it might be like to have your village destroyed in a bomb attack, or your sea-level island at risk of climate change, and the feeling of sympathy prompts a reaction. "It is an effort to mitigate the suffering of strangers. It is evidence of the genuine importance of global civil society and the real influence of international norms on the conduct of states" (Calhoun 2008: 73-74). Craig Calhoun suggests that what is new about views of being sympathetic, or having responsibilities to others, is the idea that a humanitarian "emergency demands a response, including a response from distant strangers. This goes beyond mere sympathy" (2008: 74) of warm feelings. Rather, it endorses a cosmopolitan belief that despite varying locations and differing faiths, we belong to a community of humanity where we enter relationships of mutual respect (Kwame 2006), that for many women-of-faith peacebuilders are associated with the responsibilities to others that they have taken on board.

Women-of-faith tend to express a distinct slant on sympathy. It is fascinating to read how Ana Maria Tepedino from Brazil suggests that in the struggle for justice, the starting point of her theology is the "practice of tenderness" (1988: 166). She explains this further, that a sympathetic sensitivity to the pain of others:

> calls women to suffer with, to feel with, to be in solidarity with, to be more open to the problems of others, to understand the values of sharing in the struggle for better living conditions – and also to transmit the faith characterized by the struggle for justice. (Tepedino 1988: 167)

Tepedino suggests that women in Latin America "do theology with passion.... Trying to put together rationality, scientific precision, and relationality. They accomplish this ministry with compassion, with sensibility for others' pain" (1988: 171). *Relational sympathy is a powerful tool of peacebuilding.* It isn't that men don't exhibit it because some do. It is that more women seem to build it explicitly and proudly into their everyday practices.

Charity and sympathy are related to empathy; so how do they differ? With *empathy,* there is an attempt *to identify with similar emotions,* whether this is grief, anger, desperation, fear, or shame. Christine Sylvester defends a position of what she calls "empathetic cooperation," which she describes "as a feminist method for managing, working with, respecting, and surpassing rigid standpoints, positions, and issues without snuffing out difference" (2002: 244). Again, note the attention given to the importance of moulding differences in respectful ways. In Sylvester's process of "positional slippage" one isn't dogmatically claiming to be right, which obviously is always a danger when dealing with religion and faith; instead, there is a careful listening to the concerns, fears, and agendas of others, seriously taking on board their concerns rather than dismissing them (2002: 247). Sometimes, empathy prompts a change of heart or mind, or an altered response. Sylvester clarifies further, that "empathy taps the ability and willingness to enter into the feeling or spirit of something and appreciate it fully in a subjectivity-moving way" (2002: 256). Building on these ideas, Laura Sjoberg presents "empathetic cooperation as a feminist security ethic" (2006: 46) that tries to understand where those we may view as opponents are coming from, by attending "to both justice and care" (2006: 48).

Empathy can only happen when we take on board the struggles of others by listening with an open attitude to what they have to say, without always wanting to push the conversation, direct the flow, or break through to a foregone conclusion. Listening "is attending to a sharp sense of what things mean" (Lederach 2005: 70). This is what Cynthia Cockburn calls "deep dialogue," which involves "careful listening, understanding different experiences and acknowledging different points of view" (2004: 150). Marc Gopin expresses this beautifully when he writes that "the ability to listen to the soul of the other in silence emerges from the discipline of humility" as a form of compassionate listening (2003: 257).

Such an empathetic approach permits negotiation and respectful cooperation with others who have utterly different religious beliefs or faith practices. The respect can only extend to practices that are respectful of human dignity and do not harm others. It does not discard the emotions that are involved in being empathetic, as realist international relations does. This practice of attentiveness to the particularity of other's needs is a way of "being open to entering another's world" (Wibben 2011: 105), not avoiding it as is more typical. Obviously dealing with the obstacles that remain between former enemies in violent conflicts is daunting. However, as an ideal, or a strategic inclination, empathetic cooperation is a guide to direct interactions in breaking down some of the massive hostilities of distrust between groups from different ethno-religious or ideological backgrounds.

Compassion

Charity, sympathy, and empathy are linked. How does compassion stand out? Importantly,

> who are the mercy-givers, digging to find wellsprings of compassion that do not run dry? Who scours our hearts, succours them, and breaks them wide open, stretching them to include others – more and more others? Who makes sacred space out of every landscape, alleyway, old battleground, rain forest, reclaimed and redistributed land, reservation, war-torn and destroyed region, desecrated wasteland – seeking to remind us that all ground is holy, that *here* is holy. (McKenna 2010: xii)

This chapter demonstrates that many women-of-faith peacebuilders practice this *deep compassion*. For example, Amy Caiazza (2006) and the Institute for Women's Policy Research conducted interviews from 2003 with sixty-eight American women and seven men whose activist roles in interfaith organizations were directed to issues of social justice. Caiazza summarizes the central underlying values behind their activism as "stewardship; love, peace, and compassion; interconnectedness; and basic worth and dignity" (2006: 6).

Where empathy sympathetically identifies with others' emotional responses to injustices and suffering, compassion feels pain and *responds* appropriately (Porter 2006). It is possible to feel sympathy, even to empathize emotionally, but do nothing else to alleviate someone's pain. I argue that *compassion is the act of response to suffering*. Thus, compassion is a crucial component to peacebuilding. Scott Appleby, supporting a comprehensive understanding of peace, highlights the multifaceted, continuing, long-term nature of peacebuilding, which he says, "is the envisioning, nurturing, and sustaining of compassion-filled human relationships that are essential to human flourishing" (in Marshall and Hayward 2010: 7).

The concept of *ubuntu* (humanness), present in Bantu languages in East, Central, and South Africa, includes compassion and *urumwe* (interconnectedness). *Ubuntu* "is a concept that encompasses being human, humane, relational, and respectful of the dignity of human beings and other creatures, and awareness of the interconnectedness of humanity, the Earth, and other life forces" (Mwaura 2012: 273). Additionally, *ubuntu* is an ethical and religious worldview that "expresses respect, empathy, compassion for others, reciprocity, solidarity, justice, accountability, and mutual responsibility" (Mwaura 2012: 271). Desmond Tutu reflects on the progress made during his lifetime but says that for all the cleverness of modern-day inventions, we've failed in one very important area "to grasp our need for each other" (2016: 102). Drawing on principles of *ubuntu*, he describes this need clearly:

> that those people, over there, whether they worship in synagogues or mosques or temples or churches, are actually our sisters and brothers. That we are made for each other. That we are inter-dependent. That we are born for goodness, and for love. All of us. And that we are all vulnerable. (Tutu 2016: 102)

In explaining *ubuntu*, Tutu says that it "speaks to our co-ownership, co-existence, and co-stewardship of our world. A person is a person through other persons" (2016: 103). He suggests that the compassion that we have inside us diminishes when we are prejudiced against others.

The Charter for Compassion, released in November 2009 is a cooperative effort to restore compassionate thinking and action to moral, religious, and political life. It confirms that the principle of compassion is central to all religious, ethical, and spiritual traditions. Thus, it calls "upon all men and women to restore compassion to the centre of morality and religion – to return to the action principle that any interpretation of scripture that breeds violence, hatred or disdain is illegitimate." *In a compassionate community, people are motivated by compassion to accept the responsibility for care.* There are countless examples of this compassionate, responsibility to care for others, as demonstrated by women-of-faith peacebuilders.

For example, Mary Novak works with Catholic women peacebuilders in Kenya. She says that it is their vocation that fosters compassion. Their simple lifestyle frees them to be available for attending compassionately to the vulnerable. These women are comfortable with ambiguity and long-term horizons, their invisibility "gets them into places that boggle my mind. They can sneak into places and do their activism because they are not seen as threatening" (Novak in Love 2015: 49). This isn't to make a virtue of women's exclusion from leadership structures, rather, it is to extract the benefits of not being obligated to seek permission or fulfil hierarchical expectations. Novak maintains that these women-of-faith peacebuilders "are particularly attuned to advancing participation because they immerse themselves in peoples' lives, gaining the asset of lived experience and special sensitivities to power and group dynamics" (in Love 2015: 15). Similarly, Sister Mary Goretti Kisakye reminds Ugandan women faith leaders that they "are able to bring others around to their point of views because they genuinely understand and care about where others are coming from so that the people they are leading feel more understood, supported, and valued" (in Gueskens et al. 2010: 4). *Compassion involves a response to vulnerability, suffering, and injustices.* Usually, it begins with listening to a story.

Listening in Open Dialogue

It might seem strange to discuss the importance of listening in a process of open dialogue under a section on compassion. I've already noted Sylvester's notion of empathetic cooperation as a listening process of dialogue across differences. However, I argue that listening, *hearing what the other says*, can be an *act of compassion*, a way to *demonstrate respect*. I refer here to *deep listening*, to trying to grasp what the other is saying, in a way that shows that one is concerned by the story being told, and seeking to ascertain what this person or group requires to alleviate their pain. Many women develop these skills of *artful listening* because they are immersed in daily activities where listening and responding to calls of need are essential for everyday survival, whether in the market place, labouring around cooking pots, or keeping extended families together in very difficult situations. Through these everyday, ordinary, but necessary activities, women assume the responsibilities of care. In fact, it is possible to argue that such practices of attentive listening highlight responsibilities to others as an expression of ethical choice and compassion.

There are always major obstacles to open dialogue. Extremists, fundamentalists, and all who remain intolerant to anyone holding a different view rarely engage in open dialogue, because if they're right, everyone else must be wrong. This refusal to embrace difference remains a chief hurdle in situations where religious extremism results in violent acts of atrocities. Hence *the open dialogue I refer to is one where there is a willingness to listen*, whether this is in a formal peace process, or in the many informal avenues of discussions within post-war transitional justice. Some men actively engage in open, respectful dialogue. Yet many men are so accustomed to expressing the dominant voice, that they talk over others, and thus cannot, or choose not, to hear others' voices. Many women are used to listening, but not to voicing their concerns.

Noting these qualifications, I highlight the *compassionate listening* that women-of-faith engage in as intrinsic to their *practices of just peace.* These practices require *space to express voice.* Nicola Slee, in describing the location in which feminist researchers conduct practical theology, suggests that we draw on inner resources of "justice-seeking compassion" (2013: 17). She also emphasizes the holistic richness of deep compassionate listening.

> We listen with our bodies, paying attention to feeling, memory, desire. We listen with emotional as well as intellectual intelligence, on the look-out for patterns, residences, allusions... We listen to tone of voices, sighs, stutters, laughter, tears, pauses, silences, body language, facial expression, the mood of the encounter, how it starts, shifts, changes, moves, circles, ends... using our feelings as a clue to how the other may be feeling. (Slee 2013: 18-19)

I turn now to some examples of *women peacebuilders as story-tellers, and as compassionate listeners.*

Sometimes cross-border forums and solidarity visits to other countries are extremely helpful in providing opportunities to network and express personal experiences of suffering, struggle, and hope, thereby fostering not only greater understanding of differences and similarities, but also, a greater sense of compassion. For example, a cross-learning project brought together representatives from Northern Ireland, Timor-Leste, and Liberia to share experiences of the post-conflict period and to discuss what was needed to inform their respective NAPs on UNSCR 1325. The first meeting in Belfast during 2009 focused on women's participation in the political process; the next gathering was in Dili, 2009, and examined the prevention of violence; and in 2010, participants met in Liberia to explore how best to engender the peacemaking, peacekeeping, and peacebuilding processes, with attention on the protection of women and girls (Porter and Mundkur 2012:

117, 165-166). While not explicitly an inter-faith project, each country is strongly influenced by its religious faith, and the example highlights the benefits of international exchanges in fostering open dialogue with women who value their faith.

What is needed for open deliberation, one that gives space to the speaker and permits non-judgemental listening? María Pilar Aquino suggests that: "from an intercultural feminist perspective, the renunciation of conceptual absolutisms and doctrinal dogmatisms is essential for making egalitarian communication and open deliberation possible" (2007: 18). Absolutism and dogmatism are part of fundamentalism, when neither egalitarian communication nor open deliberation are possible and violence results. However, documented case studies of open dialogue in Burundi, Colombia, Nepal, and Uganda during 2011-2013, show that "approaches that result in positive transformations seem most often to be characterized by inclusivity, dialogue, and empowerment" (Myrttinen, Naujoks, and El-Bushra 2014: 6). The inclusivity needs to be broad in covering age, gender, and degrees of power or powerlessness. Through inclusivity, necessary spaces for promoting capacities for dialogue are created. Dialogue promotes respect when it pursues mutual understanding with those who hold vastly different views, and thus it is undermined when a religious believer asserts their views without providing adequate reasons. "The moral value of respect implies an obligation to offer reasons to others who are of a different tradition or who may simply disagree" (Philpott 2012: 113).

What then are the distinct ways that women engage in inter-faith dialogue? Specifically, what models of dialogue do women-of-faith peacebuilders use to gain a better understanding of each other? Given that the authoritative doctrines and teachings of the dominant world religions were formulated exclusively by men who retain prime leadership positions, this authoritative expression is not a model that typically gives women voice. In contrast, an activist model of dialogue "actively seeks the transformation of the world *and* the transformation of religions" (Fletcher 2013: 174). Within this model, religion is necessarily interlinked with the social and political spheres. Jeannine Hill Fletcher cites examples as broad as the activist's focus for dialogue of the American, Christian, feminist, suffragette Elizabeth Cady Stanton who met with women of the local Jewish community to further women's well-being. Other examples include the Indian feminist Sarojini Naidu, who in the 1920s worked within the secular women's movement on behalf of women's education and rights, alongside her Muslim compatriots. From the 1970s onwards, both within the church and in academic circles, feminist theologians from across religions continue to address the suffering rooted in oppressive sexism, and the social conditions that negatively impact on poor women and women of colour "as primary foci for inter-religious dialogue" (2013: 175). One example of this activist model is the Women in Black anti-war network, demonstrating in silence against militarism and violence against women. The silence isn't passive; it is a massive loud statement. For women-of-faith, the dialogue that takes place in an activist peace model is not simply about religious beliefs and practices, but the role of just practices in sustaining or jeopardizing human well-being.

Common spaces for these open dialogues occur anywhere women gather – around meal tables, in playgrounds or kitchens, under a tree, on a mat, or at markets or in refugee camps. Helene Egnell summarizes what she believes to be the distinctive aspects of women-of-faith's dialogue, in that they include the integration of "traditional experience," "telling of life stories," and an emphasis on "faith as lived rather than as expressed in scriptures and doctrine" (2007: 161, 163). Kenyan Simiyu Wandibba, referring specifically to the capacity and moral authority of women-of-faith to promote peaceful coexistence, stresses that as primary caregivers, they have a huge interest in community stability, which is why women often take it on themselves to initiate unofficial peacebuilding practices (in Ramadhan and Mang'eni 2010: 29). For example, aware of the harms of small arms and light weapons in Angola, DRC, Rwanda, Sierra Leone, Somalia, Sudan and Uganda, programs exposing the risks by trained religious leaders have been successful in leading to a surrender of weapons.

Listening in open dialogue often occurs alongside of hospitality. I use the term broadly, as acts of welcome, generosity, kindness, openness, and human warmth. David Steele emphasizes the importance of hospitality in relations between the West and Islamic worlds where great value is placed on honour and hospitality. He identifies the importance of "recognition, identity, belonging, and community as an essential part of interfaith dialogue," and where face-to-face meetings help dispel false misinformation and help to rehumanize the other (2008: 12). In hospitality, there is the readiness to welcome the stranger. He recounts a story told by Mohammed Abu-Nimer, a Palestinian Muslim:

> When a Palestinian woman opened her door to a panic-stricken Israeli soldier after his patrol had killed a youth throwing stones as part of the *Intifada*, she served him coffee until it was safe for him to leave despite the fact that it was her son who had been killed. (in Steele 2008: 12)

Given this extreme act of violence, and the woman's intense grief, such surprising acts of welcome can be a means of beginning the journey of healing, through the restoring power of compassion.

Reconciling Relationships

Compassion is not necessary for reconciliation. However, sometimes, they coincide in something closer to mercy, a leniency that is more a form of gracious kindness. Daniel Philpott suggests that influential "advocates of reconciliation are disproportionately but not exclusively religious," and as examples he cites Anglican Archbishop Desmond Tutu of South Africa, Catholic Bishop Juan Gerardi of Guatemala, and John Baptist Odama of Uganda (2016: 21). Of course, these leading clergy are significant advocates, but I highlight the lesser-known work of women. Philpott argues that the core concept of reconciliation "is restoration of right relationship" that involves the principles and practices that lead to a "transformation of attitudes and emotions, apology, forgiveness, and healing through the public acknowledgement of suffering" (Philpott 2016: 21). Chile, El Salvador, Germany, Guatemala, Peru, South Africa, Sierra Leone, Timor-Leste, and Uganda provide examples of reconciliation. Jennifer Llewellyn and Philpott advocate "a relational concept of justice" (2014: 15) which they maintain is "not simply concerned with responding to wrongs but rather with the harm and effects of wrongs on relationships at all levels" (2014: 16). They acknowledge that most relational scholars are feminist theorists. *Many relational practitioners are women-of-faith peacebuilders.*

Other key writers include different features as part of reconciliation. For example, John Paul Lederach (2004) argues that truth, justice, mercy, and peace interact in complex ways, and the goal is to work jointly in culturally meaningful practices, places, and processes to find ways that reconciliation and just peace can flourish. Elsewhere, I argue that: "Reconciliation can be understood primarily as reconciling relationships, as a process, as a culture, or as a spectrum of possibilities" (2015: 183). First, and fundamentally, reconciliation between former antagonists who have felt the emotions of bitterness and hatred toward the other must signal the building, or rebuilding, of new and meaningful relationships. I like what Lederach says about the vision of relationships in peacebuilding that "recognizes that the well-being of our grandchildren is directly tied to the well-being of our enemy's grandchildren" (2005: 35). Second, the processes of reconciliation require the open dialogue discussed above, a massive move when communication is blocked or confused with misunderstandings. The process of reconciliation is more likely to happen when there is mutual trust, respect, and consideration of others' interests. Third, a culture of reconciliation should be embodied and visible in the way that people relate to each other without suspicion or hostility. Education can influence a positive culture. Fourth, there is a spectrum of possibilities of reconciliation, from a weak notion of coexistence where little has changed except that killings have ceased, to strong forms of decent, respectful interaction of mutual understanding, even when significant differences remain. Reconciliation in practice is demanding.

Gladys Ganiel asked faith leaders in Northern Ireland about diversity, ecumenicism, and reconciliation. She "found that amongst all expressions of Christianity, evangelical men were the least likely to have a 'high' view of reconciliation" (2013: np). Consistently, non-evangelicals "thought that group forms of reconciliation were more important than evangelicals did" (2013: np). When the responses are broken down by gender, the results are revealing. "Among non-evangelical laity, 46 percent of women and 42 percent of men had a 'high' view of reconciliation. Among evangelical laity, 47 percent of women – but just 20 percent of men – had a 'high' view of reconciliation" (2013: np). This is an extremely low figure in a place where sectarian divisions remain lethally volatile. Among male evangelicals, the figures are striking: "90 percent rated reconciliation with God as very important, 60 percent thought reconciliation between individuals is very important, but only 13 percent thought reconciliation between Catholics and Protestants in Northern Ireland is very important" (Ganiel 2013: np). For reconciliation to occur, it needs strong advocates and willingness to engage with the other.

Apology and Forgiveness

While apology and forgiveness aren't requirements of reconciliation, when they do occur, they often make it easier to reconcile. Nigel Biggar makes a very pertinent contribution to this discussion, when he maintains that "compassion is one of the basic motives behind forgiveness" (2003b: 321), and that "people who have been relieved of grievance are generally freer to take creative risks of sympathy or compassion" (Biggar 2011: 206). People forgive for a range of reasons, many in search of release from the negative emotions of bitterness and hatred that cripple one's spirit. Compassion towards the abuser who has apologized is more likely to occur for acts that have not deeply harmed one's dignity and sense of self, however, there are always exceptional cases.

Writing from an African context, Megan McKenna suggests that "75 percent of the church's populations are women…It is the women who do the work of forgiveness, reconciliation, and rebuilding of the communities among those who did the killings" (2010: 105). Some men also acknowledge wrongdoing, apologize, forgive, and are willing to be reconciled with the person who was an enemy, but in many places where the church plays a strong role, preaching on forgiveness strongly impacts the largely female congregations. Anderlini, writing mainly on women who are devout Muslims who frame their fight for gender equality within their religious beliefs, sees religion as potentially a powerful resource for "resilience, forgiveness, and reconciliation" (in Hayward and Marshall 2015: 315). We turn now to some examples.

John Steward, former manager for peacebuilding, healing, and reconciliation for World Vision Rwanda, recounts what he learnt from two Rwandan women who had both faced the person who killed their closest relative.

> They helped me to understand that forgiveness has two parts. The first is letting go of the feelings of bitterness or revenge for what happened, but the second part is in what these two women said to the killers: "What you did was wrong. What are you going to do to help repay - and help repair - some of the damage you have caused?" (Rwandan Stories)

Justice is part of the story. The Rwandan Stories website has accounts of rich stories of forgiveness told by women. For example, Alisa nearly died from her injuries. On release from hospital, she hated Hutus and wanted them to die. She tells her story, and points to Emmanuel, the person who is sitting beside her and says, "This is the man who cut me. I forgave him, and I feel that he's my brother now." For these Rwandan women, forgiveness is a strong concept and practice. It is a deliberate decision not to give in to revenge. It also includes elements of justice, healing for the harm inflicted, and is an offer of freedom for both victim and offender to pursue productive lives without being hostages to the past. Yet for Francine who lost her mother and little sisters, forgiveness doesn't seem possible. Instead, she says: "We will start drawing water together again, exchange some local gossip, sell each other grain. In twenty, fifty years' time, perhaps there will be young boys and young girls who will learn of the genocide from books only. For us, though, it is impossible to forgive."

Forgiveness is always a gift, given by the victim/survivor to the perpetrator of abuse and harm. It can never be taken for granted or assumed to be given. Ideally, I suggest that the process is three-fold (Porter 2015). First, there must be *acknowledgement of wrongdoing* and harm caused. Second, an *apology* offered is a statement of this acknowledgment. It must admit the wrongdoing; be genuine, sincere, and effective; be a truthful admission of responsibility for that hurt; be unambiguous; take ownership and responsibility for wrongdoing; be a statement of remorse or regret; be a credible promise of non-repetition; take effective consultation within an apologizing constituency; be delivered by a person with credibility as a speaker; be delivered with due respect to the dignity of victims; and consider appropriate compensation or reparations. There should be no caveats that qualify or justify actions, or misrepresent motives or facts, such as the typical "I apologize if I've hurt you," rather than admitting that wrong has been done. Emotions are a big part of an apology and need to be obvious, rather than any personal distancing. Remorse, shame, embarrassment, and pain are typical emotions. It is always important to ask what victims want to hear. Third, forgiveness by the person who has been harmed is *voluntary*. The person must be ready to do so, and sometimes, is never able to do so. Forgiveness is always a gift.

Building relationships of trust takes time. *Reconciled relationships are an important part of practising just peace.* To trust someone means that you believe they will do what they say they will do. It is to have confidence in someone, that you can rely on them to fulfil their promises. Interestingly, trust reinforces interdependence as intrinsic to being human. The more trust there is between individuals and groups, the more likely it is that reconciliation will grow. For example, Gloria Terikien attended a reconciliation ceremony in Bougainville where the BRA man who had bullied her for a year and a half in the bush attended the ceremony in traditional dress, carrying bows, arrows, and spears. When he approached her, she said to him:

> I forgive you before you even asked for it. I have put it all behind me. I am now settled down again and I do not want to think about this anymore. And I do not want to talk about it. All I want to say is "I forgive you" and put it behind me. (in Howley 2002: 12)

Crying, he begged her to forgive him. In another reconciliation ceremony between the BRA and the resistance in 1997 at Wakunai, a matrilineal society, the first speaker was a lady who was the major landowner in the area. She stood between the two groups calling them to reconciliation. She presented each group with betel nut and each person passed it on to the next person. Pigs were killed and there was an exchange of shell money. In the presence of one thousand people, fifteen BRA men and fifteen resistance fighters shook hands (Michael Lusman in Howley 2002: 115). Reconciliation must be culturally meaningful. It is an intrinsic part of peacebuilding and furthers justice between previous antagonists.

Practising Just Peace

This chapter seeks to answer the question: What is the unique contribution women-of-faith make when practising just peace? So far, I have shown that *women-of-faith are doing peacebuilding differently*, particularly in informal, less visible activities that revolve around *compassionate relationships*. "Right relationship is at the core of both just peacebuilding and the idea of positive peace" and for the women under discussion, the idea of "right relationship" flows from their religious belief in personal dignity and social humanity (Love 2015: 51). To this end, one of the most tangible aspects of peacebuilding work is restoration and repair, which of course includes the restoration of women's bodies and psyches. Many women-of-faith exert great strength and courage in restoring people's broken spirits, and in doing so, generating just peace. Chapter five examines the work of women in coalitions across faith differences. I conclude by highlighting the work of individual women-of-faith peacebuilders.

The Joan B. Kroc Institute for Peace and Justice at the University of San Diego believe that to achieve peace and justice, the voices of women affected by conflict, who courageously and creatively build communities, should be recorded, and shared. One way the Institute do this is through their Women Peacemaker Program. The program calls them "peacemakers," but I refer to them as peacebuilders to be consistent with the UN-based distinctions between peacekeepers, peacemakers, and peacebuilders used throughout the book. Four women peacebuilders are brought to the Institute annually for an eight-week residential to share their stories and have a peace writer document their narrative. These narratives include a brief biography, some background to the relevant conflict, a political timeline of key events that include personal events of the peacemaker, the individual personal story, questions, and answers from select interview questions, and a table of best practice. This chapter highlights some individual women's work. I have selected those women for whom faith is a central part of their work. Further, I have selected aspects of their work that resonate with the themes of this book.

Clearly, this doesn't do justice to their full life's work, or to other women who haven't participated in this program. For example, Flora Bagenal (2017) outlines the work of women leading the way in counter-extremism, including Fauziay Abdi Ali in Kenya, Fatima Akilu and Esther Ibanga in Nigeria, Ilwed Elman in Somalia, Ameena Hassan in Iraq, Omezzine Khelifa in Tunisia, Mariam Safi in Afghanistan, Mossarat Qadeem in Pakistan, Edit Schlaffer in Austria, and Fatima

Zaman in England. Also, the organization Tanenbaum: Combating Religious Prejudice run a "Peacemakers in Action" program where individuals who are driven by their faith to stop human suffering and promote reconciliation are nominated to receive recognition, funding, expert training, and an in-depth case study describing their work. There are notable women recipients from various faith traditions, including: Maria Ida from the Philippines, Dishani Jayaweera from Sri Lanka, Jamila Afghani and Sakena Yacoobi from Afghanistan, Betty Bigome from Uganda, Hind Kabawat from Syria, Osnat Aram-Daphna and Najeeba Sirhan from Israel and Palestine, and Nozizwe Madlala Routledge from South Africa.

Thus, I highlight only a small sample of women taken from the Women Peacemaker Program, stressing the key message that emerges from their work as it relates to the themes under discussion. It should be noted that most of the women are not specifically working to further UNSCR 1325 and its sister resolutions. Hence my summaries are extracted from their work, and I have drawn a central idea from the narratives, explaining how it relates to the WPS agenda. The key lessons drawn reinforce the arguments made in this book. I acknowledge that other readers of the narratives may extract different implications that are meaningful to them.

Integrating Justice and Peace

In Asia, *Ashima Kaul* is a grassroots peace worker raised in Kashmir as part of the ethnic minority community of Kashmir Hindu Pandits. She says: "I had to recover the dying, bullet-ridden soul of Kashmir, rebuild broken relationships, break the silence of women, give them a voice and establish new spaces for creation of a spirit of trust, solace, and healing" (in Morse 2014: 4). Her first step was to facilitate a group dialogue with Muslim and Pandit women, leading to the creation of a formal dialogue group, *Athwaas* (meaning handshake). She also founded the *Yakjah* (being together) Reconciliation and Development Network that seeks to build relationships between different religious and ethnic groups through dialogue and development projects, particularly reaching out to the youth. In working with Muslim and Hindu women, she refers to faith as an "anchor" (in Morse 2014: 43).

- Key message: The *creation of safe spaces for building relationships across different faiths is needed* to engage women in the work that facilitates the implementation of the WPS goals.

Rahina Hashmi is a human rights defender, working in Pakistan. She crafted a national Women Political School Project to train elected women leaders and formed a health network to provide reproductive health services to two million women. Through her leadership of Sisters Trust Pakistan, she works to help victims of domestic violence and girls who are trying to break free of religious fundamentalisms and forced marriages. One of the highlights of her work is "the interfaith communication she nurtured among Sunni, Shia, and Ismaili women in hope that it would influence the way the men there dealt with their 'enemies'" (Diaz 2013: 51). When asked what she felt is the key to interfaith harmony, she replied:

We need to focus more on our similarities, not on our differences. All religions —Islam, Hinduism, Christianity, Buddhism — talk of peace. No religion promotes war. That is a political use of religion. Every faith talks about peace and humanity...The world should not be divided on the basis of faith. (in Diaz 2013: 82)

In terms of peacebuilding, she stresses the need to link civil society with political leadership, defence, and security actors to encourage greater collaboration on common interests.

- Key message: When working with diverse groups, *finding the common aspirations within the WPS framework can unite women,* despite their stark religious and faith differences.

Rubina Feroze Bhatti, a Christian in majority Muslim Pakistan, is a founding member of the Taangh Wasaib Organization, a rights-based development group that addresses violence-against women, religious intolerance, and sectarianism. She works with Christians, Muslims, and Hindus. There was a change in her consciousness, what she calls an "inner earthquake of a revelation" in shifting her vision from religion, interfaith integration, and tolerance, to grasping that "women were also in need of peace" to further tolerance (in Barker 2009: 75). In defining peace, she says that:

> when people live in fear and insecurity, it generates ethno-centrism, religious intolerance, social exclusion and, finally, the underdevelopment of the country. Peace is the acceptance of each other without any discrimination, the active participation of all people in the development process and the uplifting of the entire population. (in Barker 2009: 105)

When asked about 9/11, she responded that "Anti-Americanism has increased religious intolerance more than sectarianism. It made things worse for Christians, Hindus, and other religious minorities" (in Barker 2009: 106). Religious intolerance is unfurled through blasphemy attacks. Bhatti says that "the key principle of our interfaith work is 'unity in diversity'" (in Barker 2009: 111).

- Key message: Peace and security means different things to different people in different contexts. This means *the women, peace, and security agenda must be culturally relevant.* Where ethnic and religious differences are causes of conflict, the protection from violence and promotion of rights are necessary to foster women's active participation in developing sustainable peace.

Shinjita Alam initiates peace programs in Bangladesh, training representatives from local organizations in conflict resolution, and organizes forums for interfaith dialogue between Christian Garos and Muslim Bengalis. She "began this part of the dialogue by asking them to share the key values of their religions and how they practice them. They realized they share several of the same: honesty, peace, compassion, and truth" (in Dzenovska 2008: 26). The Muslims also identified brotherhood, stressing that all Muslims are brothers. When the Garo didn't accept that, saying instead that "All human beings are our brothers," Alam confirms that this means they're all brothers or sisters of humanity. This affirmation was the beginning of opening a dialogue between once very bitter neighbours.

- Key message: In contexts where there are deep divisions, *identification of common shared values*, rather than concentrating on irreconcilable differences, is a key strategy in the initial dialogue on how best to realize the WPS goals.

Merli Mendoza provides technical support on disaster response and risk reduction to church-based social action organizations in the Catholic Caritas network in the Philippines. In the Corazon Aquino administration, she served on the Peace Commission and the National Unification Commission and assisted the Government Peace Negotiating Panel for Talks with the Communist Party of the Philippines, the New People's Arm, and the National Democratic Front. She then transitioned to the grassroots space in 1999, coordinating a national coalition for peace and security in Mindanao. In 2008, she was abducted by the militant separatist group Abu Sayyaf, and held hostage for two months. Despite this frightening experience, she is still able to say: "Peacemaking and conflict management go beyond the rational.

They touch on the sacred and the divine," and explains that "it is a combination of art and a science. It is about goodness" (in Liepold 2010: 4). When she was a hostage, in communicating with a young guard, she asked him: "Why did you go with the Abu Sayyaf?" to which he answered that the group fed him and gave him a gun which made him feel powerful, and he asked her to pray for him so he could return to his family (in Liepold 2010: 39).

On another occasion, faced with a machete at her neck, the aim to behead her, kneeling on the ground in what might be her last moments, Mendoza wondered what had brought her likely killer "to this place, ready to kill an unarmed noncombatant, a woman, a humanitarian. A question formed in her mind: *How did we end up making him into a monster?*" (in Liepold 2010: 41). A Christian, "with her next breath she heard herself apologizing: 'For all the sins that the Christians have committed against the Muslim people, I ask forgiveness'" (in Liepold 2010: 41). Even then, she was aware that she was living in what could be her last moments, and she was still able to reflect that: "I will never lose respect for the Muslim people who have welcomed me into their homes and adopted me as one of their own. Because of them I have become a better Christian" (in Liepold 2010: 41).

She explains, "every peacebuilding act is also an act of healing" (in Liepold 2010: 51). She places her calling as a peacebuilder firmly as part of her life mission, as "a call to service, a higher goal beyond yourself. It is your faith in God and faith in others that lead you on the track" (in Liepold 2010: 53). As a peacebuilding principle, she stresses that "the local context must define the engagement approach. Educate yourself and partners about the complex historical and cultural context of each situation. Learn, teach, listen, and appreciate the context" (in Liepold 2010: 55).

- Key message: Always *being amenable to try to understand the reality of the "other"* permits an open perspective on the motivations of antagonists, and thus the possibility for conflict transformation.

Further, it enables one to engage in *building trustful relationships,* even with the supposed "enemy," despite enormous differences. Meaningful insight into what is required in the WPS agenda is more likely to occur when there is the identification of local leaders who listen well to local stories and can determine a community's perceived needs and priorities. Also, *compassion contributes to unexpected changes in personal relationships.*

Liza Llesis Saway is an indigenous peacemaker in Mindanao where Muslim Moros, Christian settlers, and indigenous peoples coexist amidst armed groups fighting the government army. She is a leader in interfaith and multi-ethnic community efforts to progress peace. She says that of course everyone wants peace, but that this will not happen until everyone learns to respect and protect each other's land. "Not until everybody stops invading, intruding, corrupting, stealing and denying the inherent rights and share of other people will we achieve peace" (in Simoni 2009: 25-26). When asked to reflect on what peacemaking is, she draws strongly on her indigenous heritage to say that:

> Peacemaking is basically an effort to restore balance, which can occur among peoples, tribes, clans, families, communities, and individuals. It is a sincere attempt to connect harmoniously with fellow human beings, animals, plants, and nature. Peacemaking is also an effort to heal the wounds of conflicts, so it is like the medicine for conflict. (in Simoni 2009: 38)

She adds also that it is about the "effort to care sincerely for the people involved in a conflict. It is caring for them physically, psychologically, spiritually, and emotionally," so that in the practical caring tasks of providing food, shelter, clothes, and medicines, "we restore the harmonious connections between ourselves and nature and spirits" (in Simoni 2009: 38). In drawing on her indigenous practices, she says:

In Talaandig traditions, rituals, reflections, prayers, and mothers' negotiations are very important in practicing peacemaking and peacebuilding. It has been proven that in many negotiations, whenever we use all of those tools, conflicts can be reconciled in a more civilized manner. Calling spirits is also an elemental practice because the connections between us and the caretaker and protector spirits bring calm and peace. (in Simoni 2009: 42)

- Key message: The WPS community benefits from *listening closely to stories told by indigenous women* for whom peace and security has a practical focus that connects with nature and the provision of essential material needs. Also, *the ways that peacebuilders practice compassionate care require holistic approaches to building just peace.*

Mary Ann Arnado is a Christian advocate for the indigenous peoples of Mindanao and is involved in the Mindanao Interfaith Peoples Caucus. She told a conference of Catholics: "As a political issue, we need to take positions on the causes and the conditions that create the conflict. The church advocates forgiveness as a value of peacebuilding, but many of the people affected by the conflict are wondering, 'Where is the justice?'" (in Woodward 2005: 21), referring particularly to land ownership and use. When refused entry to the official ceasefire monitoring panels, she created an independent, community-based ceasefire monitoring group, maintaining women's "natural ability to connect and communicate with the soldiers and civilians alike" (in Woodward 2005: 24).

- Key message: Justice is a vital component of peace. *What justice means differs in different contexts.* Also, when women are refused access to official WPS processes, their alternative contributions are deeply valuable at local community levels and should be encouraged.

From the Americas, *Marta Benavides* is an activist and peace advocate in El Salvador since the 1970s, when the climate of repression was rising. She works on humanitarian aid, refugee centres for those displaced by violence, and environmentally sustainable development, and she built international networks of solidarity for a negotiated, peaceful, political solution. After the peace accords were signed in 1992, she returned from exile and founded the International Institute for Cooperation Amongst Peoples. As an ordained Baptist pastor, she fought with God over the constant struggle for peace and justice, and a message came to her that it wasn't about fighting, struggling, or building peace, she just needed to "be peace." She kept repeating the mantra of the need to be patient. The message was: "Be at peace. Practice the science of peace. Work for peace in a scientific way. Understand how to manifest peace. Manifest peace in all you do. Thus, be peace. Not at peace – be. Be peace" (in Fenly 2009: 60).

Thus, she redefines peace as "a gift of the spirit. It is a given, a way of being" (in Fenly 2009: 60). She explains "that peacemaking is really about living every day the culture of peace" (in Fenly 2009: 67). She restates that the motivation for activism often comes from experiencing injustice, in her case through her family's experiences of the "oppression of women and peasants, the government's irresponsible social policies, the lack of care of Mother Earth and all of nature. I honestly can say that peacemaking has been my life – it has been at the center of everything I do" (in Fenly 2009: 68). Drawing on her indigenous heritage, she defines her faith as being rooted in the Creator Spirit. This means that in creating one's daily meaning, "peacemaking results from being peace, from living the culture of peace all the time" (in Fenly 2009: 72).

- Key message: UNSCR 1325 talks of "durable peace," and the "role of women in peacebuilding," and "peace and security." For some women-of-faith, *peace is an internal state of being*. One demonstrates it by being assured of inner peace, being peaceful towards others, and respectful of nature. This is a different yet compatible conception of peace to that presented in UN resolutions. *Sensitivity to indigenous understandings of peace is essential.* Again, the experiences of injustice and oppression are motivators for women-of-faith's activism for just peace.

Claudette Werleigh became the first female PM in Haiti in 1995, where she always sought to be cooperative rather than confrontational. She was Secretary-General of the Catholic peace movement Pax Christi International from 2007-2010, where her work took her to many conflict areas. She worked in popular education, placing particular emphasis on educating women, knowing how this "would strengthen the community. It was a specific strength that was hard for her to pinpoint, but Werleigh was convinced that women's contributions were not only valuable, but unique" (Das 2011: 46). When asked to explain her understanding of peace, she replied:

> Peace is the result of a combination of factors: satisfaction of basic needs; harmonious relationships; acceptance of differences (tolerance); respect; existence (and perception of the prevalence) of justice, fairness, and equity; good governance; and freedom of expression. There is no ready-to-use formula to put an end to violent conflicts — not just one magical, unique, and universal way to build peace. (in Das 2011: 65)

- Key message: *Peace is understood in rich, holistic, multidimensional ways* that WPS strategies should note.

From Africa, *Sister Pauline Silver Acayo*, mentioned in the previous chapter, was raised in a strong Catholic family in Uganda. From an early age, the teachings of her parents influenced her to "Be peaceful with others. Be peaceful in yourself" (in Noma 2005: 11). As well as these simple words, more complex ideas like "If ever someone does wrong to you, never, never, pay it back with wrong. Always pay someone who has done wrong to you with good" took root in her life, particularly as she observed her mother living closely to these ideas (in Noma 2005: 11). Acayo entered the Little Sisters of Mary Immaculate in Gulu as an eighteen-year-old. In her work, there were many encounters with rebels, one when she was teaching in a secondary school and fifty-one girls were abducted, some could escape and return, and one became a bush leader. By 2001, Acayo stopped teaching to commit fully to peacebuilding in northern Uganda. She works particularly with returnees, understanding that many of the young men participated unwillingly in killing activities, aware that if they didn't kill, they would be killed. After a cleansing ritual:

> To the returnees, she speaks words of comfort and courage: "You are not an outsider. You should feel free to be a part of the community. Join us and do not be afraid." To the community, she implores: "Accept the returnees as your own children. Forgive. It will be difficult. Reconciliation does not take place in a day; it is a process. If you welcome them and eat with them, that is already the beginning of reconciliation." (in Noma 2005: 39)

Her words appeal to both Acholi culture and Christian spirituality. She acknowledges that obstacles to reintegration involve both attitudes of the community, and the trauma suffered by the returnees. She trains "caregivers" to work with these returnees, but the trauma is severe, the acts of violence committed horrendous. With colleagues from Catholic Relief Services and the Justice and Peace Commission, Acayo started peace clubs where students learn how to implement peace in their communities. Voluntarily, students extend this beyond schools to IDP camps and prisons. She is part of the Acholi Religious Leaders Peace Initiative, conveying messages between the LRA and the government.

- Key message: Reintegration of those who have committed appalling harms is always going to be traumatic for the accepting community and for the returnee, even those who are remorseful in facing the consequences of their acts. *Women-of-faith who can involve traditional indigenous practices alongside newer religious customs assist the complex connections between acknowledgement of wrongdoing, apology, forgiveness, and reconciliation.*

Margaret Arach Orech is the founder of the Ugandan Landmine Survivors Association. She is a survivor of a landmine explosion and attack by rebels of the LRA. Her work with communities affected by the conflict includes encouraging dialogue between survivors of violence and former rebels.

> In one case, she came face-to-face with a young man who was part of the group responsible for the attack that nearly killed her. Showing him compassion upon his expression of remorse, she helped organize a traditional cleansing ceremony to help him begin his slow journey to recovery. (Ruttenberg 2004: 4)

Orech is also a commissioner for the Interfaith Action for Peace in Africa. She suggests that the principal objective of this organization "is to look for African solutions to issues of peace, particularly using a faith-based approach, including the African traditional religions, which all talk about peace" (2014: 59). She is explicit that it was her faith that helped "her transition from victim to survivor" (2014: 44). Wearing a manufactured limb, she can encourage women who also are landmine survivors to "access medical care, peer-to-peer networks, livelihood support and, most importantly, the courage within themselves to live their lives in hope, forgiveness, resilience, and faith" (2014: 47). Reflecting on forgiveness, she said, she also associates her faith with her ability to forgive:

> I realized that one bitter feeling and one moment of anger adds on more, so I was just piling it on. But then when I got rid of

a little bit of it, I started offloading all the anger and bitterness. And I was free. (in Ruttenberg 2014: 57)

- Key message: The identification of local women leaders who have suffered in similar ways to other local women assists progress of the WPS agenda. *This identification is embodied sympathy, empathy, and compassion in action.* Many women are explicit that it is their faith that helps them to function as healed survivors and as respected local leaders.

Valiba Kebeh Flomo was a women's officer in the Lutheran Church in Liberia's Trauma Healing and Reconciliation Program, supervising psychosocial services to war-affected women and girls. She was a founding member of the Christian Women Peace Initiative which inspired the creation of the Muslim Women for Peace, two groups which merged to become the Liberian Women Mass Action for Peace, discussed in other chapters. With Leymah Gbowee as mentor, she listened to many testimonies of traumatized women.

> Seeing the anger and hurt in the women and identifying with them, she said to herself, "If women are the primary victims of violence they should get involved, because the one that feels the pain knows how to describe it to people. If we work through these women we can succeed in stopping the violence." (in Koenders 2010: 29)

Flomo explained her view to Gbowee and their colleagues:

> We mobilize women. We use white clothes to show our commitment to peace. We will go in the streets, we will sing peaceful songs telling our children to come home, telling our children to lay down their guns, and that we still have space for them to come back to us. (in Koenders 2010: 30)

On the first day, over five-hundred Christian women met to organize. Many women expressed hesitation that some individuals were seeking personal or political gain. On being reassured that Flomo and Gbowee had a religious and traditional background, they felt more open to support the movement. The Christian Women Peace Initiative began. The one Muslim woman present was Asatu.

> Fear divided the Christian and the Muslim women, forming a gap that had to be bridged for the sake of peace. Working with the groups separately and repeating the messages *In time of war, women and children suffer most and the bullet cannot pick and choose. Once it is in the air it is not looking for a Christian, it is not looking for a Muslim. It comes to anyone,* more and more women came to see the importance of collaboration. (in Koenders 2010: 34-35)

In one meeting, one pregnant woman cried out in pain. Many women rushed to her. Gbowee pointed out that no one stopped to see if she was Christian or Muslim. The point about a shared concern was reiterated – of suffering through the violence and the common desire for peace. To maintain peace, they began the Peace Hut Talks where women meet to discuss issues that might threaten peace like lack of jobs, and the need for schools, health clinics, and safe drinking water.

- Key message: *Empathetic identification with fellow sufferers is a powerful uniting force across religious differences.* Spaces where the building of trust can flourish are needed in inter-faith dialogue. For women, these must feel like *safe spaces.* Peace is viewed holistically in terms of having a context in which to realize everyday needs.

From Europe, *Sabiha Husić* is an Islamist theologian and inter-religious peacebuilder. Since 2007, she has been the director of Medica

Zenica in Bosnia-Herzegovina, an NGO mentioned in other chapters, providing psychosocial and medical support to women and children victims of war and post-war violence, including sexual violence, domestic violence, torture, and trafficking. She was first aware of the NGO when, displaced herself, she witnessed their work in the refugee camp she was in, and "the approach toward women which I saw there gave me the reason to live, and my willingness to help other people was even bigger" (in Rokhideh 2013: 4). In the post-war climate, Husić works for reconciliation, bringing together women from all communities for training on stress and trauma, dialogue, and conflict resolution. Along with two women from Switzerland, she leads the European Project for Interreligious Learning, which unites Christian and Muslim women from five countries to promote understanding and tolerance, including Serbian Orthodox Christians, Catholic Croats, and Muslim Bosnians. This project seeks to build peaceful religious communities, to create mutual respect and cooperation. In reflecting on the role of religion in Bosnian life, she says:

> If women recognize religion as an important coping mechanism, it is important that we help them be free to express their beliefs. We know that trauma destroys three pillars: One is the picture about myself, the second is the picture about others, and the third is the belief in natural powers, the universe, or God. (in Rokhideh 2013: 55)

Her view is that if a woman has an undestroyed faith in God, then the healing of self-dignity and belief in others can draw strength from this faith. She met with authorities in the Islamic community, convincing them to endorse a document widely published to say that people should be respectful of all who had been raped, to allow these women and girls to enter their healing process in their communities without fear, stigmatization, or guilt.

- Key message: *Faith is an intrinsic part of many people's lives.* Drawing on the strengths and positive dimensions within faiths, permits a greater acceptance of the requirements of the resolutions related to women, peace, and security.

In the Middle East, *Rashad Zaydan* from a devout Muslim family in Iraq is a pharmacist. After the US occupation in 2003, she founded a Knowledge for Iraqi Women Society which seeks to bring hope and empowerment, especially to widows and orphans, through the provision of humanitarian aid, education, and economic, social, and medical programs. When asked how it came about, she explains that initially she was receiving people in her house when the demands escalated. She negotiated with other educated professional women to help other women. They didn't have a fixed plan. "Everything started based on need" (in Pugh 2011: 118). In explaining how her Islamic faith enabled her to go where there was heavy fighting, such as to Fallujah, Abu Ghraib, and Ninawa, Zayden says,

> We were just thinking that it is our duty. It is our job to go. Those people needed our help. We were thinking, we are educated women, we have our families, so let's go and look after those people who lost their families. Let's try to absorb this hate they have inside by supplying their daily needs. We were not giving them much, just simple things but with a very compassionate word so they can feel another's feelings and they can change. (in Pugh 2011: 122)

Like others above, she talks of inner peace, saying that there is an understanding in the Islamic religion that:

> You cannot change the community unless you change yourself. You cannot make the peace outside unless you bring it to yourself. I cannot be in tension and be nervous and impatient and not have faith, and still make peace with the other. I have to practice

it for myself. And from my experience, religion has had much effect on helping me be more patient, to absorb the shock of working in this world and to not be afraid of many things. I just believe that life is in the hands of God. (in Pugh 2011: 122)

- Key message: *Compassionate attention to people's immediate everyday needs is a vital aspect of the just peace.* Faith provides the courage for women-of-faith to initiate practical ways to understand what is needed to alleviate suffering in response to people's pain.

These examples of ways that women-of-faith practice just peace are inspirational. Responding to immediate practical concerns, these women *listen attentively, organize cooperatively,* and *attend with compassion* to traumatized, needy people. I conclude that women-of-faith's contribution to practices of just peace *is* different.

***

This chapter explains what is distinctive about the role women-of-faith play in practising just peace. I show that women-of-faith practice peacebuilding with a heightened sense of *relationality*, which views *connectedness* as the starting point for sensitivity to the need to be inclusive and respectful to those of different faiths. I link this inclusivity to feminist notions of equality and justice. I argue that *compassion* is a guiding principle and practice for many women-of-faith peacebuilders. For these women, the rationale for compassion emerges from within faith traditions, and greatly assists their *listening in open dialogue*, a practise that is an integral part of peacebuilding. *It is the response to suffering that demonstrates compassion.* I then show that the building or restoring of constructive relationships that are fundamental to reconciliation is an idea that is firmly positioned within secular and faith traditions. This means that there are many amazing examples of women-of-faith who are willing to reconcile with those who appear, given the context of war, to be irreconcilable. A range of examples of women-of-faith who practice just peace, brought from the Women Peacemaker Program, show that abundant lessons can be drawn from these narratives. Many women define justice in culturally contextual ways that translate practically. For example, the measure of just peace is often viewed pragmatically, so that *when people's everyday needs are met, a just peace is more likely to occur.* The conclusion that follows, summarizes the book's main findings.

Conclusion

Throughout this book, I provide instances of ways in which women-of-faith peacebuilders make a major contribution in local communities to fostering good relationships, transforming conflict in non-violent ways, dealing with the traumatized effects of violent conflict, and creating situations where peace is built and sustained. For these women, self-claimed faith, justice broadly construed, and sustainable peace, are intrinsically connected. Additionally, I argue that feminist women-of-faith peacebuilders make a significant impact in transforming socio-political contexts, because they address the structural root causes of gender inequality, injustice, and oppression.

The book utilizes a two-prong framework. First, the fact that "more than 80 percent of the world identifies as religious," and religious actors "help shape a community's attitudes and behaviours," often on the front lines of conflict (Cox et al. 2017: 1), is of great significance, but rarely discussed in scholarship on the politics of peacebuilding. I show that there is a resurgence of religion in global politics, particularly post-9/11. Despite the West considering itself to be secular, there are increasing tendencies for religion to have an impact on policies, laws, and in the USA when President Trump was in power, the choice of individuals who are appointed to influential positions. In the Global South, where ethnic differences frequently collide with religious ones, religious texts are used as a rationale to justify violence toward the "other." Further, the rise of religious fundamentalisms leads to violent extremism, and acts of terrorism manifest in many parts of the world. Yet there is a massive contradiction – despite the use of diverse religious scriptures to justify violent conflict, all religions have visions of peace and respect for life. Hence, my emphasis is less on formal religion, but rather, on women whose *personal faith* motivates them to work for just peace.

The second part of the framework for the book is the women, peace, and security agenda, especially as it relates to UNSCR 1325 and its sister resolutions. I demonstrate that while UNSCR 1325 does not mention religion or faith, many states' national action plans recognize how important it is to have local religious or faith-based leaders who are esteemed in their communities to stress that sexual violence against women and girls is wrong. However, while the protection and prevention pillars of this resolution are critical, I illustrate how there remains an under-emphasis on two other pillars, namely participation and prosecution. Accordingly, I reveal a major weakness of these national plans that tend not to accentuate how local faith-based leaders can encourage the increased participation of women in decision-making on peace and security matters. A prime reason for the reluctance to do so lies in prevalent patriarchal attitudes toward women and girls that place them under cultural constraints of subjection and submission to male leadership, which are justified by selective readings of diverse scriptural texts.

Hence, the prime argument in this book is that the vast community of women and men who are working to improve gender equality and justice in places where violence has ravaged lives, would benefit from drawing on, and learning from, the considerable experiences and expertise of local women-of-faith peacebuilders. There is justified criticism on UNSCR 1325 and its sister resolutions in signalling great promises of change, but too frequently, remaining as grand rhetorical statements. Throughout this book, I argue that women-of-faith peacebuilders are a rich resource to assist the implementation of these resolutions, because they have an intimate grasp of local customs, and thus know what is needed for changes to occur, because each locale has its distinctive needs. Yet, sadly, what these peacebuilders often lack is the authority to instigate these changes. Regarding authority, I also show that some senior women in traditional church structures, particularly in the Catholic Church, utilize their lack of a formal role to bypass the need for obtaining approval from those in authority positions. This is where the international community of policy-makers, aid and development workers, human rights activists, and practitioners, UN and NGO workers, and academics conducting fieldwork on WPS issues, can act as brokers to connect more with local women-of-faith, and develop capacities and community-based strategies that link local women's work with local male champions of gender equality. Sometimes, these champions will not be present. Ongoing resources constantly are needed to sustain such strategies, whilst heeding community needs, expressed by neighbouring people.

As noted, many religions have conservative tendencies in terms of suppressing women's participation in public life. I offer a note of caution in preceding chapters that it cannot be assumed that all women-of-faith peacebuilders are working specifically to further gender equality, or the requirements of UNSCR 1325. Many participate in caring practices such as healthcare, education, development, and trauma healing, and do not view their roles as necessarily furthering feminist aims. However, I show that unintentionally, their work often assists the building of gender equality which is recognized as a crucial component to sustainable peace. The *Global Peace Index 2016* acknowledges that gender equality is "a component of positive peace" (2016: 53) because it reflects "societies that uphold acceptance of the rights of others" (2016: 56). Frequently, fragile and conflict states struggle to meet targets related to gender parity.

Another major strand of my argument is that women-of-faith peacebuilders who identify as feminists, have massive potential to instigate radical social and political change. Examples demonstrate that the primary reason for this potential is the way these women are driven by their faith to work tirelessly to overcome injustices and all forms of oppression that men and women experience. To this end, I maintain that feminist women-of-faith actively pursue a transformative praxis as a manifestation of *justice in practice*.

Thus, I show why viewing women-of-faith as transformative agents requires a narrative understanding of agency to comprehend their activism. Women typically are immersed in webs of relationships that define their sense of selfhood. The telling of personal stories emerges through ordinary encounters within these webs. Hence, in the examples used, I give priority to first-hand accounts of everyday, local experiences that reveal insights into the situatedness of diverse, complex, lived stories. I highlight four main examples of these distinctive activities.

First, I explain that there is little participation by any women, let alone women-of-faith in the formal Track one roles in peace processes. This is a major lack, especially in places where religion is a major contributor in forming social and political views that influence policies, laws, and practices. I also stress how this function of religion can be harmful in dividing groups into a "them" and "us" mentality, or it can help to build peace in stressing common humanity, despite stark differences. With this latter function, in informal activities, women play crucial roles in lobbying for change, trying to influence their male relatives to lay down arms, and in working to transform conflict through non-violent means at grassroots level. Controversially, women often use their symbolic roles as mothers, not just as biological mothers, but as spiritual mothers of the earth, or to the connectedness of human life, to appeal to (mainly) men, viewed as "sons" to cease fighting. While this might reflect gendered stereotypes, the symbolism cannot be dismissed lightly, because in many cultures, it is the mothering role, conceived broadly, that gives women not only their social status, but also, the authority to speak out. This influence should be linked with gender equality.

Second, I reveal how and why women-of-faith show strengths in building coalitions across major ethnic, cultural, and religious differences. In doing so, they do not disregard their different beliefs, but they refuse to allow these differences to obstruct the pressing, pragmatic need to build human security, whether this is finding food, shelter, economic skills, education, healthcare, or trauma counsel, as part of their peacebuilding. The strength comes in finding commonalities across diverse individuals and groups, not in stressing the controversial differences. Often these commonalities revolve around shared insecurities, loss, and grief, and meeting essential human needs. Further, I argue that pragmatism is neither abstract, nor instrumental, rather, it comes from valuing everyday life, and accepting the responsibility to meet basic human necessities, and care for those who are suffering.

Third, I provide examples of women-of-faith's work with victims of sexual violence. Despite resolutions condemning this prevalent violence, the gross violations continue. As mentioned, about a third of national action plans include references to engaging religious or faith-based leaders in condemning sexual violence, and in welcoming those women who have been violated, back into families and communities. Trafficking for sexual purposes is part of this story and is the justice cause chosen by some Western churches. Each individual rescue gives a person freedom. However, while immediate protection is crucial, the long-term strategy of prevention must address the structural injustices of globalized, capitalist labour markets, and vulnerability of women from conflict zones, as well as patriarchal reasons for the demand.

The fourth example I use is the unique way that women-of-faith practice peacebuilding. *The distinctive skills of women-of-faith are inclusivity to difference, attentive listening to victims' stories, and a demonstration of compassion.* These are skills that feminist writers of justice and care also emphasize. But, in the examples of individual women highlighted, whether these women self-identify as feminist or simply as women-of-faith, it is their faith that is the prime motivator for their peacebuilding, in integrating justice and compassion. Telling the stories of these women's work is important because it is rarely done, and their work is extremely valuable, and should be recognized.

Are these messages likely to take hold beyond feminist academia, and the broad-based WPS practitioner community? I would like to think so. Jimmy Carter (2009), President of the US from 1977 to 1981, writes that the influential group of Elders, founded by the late Nelson Mandela, "are deeply committed to challenging injustice wherever we see it." This independent group of global leaders work together for peace and human rights. In 2023, with Mary Robinson the Chair, there are thirteen major leaders, with three Elder Emeritus. In appealing to the responsibilities of religious and traditional leaders to ensure equality and human rights, Carter declares their statement that: "The justification of discrimination against women and girls on grounds of religion or tradition, as if it were prescribed by a Higher Authority, is unacceptable," and the statement asks leaders of all religions to courageously "acknowledge and emphasize the positive messages of dignity and equality that all the world's major faiths share" (Carter 2009). Pope Francis, stressing women's contribution to listening, welcoming, and opening themselves to others, states that "women have the right to be actively involved in all areas," including involvement "in exchanges at the religious level, as well as those at the theological level" (in Catholic News Agency 2017). While these statements are appreciated, they clash with the Catholic church's prohibition on women's leadership.

To conclude, the women, peace, and security agenda is understandably, and appropriately, a secular one. However, its application has massive implications in countries where religion plays a significant part of being accepted in communities. Within the broad-church community of activists working to progress this agenda, some individuals have varying degrees of religious faith, but they do not necessarily connect this faith explicitly in their work. Some feminists see religion solely as a source of oppression, and in vocalizing their views, they run the risk of suppressing those feminists who value their personal faith. Inclusivity of diverse differences strengthens the likelihood of success of this agenda.

This book confirms that: *women-of-faith peacebuilders and feminist women-of-faith peacebuilders make major contributions to attentive, relational, compassionate, and community-based peacebuilding.*

References

A21. 2017. *Abolish Slavery Everywhere, Forever: Freedom Report 2016*, A21: USA.

---.2016. *Abolishing Injustice in the Twenty-first Century.* http://www.a21.org/index.php?linkid=2319 accessed 28 September 2016.

Ackerman, Denise M. 2012. "Interrupting 'Global-Speak': A Feminist Theological Response from Southern Africa to Globalization." In *The Oxford Handbook of Feminist Theology*. Eds. Mary McClintock Fulkerson and Sheila Briggs. Oxford: Oxford University Press, 212-238.

Ahmed Aziza and Seshu, Meena. 2015. "We Have the Right Not to be 'Rescued'." In *Global Human Trafficking. Critical Issues and Contexts*, Ed. Molly Dragiewicz, London: Routledge, 169-180.

Alderton, Margot, ED. 2016. *Women and Violent Radicalization in Jordan*, Amman: UN Women.

Alidou, Ousseina. 2005. *Engaging Modernity: Muslim Women and Politics of Agency in Postcolonial Niger*, Madison: University of Wisconsin Press.

Althaus-Reid, Marcella. 2012. "Doing a Theology From Disappeared Bodies: Theology, Sexuality, and the Excluded Bodies of the Discourses of Latin American Liberation Theology." In *The Oxford Handbook of Feminist Theology*. Eds. Mary McClintock Fulkerson and Sheila Briggs. Oxford: Oxford University Press, 441-455.

Amoah, Elizabeth. 2012. "Theological Perspective on Mutual Solidarity in the Context of Globalization: The Circle's Experience." In *The*

Oxford Handbook of Feminist Theology. Eds. Mary McClintock Fulkerson and Sheila Briggs. Oxford: Oxford University Press, 239-249.

Anderlini, Sanam, Naraghi. 2016. "Uncomfortable Truths, Unconventional Wisdoms. Women's Perspectives on Violent Extremism and Security Interventions," March 2016, No. 1, Washington DC: Women's Alliance for Security Leadership.

---. 2007. *Women Building Peace: What They Do, Why It Matters.* Boulder, COLO: Lynne Rienner.

Andrees, Beate. 2014. "Why Definitions Matter," International Labour Organization. 3 February 2014. http://www.ilo.org/global/about-the-ilo/newsroom/comment-analysis/WCMS_234854/lang--en/index.htm accessed 15 September 2015.

Apawo Phiri, Isabel. 2005. "The Circle of Concerned African Women Theologians: Its Contribution to Ecumenical Formation." *The Ecumenical Review* 57(1): 34-41.

Appleby, R. Scott. 2003. "Religion as an Agent of Conflict Transformation and Peacebuilding." In *Turbulent Peace: The Challenges of Managing International Conflict.* Eds. C. A. Crocker, F. O. Hampson, and P. Aall, Washington, DC: United States Institute of Peace: 821-840.

Aquino, María Pilar. 2012. "Theology and Identity in the Context of Globalization." In *The Oxford Handbook of Feminist Theology.* Eds. Mary McClintock Fulkerson and Sheila Briggs. Oxford: Oxford University Press, 418-440.

---. 2011. "Religious Peacebuilding," In *The Blackwell Companion to Religion and Violence.* Ed. Blackwell Publishing Ltd. Published.

---. 2010. "Analysis, Interconnectedness and Peacebuilding for a Just World." In *New Feminist Christianity: Many Voices, Many Views,* Eds. Mary E. Hunt and Neu, Diann L. Woodstock Vt: SkyLight Paths Publishing, 41-51.

---. 2009. "Theological Vision and Praxis for Liberation: Facing Destructive Conflict." *Journal of Feminist Studies in Religion* 25(1): 201-207.

---. 2007. "Feminist Intercultural Theology. Toward a Shared Future of Justice." In *Feminist Intercultural Theology. Latina Explorations for a Just World*. Eds. María Pilar Aquino and Maria José Rosaldo-Nunes. Maryknoll, NY: Orbis Books, 9-28.

---. 2002. "Latina Feminist Theology: Central Features." In *A Reader in Latina Feminist Theology*, Eds. María Pilar Aquino, Daisy L. Machado, and Rodríguez, Jeanette, Austin: University of Texas Press, 133-160.

Aquino, María Pilar, Machado, Daisy, L. and Rodríguez. Jeannette 2002. *A Reader in Latina Feminist Theology*, Austin: University of Texas Press.

Aune, Kristin. 2015. "Is Secularism Bad For Women?" *OpenDemocracy*, 30 March 2015.

AWID, 2016. "The Devil is in the Details: At the Nexus of Development, Women's Rights, and Religious Fundamentalisms." Toronto: Association for Women's Rights in Development.

Ayoob, Mohammed. 2011. *The Many Faces of Political Islam. Religion and Politics in the Muslim World*. Ann Arbor: The University of Michigan Press.

Bagenal, Flora. 2017. "10 Women Leading the Way in Counter-Extremism," 1 March 2017, *News Deeply: Women and Girls*.

Balchin, Cassandra. 2011. *Towards a Future Without Fundamentalisms: Analyzing Religious Fundamentalist Strategies and Feminist Responses*. Toronto: Association for Women's Rights in Development.

Banchoff, Thomas and De Gioia, John J 2016, "The Berkeley Centre at Ten." In *Religion, Peace, and World, Affairs: The Challenges Ahead. Berkeley Centre Ten-Year Anniversary Essays*, Ed. E. Taylor, Washington DC: Georgetown University, 5-8.

Barker, Kaitlin. 2009. "Harmony in the Garden: The Life and Work of Robina Feroze Bhatti of Pakistan." Ed. Emiko Noma, San Diego, CA: University of San Diego.

Barnett, Michael and Weiss, Thomas. 2008. "Humanitarianism: A Brief History of the Present." In *Humanitarianism in Question: Politics, Power, Ethics*. Eds. Michael Barnett and Thomas Weiss, Ithaca: Cornell University Press, 1-48.

Basini, Helen and Ryan, Caitlin, 2016. "National Action Plans as an obstacle to meaningful local ownership of UNSCR 1325 in Liberia and Sierra Leone. *International Political Science Review*, 37(3): 390-403.

Basu, Soumita. 2016. "The Global South Writes 1325 (too)." *International Political Science Review*, 37(3): 362-374.

Beckford, James. 2014. "Re-Thinking Religious Pluralism." In *Religious Pluralism*. Eds. G. Giordan and E. Pace. Berne: Springer International Publishing, 15-29.

Bedford, Nancy E. 2012. "The World Palpitates: Globalization and the Religious Faith and Practices of Latin American Women." In *The Oxford Handbook of Feminist Theology*. Eds. Mary McClintock Fulkerson and Sheila Briggs. Oxford: Oxford University Press, 180-194.

Bell, Christine and Catherine O'Rourke. 2010. "Peace Agreement or Pieces of Paper? The Impact of UNSC Resolution 1325 on Peace Processes and their Agreements." *International and Comparative Law Quarterly* 59 (4): 941-980.

Bellin, Eva. 2008. "Faith in Politics: New Trends in the Study of Religion and Politics." *World Politics* 50(2): 315-347.

Bennett, Olivia, Bexley, Jo, and Warner, Kitty. Eds. 1995. *Arms to Fight, Arms to Protect: Women Speak out About Conflict*, London: Panos Publications Ltd.

Bercovitch, Jacob and Kadayifci-Orellana, S. Ayse. 2009, "Religion and Mediation: The Role of Faith-Based Actors in International Conflict Resolution." *International Negotiation* 14(1): 175-204.

Bernstein, Elizabeth. 2010. "Militarized Humanitarianism Meets Carceral Feminism: The Politics of Sex, Rights, and Freedom in Contemporary Antitrafficking Campaigns," *Signs* 36(1): 45-71.

----. 2007. "The Sexual Politics of the 'New Abolitionism'." *A Journal of Feminist Cultural Studies* 18(3): 128-151.

Bernstein, Sarah. 2012. "Is 'Interreligious' Synonymous with 'Interfaith'? The Roles of Dialogue in Peacebuilding." In *Peacebuilding and Reconciliation: Contemporary Themes and Challenges* Eds. Marwan Darweish and Carol Rank. London: Pluto Press, 105-118.

Berry, Jan. 2013. "From Privacy to Prophecy: Public and Private in Researching Women's Faith and Spirituality." In *Explorations in Practical, Pastoral and Empirical Theology: Faith Lives of Women and Girls: Qualitative Research Perspectives.* Eds. Slee, Nicola, Porter, Fran & Phillips. Farnham: Ashgate, 25-36.

Biggar, Nigel. 2011. "Mounting the Icepacks of Enmity: Forgiveness and Reconciliation in Northern Ireland," *Studies in Christian Ethics* 24 (two): 199-209.

--- 2003a. "Making Peace or Doing Justice: Must We Choose?" In *Burying the Past. Making Peace and Doing Justice After Civil Conflict.* Ed. Nigel Biggar, Washington DC: Georgetown University Press, 3-24.

--- 2003b. "Conclusion." In *Burying the Past. Making Peace and Doing Justice After Civil Conflict.* Ed. Nigel Biggar, Washington DC: Georgetown University Press, 307-324.

Blanch, Andrea and Rozenman, Elana. 2008. "Women's Interfaith Leadership Development." *Report on Workshop, Centre for Religious Tolerance*, 9-11 September 2007, Amman, Jordan.

Bloom, Linda. 2014. "Talking About 'The Things That Make for Peace'," *New York United Methodist News Service*, September 19, 2014.

Boden, Alison. 2013. "The Arab Spring and Women's Rights." *Liechtenstein Institute on Self-Determination*, The United Nations, New York. 22 January 2013.

Bordeau, Catherine, Davila, Emily, Killeen, Alison and Stone, Kathleen. 2008. *Faith at the UN: Gender in the Church. Ecumenical Women's* UN: New York.

Bouta, Tsjeard, Kadayifci-Orellana, A. Ayse, and Abu-Nimer, Mohammed. 2005. *Faith-Based Peacebuilding: Mapping and Analysis of Christian, Muslim and Multi-Faith Actors.* The Hague: Netherlands Institute of IR, Clingendael.

Boutros-Ghali, Boutros. 1992. *An Agenda for Peace: Preventive Democracy, Peacemaking and Peacekeeping.* New York: United Nations.

Braidotti, Rosi. 2008. "In Spite of the Times. The Postsecular Turn in Feminism." *Theory, Culture, and Society,* 25(6): 1-24.

Brison, Karen. 2007. *Our Wealth is Loving Each Other: Self and Society in Fiji.* Lanham, MD: Lexington Books.

Brown, Katherine E. 2015. "Religion." In *Gender Matters in Global Politics. A Feminist Introduction to International Relations.* Ed. Laura J. Shepherd. London: Routledge 298-308.

Brysk, Alison. 2011. "Sex and Slavery? Understanding Private Wrongs," *Human Rights Review* 12: 259-270.

Caiazza, Amy. 2006. *Called to Speak. Six Strategies That Encourage Women's Political Activism. Lessons from Interfaith Community Organizing.* Washington DC: Institute for Women's Policy Research.

Caine Christine, http://www.christinecaine.com/content/about/gjegfk accessed 15 September 2015.

Calhoun, Craig. DATE "The Imperative to Reduce Suffering: Charity, Progress, and Emergencies in the field of Humanitarian Action." In *Humanitarianism in Question: Politics, Power, Ethics.* Eds. Michael Barnett and Thomas Weiss, Ithaca: Cornell University Press, 73-97.

Carlson, John D. 2011. "Religion and Violence: Coming to Terms with Terms." In *The Blackwell Companion to Religion and Violence.* Ed. Andrew R. Murphy. Blackwell Publishing Ltd. Published, 7-22.

Carrington, Kerry. 2015. *Feminism and Global Justice.* London: Routledge.

Carter, Jimmy. 2009. "Losing my Religion for Equality," *The Age,* 5 July 2009.

Charlesworth, Hillary. 2008. "Are Women Peaceful? Reflections on the Role of Women in Peacebuilding," *Feminist Legal Studies* 16 (3): 347-361.

Cockburn, Cynthia. 2004. *The Line. Women, Partition and the Gender Order in Cyprus,* London: Zed Books.

—— 1998. The Space between Us. Negotiating Gender and National Identities in Conflict, London: Zed Books.

Cohn, Carol, Kinsella, Helen and Gibbings, Sheri. 2004. "Women, Peace, and Security," *International Feminist Journal of Politics* 6 (1): 130-140.

Coomaraswamy, Radhika. 2015. *Preventing Conflict, Transforming Justice, Securing the Peace. A Global Study on the Implementation of UNSCR 1325.* New York: UN Women.

Cooper, Thia. 2011. "Liberation Theology and the Spiral of Violence." In *The Blackwell Companion to Religion and Violence.* Ed. Andrew R. Murphy, Blackwell Publishing Ltd., 541-553.

Copeland, M. Shawn. 2010. *Enfleshing Freedom. Body, Race, and Being.* Minneapolis, MN: Fortress Press.

Corcoran-Nantes, Yvonne. 2005. *Lost Voices: Central Asian Women Confronting Transition.* London: Zed Books.

Corey, Benjamin. 2015. "Why Sex Still Dominates Christian Focus on Human Trafficking." *Pantheos:Hosting the Conversation on Faith,* 11 August 2015. http://www.patheos.com/blogs/formerlyfundie/why-sex-still-dominates-christian-focus-on-human-trafficking/ accessed 28 September 2016.

Darby, John & Mac Ginty, Roger. Eds. 2008. *Contemporary Peacemaking: Conflict, Peace Processes and Post-War Reconstruction.* Basingstoke: Palgrave Macmillan.

Das, Bijoyeta. 2011. "Building Bridges, Building Peace: The Life and Work of Claudette Werleigh of Haiti," Ed. Kaitlin Barker Davis, San Diego, CA: University of San Diego.

de Jonge Oudraat, Chantal & Brown, Michael, E. 2016. "Women, Gender, and Terrorism: The Missing Links," *WIIS POLICYbrief*, 1 August 2016, Washington DC: Women in International Security.

de Jonge Oudraat, Chantal, Stojanović-Gajić, Sonja, Washington, Carolyn, and Stedman, Brooke. 2015. "The 1325 Scorecard. Gender Mainstreaming: Indicators for the Implementation of UNSCR 1325 and its Related Resolutions." Washington DC: Women in International Security.

Diamond, Louise, 2016. "The Inner Spirit of Peacemaking: A New Training Imperative." In *Faith and Practice in Conflict Resolution: Toward a Multidimensional Approach*, Ed. Rachel M. Goldberg, Boulder, COLO: Lynne Rienner, 167-178.

Diaz, Pablo, Castillo. 2010. *Women's Participation in Peace Negotiations: Connections Between Presence and Influence.* New York: UNIFEM.

Diaz, Pablo, Castillo and Tordjman, Simon, 2012. *Women's Participation in Peace Negotiations: Connections Between Presence and Influence.* New York: UN Women.

Diaz, Sue. 2013. "Standing With Our Sisters: The Life and Work of Rehana Hashmi of Pakistan," Ed. Emiko Noma, San Diego, CA: University of San Diego.

Dikken, Bülent & Lausten, Carston Bagge. 2005. "Becoming Abject: Rape as a Weapon of War," *Body and Society*, 11(1): 111-128.

Dobson, Stephanie. 2012. "Reconciling Local with Global: New Zealand Muslim Women Articulating Faith in their Lives," *The Asia Pacific Journal of Anthropology.* 13 (3): 228-244.

Douglas, Kelly Brown. 2005. *What's Faith Got to do With it? Black Bodies/ Christian Souls.* Maryknoll, NY: Orbis Books.

Dzenovska, Ilze, 2008. "The Candle of Bangladesh; The Life and Work of Shinjita Alam," Ed. Emiko Noma, San Diego, CA: University of San Diego.

Eck, Diane. Nd. The Pluralism Project, Harvard University, http://www.pluralism.org/ (2 Sep 2015).

Edet, Rosemary and Ekeya, Bette. 1988. "Church Women of Africa: A Theological Community." In *With Passion and Compassion. Third World Women Doing Theology*. Eds. Virginia Fabella and Mercy Amba Oduyoye. Maryknoll, NY: Orbis Books, 3-13.

Edwards, Sarah, 2012. *All Change. Preventing Trafficking in the UK. Devolved Policies*. London: Anti-Slavery International for the Anti-Trafficking Monitoring Group.

Egnell, Helene. 2007. *Other Voices: The Study of Christian Feminist Approaches to Religious Plurality East and West*. Uppsala: Studia Missionalia Svecana.

El Bushra. Judy. 2007. "Feminism, Gender, and Women's Peace Activism," *Development and Change* 38: 131-147.

Elenes, C. Alejandra, 2014. "Spiritual Roots of Chicana Feminist Borderland Pedagogies." In *Fleshing the Spirit: Spirituality and Activism in Chicana, Latina, and Indigenous Women's Lives*. Eds. Elisa Facio, and Irene Lara, Irene, Tucson: University of Arizona Press. 43-58.

Evans, Mark. 2012. "'Just Peace'. An Elusive Ideal." In *Ethics Beyond Wars End*, Ed. Eric, Patterson, Washington: Georgetown University Press, 197-219.

FemLINK Pacific. 2014. "Actions and Impacts for a Peaceful Pacific: 2015 and Beyond," Suva: FemLINK Pacific.

Fenley, Leigh. 2009. "Being Peace: The Life and Work of Marta Benavides of El Salvador," Ed. Emiko Noma, San Diego, CA: University of San Diego.

Finlayson, Lorna. 2016. *An Introduction to Feminism*, Cambridge: Cambridge University Press.

Fletcher, Jeannine Hill. 2013. "Women in Inter-Religious Dialogue." In *The Wiley-Blackwell Companion to Inter-Religious Dialogue*. Ed. Catherine Cornille, Hoboken, NJ: John Wiley & Sons, Ltd., 168-183

Freston, Paul. 2008. "Protestantism." In *Routledge Handbook of Religion and Politics*. Ed. Jeffery Haynes, London: Routledge, 26-46.

Friedlander, Peter. 2008. "Buddhism and Politics." In *Routledge Handbook of Religion and Politics*, Ed. Jeffery Haynes, London: Routledge, 11-25.

Galtung, Johan. 1964. "An Editorial." *Journal of Peace Research* 1(1): 1-4.

Ganiel, Gladys. 2013. "Are Evangelical Men Ready for Reconciliation?" 18 November 2013, *Contemporary Christianity: Biblical Faith for a Changing World*, http://www.contemporarychristianity.net/website/are-evangelical-men-ready-for-reconciliation/

Gardam, Judith and Jarvis, Michelle. 2000. "Women and Armed Conflict: The International Response to the Beijing Platform for Action." *Columbia Human Rights Law Review* 32: 1-65.

Garrod, Joan and Jones, Marsha. 2009. *Religion and Belief.* Houndmills, Basingstoke: Palgrave Macmillan.

Gbowee, Leymah with Mithers, Carol. 2011. *Mighty be our Powers. How Sisterhood, Prayer, and Sex Changed a Nation at War*, New York: Beast Books.

George, Nicole. 2016. "Institutionalising Women, Peace, and Security in the Pacific Islands: Gendering the 'Architecture of Entitlements'?" *International Political Science Review* 37(3): 375-389.

---. 2015. "'Starting with a Prayer': Women, Faith, and Security in Fiji," *Oceania* 85 (1): 119-131.

---. 2014. "Promoting Women, Peace, and Security in the Pacific Islands: Hot Conflict/slow Violence," *Australian Journal of International Affairs* 68 (3): 314-332.

---. 2011. "Pacific Women Building Peace: A Regional Perspective," *The Contemporary Pacific* 23 (1): 37-71.

George, Nicole and Doerksen, Chantelle. 2016. "Gender and Peacebuilding: Hybridity and Friction in the Pacific Islands." In *Practical Approaches to Peacebuilding. Putting Theory to Work*, Eds. Pamina Firchow and Harry Anastasiou, Boulder, COLO: Lynne Rienner Publishers, 81-107.

Gerhardt, Elizabeth. 2014. *The Cross and Gendercide: A Theological Response to Global Violence Against Women and Girls.* Downers Grove, IL: IVP Academic.

Global Slavery Index 2016 http://www.globalslaveryindex.org/ accessed 29 September 2016.

Gilligan, Carol. 1982. *In a Different Voice: Psychological Theory and Women's Development,* Cambridge: Cambridge University Press.

Goldberg, Rachel, M. Ed. 2016. *Faith and Practice in Conflict Resolution: Toward a Multidimensional Approach,* Boulder, COLO: Lynne Rienner.

Gopin, Marc. 2003. "Religion as an Aid and a Hindrance to Postconflict Work." In *Imagine Coexistence. Restoring Humanity After Violent Ethnic Conflict,* Eds. Antonia Chayes and Martha Minow, San Francisco, CA: Jossey-Bass, 252-266.

Gouws, Amanda. 2015. "Unpacking the Difference Between Feminist and Women's Movements in Africa," *The Conversation,* 9 August 2015.

Govier, Trudy. 2002. *Forgiveness and Revenge.* London: Routledge.

Greiff, Shaina. 2010. "No Justice in Justifications: Violence Against Women in the Name of Culture, Religion, and Tradition," The Global Campaign to Stop Killing and Stoning Women and Women Living Under Muslim Laws, March 2010.

Grey, Mary. 2010. "Sustaining Hope when Relationality Fails: Reflecting on Palestine – a case Study." In *Through Us, With Us, In Us: Relational Theologies in the Twenty-First Century.* Eds. Lisa Isherwood and Elaine Bellchambers, Norwich: SCM Press, 87-106.

Griffen, Arlene. 2006. "Introduction." In *Lalanga Pasifika, Weaving the Pacific. Stories of Empowerment from the South Pacific.* Ed. Arlene Griffen, Suva: University of the South Pacific, 1-20.

Groody, Daniel G. 2007. *Globalization, Spirituality, and Justice. Navigating the Path to Peace.* Maryknoll, NY: Orbis Books.

Guelke, A. 2008, "Negotiations and Peace Processes." In *Contemporary Peacemaking. Conflict, Peace Processes and Post-war Reconstruction.* Eds. J. Darby & R. Mac Ginty, Houndmills, Basingstoke: Palgrave MacMillan, pp. 63-77.

Gueskens, Isabelle, Gosewinkel, Merle and de Vries, José. Eds. 2010. *Faith-based Peacebuilding: The Need for a Gender Perspective.* Alkmaar: International Fellowship of Reconciliation.

Hammond, Laura. 2008. "The Power of Holding Humanitarianism Hostage and the Myth of Protective Principles." In *Humanitarianism in Question: Politics, Power, Ethics.* Eds. Michael Barnett and Thomas Weiss, Ithaca: Cornell University Press, 172-195.

Harrison, Beverly Wildung. 2004. *Justice in the Making: Feminist Social Ethics.* Louisville, KY: Westminster John Knox Press.

Hauerwas, Stanley and Jones, Gregory. Eds 1997. *Readings on Narrative Theology.* Eugene Oregon: Wipf & Stock Publishers.

Hauss, Charles. 2010. *International Conflict Resolution,* (2nd ed.) New York: Continuum.

Haynes, Dina. 2017. "The Wastefulness of Human Trafficking Awareness Campaigns," *OpenDemocracy,* 15 March 2017.

Haynes, Jeffrey. 2008. "Introduction." In *Routledge Handbook of Religion and Politics.* Ed. Jeffery Haynes, London: Routledge, 1-7.

Hayward, Susan. 2015. "Women, Religion, and Peacebuilding." In *the Oxford Handbook of Religion, Conflict, and Peacebuilding,* Eds. Atalia Omer, R Scott Appleby and David Little, Oxford: Oxford University Press, 307-332.

Hayward, Susan and Marshall, Katherine. 2015. "Religious Women's Invisibility. Obstacles and Opportunities." In *Women, Religion and Peacebuilding. Illuminating the Unseen.* Eds., Susan Hayward and Katherine Marshall, Washington DC: United States Institute of Peace Press, 1-27.

Heathcote, Gina and Otto, Dianne, Eds. 2014. *Rethinking Peacekeeping, Gender Equality, and Collective Security.* Basingstoke: Palgrave Macmillan.

Heugh, Kathleen. 2011. "Discourses From Without, Discourses from Within: Women, Feminism and Voice in Africa." *Current Issues in Language Planning* 12 (1): 89-104.

Heyward, Carter. 2010. "Breaking Points: Shaping a Relational Theology." In *Through Us, With Us, In Us: Relational Theologies in the Twenty-First Century.* Eds. Lisa Isherwood and Elaine Bellchambers, Norwich: SCM Press, 9-32.

Heyzer, Noeleen. 2006. "Combating Trafficking in Women and Children. Over Gender and Human Rights Framework." In *Engendering Human Security. Feminist Perspectives.* Eds. Thanh-Dam Truong, Saskia Wieringa and Amrita Chhachhi. London: Zed Books Ltd. 101-123.

Höglund, Anna T. 2003. "Justice for Women in War? Feminist Ethics and Human Rights for Women." *Feminist Theology* 11 (3): 346-361.

Howley, Pat. 2002. *Breaking Spears and Mending Hearts. Peacemakers and Restorative Justice in Bougainville.* London: Zed Books.

Hudson, Heidi. 2016a. "A Double-edged Sword of Peace? Reflections on the Tension between Representation and Protection in Gendering Liberal peacebuilding," *International Peacekeeping* 19 (4): 443-460.

--- 2016b. "Subversion of an Ordinary Kind: Gender, Security and Everyday Theory in Africa." In *Africa in Global International Relations: Emerging Approaches to Theory and Practice.* Eds. Paul-Henri Bischoff, Kwesi Aning and Amitav Acharya. London: Routledge. 43-63.

--- 2005. "Doing Security as Though Humans Matter: A Feminist Perspective on Gender and the Politics of Human Security," *Security Dialogue,* 36(2): 155-174.

Husić, Sabiha, Duraković-Belko, Elvir, Šiljak, Irma, Hauser, Monika, Lindorfer, Simone, Wienberg, Kirsten & Griese, Karin. 2014. *"We are Still Alive" Research on the Long-Term Consequences of War Rape and Coping Strategies of Survivors in Bosnia and Heregovina.* Sarejevo: Medica Zenica & Medica Mondiale.

Hussein, Shakira. 2009. "Women's Engagement with Islam in South and Southeast Asia." In *Gender and Global Politics in the Asia-Pacific.* Eds. Bina D'Costa and Katrina Lee-Koo. New York: Palgrave Macmillan. 143-156.

Ibanga, Esther. 2015. "Uniting Christian and Muslim Women in Nigeria is Imperative to Build a Bridge Toward Peace," *Global Post,* 20 March 2015.

IEP. 2015. *Five Key Questions Answered on the Link Between Peace and Religion.* Sydney, New York, and Oxford: Institute for Economics and Peace.

International Labour Organization. 2016. "Forced Labour, Human Trafficking, and Slavery." http://www.ilo.org/global/topics/forced-labour/lang--en/index.htm accessed 28 September 2016.

Israel-Cohen, Yael. 2012. *Between Feminism and Orthodox Judaism: Resistance, Identity, and Religious Change in Israel.* Leiden: Brill.

Johnson, Lydia. 2003. "'Weaving the Mat' of Pacific Women's Theology: A Case Study in Women's Theological Method." In *Weavings: Women Doing Theology in Oceania.* Eds. Lydia Johnson and Joan Alleluia Filemoni-Tofaeono. Suva: Weavers, South Pacific Association of Theological School and University of the South Pacific, 10-22.

Jones, Nicola, Cooper Janice, Presten-Marshall, Elizabeth & Walker, David, 2014. "The Fallout of Rape as a Weapon of War," June 2014, London: Overseas Development Institute.

Jones, Serene. 2012. "Feminist Theology and the Global Imagination." In *The Oxford Handbook of Feminist Theology.* Eds. Mary McClintock Fulkerson and Sheila Briggs. Oxford: Oxford University Press, 23-50.

Jordan, Ann. 2004. "Women and Conflict Transformation: Influences, Roles, and Experiences." In *Development, Women, and War: Feminist Perspectives.* Eds. Haleh Afshar and Deborah Eade, Oxford: Oxfam, GB,133-151.

Joshi, Sushma. 2015. "'You'll Know What we are Talking About When you Grow Older': A Third Wave Critique of Anti-trafficking Ideology, Globalization and Conflict in Nepal." In *Defending Our Dreams. Global Feminist Forces for a New Generation.* Eds., Shamillah Wilson, Anasuya Sengupta and Kristy Evans. London: Zed Books, 79-94.

Juergensmeyer, Mark. 2003. *Terror in the Mind of God: The Global Rise of Religious Violence.* 3rd ed. Berkeley: University of California Press.

Kadayifci-Orellana, S. Ayse. "Muslim Women's Peacebuilding Initiatives." In *Women, Religion and Peacebuilding. Illuminating the Unseen.* Eds. Susan Hayward and Katherine Marshall, Washington DC: United States Institute of Peace Press, 71-95.

---2013. "Inter-Religious Dialogue and Peacebuilding." In *The Wiley-Blackwell Companion to Inter-Religious Dialogue.* Eds. Catherine Cornille. Chichester, John Wiley & Sons, Ltd. 149-167.

Kang, Namsoon. 2004. "Who/What is Asian? A Postcolonial Theological Reading of Orientalism and Neo-Orientalism." In *Postcolonial Theologies. Divinity and Empire.* Eds. Catherine Keller, Michael Nausner and Mayra Rivera, St Louis, MA: Chalice Press, 100-117.

Karam, Azza. 2014. "Religion and Development Post-2015: Report of a Consultation Among Donor Organizations, United Nations Development Agencies and Faith-Based Organizations." New York: UNFPA.

Katano, Atsuhiro. 2008. "Conflict Prevention and Peacebuilding." In *Routledge Handbook of Religion and Politics.* Ed. Jeffery Haynes, London: Routledge, 350-365.

Keller, Catherine, Nausner, Michael and Rivera, Mayra. 2004. "Introduction. Alien/Nation, Liberation, and the Postcolonial Underground." In *Postcolonial Theologies. Divinity and Empire.* Eds. Catherine Keller, Michael Nausner and Mayra Rivera, St Louis, MA: Chalice Press, 1-19.

Kerner Furman, Frida, 2011. "Religion and Peacebuilding: Grassroots Efforts by Israelis and Palestinians," *Journal of Religion, Conflict, and Peace,* 4, 2, online http://www.religionconflictpeace.org/

volume-4-issue-2-spring-2011/religion-and-peacebuilding-grass-roots-efforts-israelis-and-palestinians

Kisakye, Mary Goretti. 2010. "A Dialogue Report on the Role of Uganda Women of Faith Network Participation in National Leadership." *Inter-Religious Council of Uganda*, 6 October 2010, Kampala, Uganda.

Kleck, Monika. 2006. "Working with Traumatized Women." In *Peacebuilding and Civil Society in Bosnia-Herzegovina. Ten years After Dayton.* Ed. Martina Fischer. Berlin: LIT VERLAG, 343-355.

Kurtzer-Ellenbogen, Lucy. 2015. "Jewish Women in Peacebuilding: Embracing Disagreement in the Pursuit of 'Shalom'." In *Women, Religion and Peacebuilding. Illuminating the Unseen.* Eds., Susan Hayward and Katherine Marshall, Washington DC: United States Institute of Peace Press, 113-125.

King, Ursula. 2011. "Reflections on Peace, Women, and the World's Faiths." *Dialogue and Alliance: Women of Faith and Peacebuilding*, 25(1): online http://www.upf.org/resources/speeches-and-articles/4093-u-king-reflections-on-peace-women-and-the-worlds-faiths

Kirby, Paul and Shepherd, Laura J. 2016. "The Futures Past of the Women, Peace, and Security Agenda," *International Affairs* 92 (2): 373-392.

Koenders, Sara. 2010. "The Bullet Cannot Pick and Choose: The Life and Peacebuilding Work of Vaiba Kebeh Flomo of Liberia." Ed. Emiko Noma, San Diego, CA: University of San Diego.

Kurtz, Lester R. 2012. *Gods in the Global Village. The World's Religions in Sociological Perspective.* 3rd ed. Los Angeles, CALIF: Sage.

Kwame, Anthony Appiah. 2006. *Cosmopolitanism: Ethics in a World of Strangers.* New York: W.W. Norton.

Lara, Irene & Facio, Elisa, 2014. "Introduction: Fleshing the Spirit, Spiriting the Flesh." In *Fleshing the Spirit: Spirituality and Activism in Chicana, Latina, and Indigenous Women's Lives.* Eds. Elisa Facio, and Irene Lara, Tucson, US: University of Arizona Press, 3-17.

Lederach, John Paul, 2005, *The Moral Imagination. The Art and Soul of Building Peace*. New York, NY: Oxford University Press.

---. 2004. *Building Peace: Sustainable Reconciliation in Divided Societies*. Washington, DC: United States Institute of Peace Press.

Lempereur, Alain & Colson, Aurélien Michele, 2010. *The First Move. A Negotiator's Companion*. London: Wiley.

Liepold, Mary. 2010. "The Power of the Powerlessness: The Life and Work of Merlie 'Milet' B Mendoza of the Philippines." Ed. Emiko Noma, San Diego, CA: University of San Diego.

Little, David and Appleby, Scott. 2004. "A Moment of Opportunity? The Promise of Religious Peacebuilding in an Era of Religious and Ethnic Conflict." In *Religion and Peacebuilding*, Eds. Harold Coward and Gordon S. Smith, Albany, State University of New York Press, 1-23.

Llewellyn, Jennifer J. and Philpott, Daniel. 2014. "Restorative Justice and Reconciliation: Twin Frameworks for Peacebuilding." In *Restorative Justice, Reconciliation, and Peacebuilding*, Eds. Jennifer J. Llewellyn and Daniel Philpott, New York, NY: Oxford University Press, 14-36.

López, Maricel Mena. 2012. "Globalization and gender Inequality: A Contribution from a Latino Afro-Feminist Perspective." In *The Oxford Handbook of Feminist Theology*. Eds. Mary McClintock Fulkerson and Sheila Briggs. Oxford: Oxford University Press, 157-179.

Love, Maryann Cusimano. 2015. "Catholic Women Building Peace: Invisibility, Ideas, and Institutions." In *Women, Religion and Peacebuilding. Illuminating the Unseen* Eds. Susan Hayward and Katherine Marshall, Washington DC: United States Institute of Peace Press, 41-69.

Maka, Lia. 2006. "*Ta Fihi*: From Tangled Web We Weave Ane." In *Lalanga Pasifika, Weaving the Pacific. Stories of Empowerment from the South Pacific*, Ed. Arlene Griffen, Suva: University of the South Pacific, 21-102.

Marshall, Katherine, 2016. "Looking Back, Looking Ahead: Webs that Connect Development, Peace, and Religion." In *Religion, Peace, and World, Affairs: The Challenges Ahead. Berkeley Centre Ten-Year Anniversary Essays*, Ed. E. Taylor, Washington DC: Georgetown University, 52-55.

Marshall, Katherine and Hayward, Susan. 2011 "Women in Religious Peacebuilding," *PeaceWorks* Washington DC: United States Institute of Peace.

--- 2010. "Women, Religion, and Peace: Exploring an Invisible Force," *World Faiths Development Dialogue, Berkeley Center for Religions, Peace, and World Affairs and the United States Institute for Peace*, December 2010.

Martín-Muñoz. 2010. "Unconscious Islamophobia," *Human Architecture: Journal of the Sociology of Self-Knowledge* 8(2): 21-28.

McGinty, Anna Mansson. 2012. "'Faith Drives Me to be an Activist': Two American Muslim Women on Faith, Outreach, and Gender," *The Muslim World* 102(2): 371-389.

McGrory, Jane. 2008. *Faithful Peace, Peaceful Faith: The Role of Women of Faith in Building Peace*, London: Progressio.

McKenna, Megan. 2010. *This Will be Remembered of Her: Stories of Women Reshaping the World*. Grand Rapids, MICHIGAN: Will B. Eerdmans Publishing Company.

Medie, Peace, 2016, "Invest in Women's Organization for a Change," https://wilpf.org/invest-in-womens-organisations-for-a-change/ accessed 8 November 2018.

Meeker, Joy. 2016, "Staying With Emotions in Conflict Practice: Opening a Space In-Between." In *Faith and Practice in Conflict Resolution: Toward a Multidimensional Approach*, Ed. Rachel M. Goldberg, Boulder, COLO: Lynne Rienner, 113-130.

Mehta, Ritambhara. Nd. "UNSC Resolution 1325: Women and Conflict (From a South Asia Perspective)." www.peacewomen.org accessed 11 November 2015.

Meintjes, Sheila, Pillay, Anu and Turshen, Meredith. Eds. 2001. *The Aftermath. Women in Post-Conflict Transformation*. London: Zed Books.

Minwalla, Sherizaan. 2016. "Yazidi Women and Girls Resist ISIS in Creative Ways," Blog 4 October 2016, *Women's Media Centre*, Women Under Siege Project.

Morgain, Rachel. 2015. "'Break Down These Walls': Space, Relations, and Hierarchy in Fiji and Evangelical Christianity," *Oceania* 85(1): 105-118.

Morgain, Rachel and Taylor, John. 2015. "Transforming Relations of Gender, Person, and Agency in Oceania," *Oceania* 85(1): 1-9.

Morse, Alison. 2014. "A Slow Bloom: The Life and Work of Ashima Kaul of India (Kashmir)," Ed. Kaitlin Barker Davis, San Diego, CA: University of San Diego.

Murabit, Alaa. 2015. "Reclaiming Faith," *The Forum on Women, Religion, Violence and Power*, https://forumonwomen.wordpress.com/2015/02/05/reclaiming-faith/
accessed 3 September 2015.

Mukansengimana-Nyirimana, Rose and Draper, Jonathan, 2013. "The Peace-Making Mother: Reading John 2:1-12 in the Context of Rwandan Post-Genocide Women," *Scriptura* 112 (2): 1-16.

Murabit, Alaa. 2015a. "What My Religion Really Says About Women," TEDWomen May 2015.

--- 2015b "Reclaiming Faith," February 5 2015, *The Forum on Women, Religion, Violence, and Power at the Carter Centre*, http://forumonwomenblog.cartercenter.org/2015/02/05/reclaiming-faith/ accessed 3 September 2015.

Mwaura, Philomena, N. and Parsitau, Damaris, S. 2016. "Perceptions of Women's Health and Rights in Christian New Religious Movements in Kenya." In *African Traditions in the Study of Religion in Africa*. Eds. Adogame, Afe, Chitandra Ezra, and Bateye, Bolai. London: Routledge, 175-185.

Mwaura, Philomena Njeri. 2012. "Woman Lost in the Global Maze: Women and Religion in East Africa Under Globalization." In *The

Oxford Handbook of Feminist Theology. Eds. Mary McClintock Fulkerson and Sheila Briggs. Oxford: Oxford University Press, 250-279.

Myrttinen, Henri, Naujoks, Jana and El-Bushra, Judy. 2014. "Re-Thinking Gender in Peacebuilding," London: International Alert.

Nickerson, Colin. 2015. "Four Courageous Women Who Are Making a Difference," *The Boston Globe,* 17 February 2015.

Ní Aoláin. Fionnuala. 2016. "The 'War on Terror' and Extremism: Assessing the Relevance of the Women, Peace, and Security Agenda," *International Affairs* 92 (2): 275-291.

--- 2006. "Political Violence and Gender during Times of Transition," *Columbia Journal of Gender and Law* 15(3): 829-849.

Noma, Emiko. 2005. "Born in the Borderlands, Living for Unity: The Story of a Peacebuilder in Northern Uganda. A Narrative of the Life and Work of Sister Pauline Silver Acayo." Ed. Shelley Lyford, San Diego, CA: University of San Diego.

Nussbaum, Martha C. 1999. *Sex and Social Justice.* New York, NY: Oxford University Press.

Ogega, Jacqueline and Marshall, Katherine. 2015. "Strengthening Religious Women's Work for Faith." In *Women, Religion and Peacebuilding. Illuminating the Unseen.* Eds. Susan Hayward and Katherine Marshall, Washington DC: United States Institute of Peace Press, 283-297.

Olonisakin, 'Funmi, Barnes, Karen, and Ikpe, Eka, Eds., 2011. *Women, Peace and Security: Translating Policy into Practice,* New York: Routledge.

Oliver, Angela, Karam, Azza, and Levy, Elisa. Eds. 2004. *Women of Face: Transforming Conflict. A Multi-Religious Training Manual.* New York: World Conference of Religions for Peace.

Omer, Atalia. 2015. "Religion, Conflict, and Peace building: Synthetic Remarks." In *the Oxford Handbook of Religion, Conflict, and Peacebuilding.* Eds. Atalia Omer, R Scott Appleby and David Little, Oxford: Oxford University Press, 678-700.

O'Reilly, Marie. 2015 "Why Women? Inclusive Security and Peaceful Societies," Washington DC: Inclusive Security.

O'Rourke, Catherine. 2013. *Gender Politics and Transitional Justice.* London: Routledge.

Pankurst, Donna. Ed. 2008. *Gendered Peace: Women's Struggles for Post-War Justice and Reconciliation.* New York: Routledge.

Paris, Roland. 2004. *At War's End: Building Peace After Civil Conflict.* Cambridge: Cambridge University Press.

Peskowitz, Miriam, Aquino, María Pilar, Davaney, Sheila Greeve, Lewis, Nantawan, B., Townes, Emilie, M. and Plaskow, Judith. 1995. "What's in a Name? Exploring the Dimension of What 'Feminist Studies in Religion Means'," *Journal of Feminist Studies in Religion* 11 (1): 111-136.

Pew Research Centre website. http://www.globalreligiousfutures.org/ accessed 27 April 2016.

Pettman, Jan Jindy. 1996. *Worlding Women. A Feminist International Politics.* London: Routledge.

Phelps, Teresa Godwin. 2004. *Shattered Voices. Language, Violence, and the Work of Truth Commissions,* Philadelphia, PENN: University of Pennsylvania Press.

Philpott, Daniel. 2016. "An Age of Mercy." In *Religion, Peace, and World, Affairs: The Challenges Ahead. Berkeley Centre Ten-Year Anniversary Essays,* Ed. E. Taylor, Washington DC: Georgetown University, 19-22.

---. 2012. *Just and Unjust Peace. An Ethic of Political Reconciliation,* New York, NY: Oxford University Press.

---. 2009. "Has the Study of Global Politics Found Religion?" *Annual of Political Science* 12: 183-202.

---. 2006. "Beyond Politics As Usual: Is Reconciliation Compatible With Liberalism?" In Daniel Philpott, Ed., *The Politics of Past Evil: Religion, Reconciliation, and the Dilemmas of Transitional Justice,* Notre Dame, IN: University of Notre Dame Press, 2006, 11-44.

Porter, Elisabeth, & Mundkur, Anuradha. 2012. *Peace and Security: Implications for Women*. Brisbane: University of Queensland Press.

Porter, Elisabeth. 2016. "Feminists Building Peace and Reconciliation: Beyond Post-Conflict," *Peacebuilding*, 4(2): 210-225.

--- 2015. *Connecting Peace, Justice & Reconciliation*. Boulder, COLO: Lynne Rienner.

--- 2013. "Rethinking Women's Empowerment," *Journal of Peacebuilding and Development*, 8(1): 1-14.

--- 2007. *Peacebuilding: Women in International Perspective*. London: Routledge.

--- 2006. "Can Politics Practice Compassion?" *Hypatia. A Journal of Feminist Philosophy*, 21(4): 97-123.

--- 2003. "Women, Political Decision-Making and Peacebuilding in Conflict Regions," *Global Change, Peace and Security*, 15(3): 245-262.

Porter, Fran, 2013. "The 'In-the Middle' God and Power in Northern Ireland." In *Explorations in Practical, Pastoral, and Empirical Theology: Faith Lives of Women and Girls: Qualitative Research Perspectives*. Eds. Nicola Slee and Anne Phillips, Farnham: Ashgate Publishing Ltd, 91-101.

Powers, Gerard, F. 2010. "Religion and Peacebuilding." In *Strategies of Peace. Transforming Conflict in a Violent World*. Eds. Daniel Philpott and Gerard F. Powers, New York, NY: Oxford University Press, 317-352.

Prasch, Allison. 2015. "Maternal Bodies in Militant Protest: Leymah Gbowee and the Rhetorical Agency of African Motherhood," *Women's Studies in Communication* 38(20): 187-205.

Pratt, Nicola and Richter-Devroe, Sophie, 2011. "Critically Examining UNSCR 1325 on Women, Peace, and Security," *International Feminist Journal of Politics* 13(4): 489-503.

Press, Robert N. 2010. "'Guided By The Hand of God': Liberian Women Peacemakers and Civil War," *The Review of Faith and International Affairs* 8(1): 23-29.

Puechguirbal, Nadine. 2010. "Discourses on Gender, Patriarchy, and Resolution 1325: A Textual Analysis of UN Documents," *International Peacekeeping*, 17(2): 172-187.

Pui-Lan, Kwok. 2012. *Globalization, Gender, and Peacebuilding. The Future of Interfaith Dialogue.* New York: Paulist Press.

---. 2010. "A Postcolonial Feminist Vision or Christianity." In *New Feminist Christianity: Many Voices, Many Views*, Eds. Mary E. Hunt and Neu, Diann L. Woodstock Vt: SkyLight Paths Publishing, 3-10.

Pugh, Nikki Ly. 2011. "Um Al-Iraq (The Date Palm Tree). The Life and Work of Dr Rashad Zaydan of Iraq," Ed. Kaitlin Barker Davis, San Diego, CA: University of San Diego.

Ramadhan, Shamsia and Mang'eni, Barasa. 2010. "African Council of Religious Leaders: The Role of Religious Leaders and Women of Faith in Peace, Conflict Transformation, and Millennium Development Goals in Africa." *A Report of a Consultative Meeting*, 19-21 November 2010, Nairobi, Kenya.

Ramsbotham, Oliver, 2010, *Transforming Violence Conflict. Radical Disagreement, Dialogue and Survival.* London: Routledge.

Razavi, Shahra and Jenichen, Anne. 2010. "The Unhappy Marriage of Religion and Politics: Problems and Pitfalls for Gender Equality." *Third World Quarterly* 31(6): 833-850.

Reid-Cunningam, Allison Ruby. 2008. "Rape as a Weapon of Genocide," *Genocide Studies & Prevention: An International Journal*, 3(3): 279-296.

Religions for Peace. 2013. *Restoring Dignity: A Toolkit for Religious Communities to end Violence Against Women.* New York: World Conference of Religions for Peace.

--- 2009. *A Guide for Building Women of Faith Networks.* New York: World Conference of Religions for Peace.

Remengesav, Debbie. 2011. "Women as Global Peacebuilders," *Dialogue and Alliance: Women of Faith and Peacebuilding* 25(1):

online http://www.upf.org/dialogue-and-alliance/3785-dialogue-a-alliance-women-of-faith-and-peacebuilding

Richmond, Oliver, P. 2009. "A Post-liberal Peace: Eirenism and the Everyday," *Review of International Studies*, 35(3): 557-580.

Robinson, Fiona. 2011. *The Ethics of Care. A Feminist Approach to Human Security*. Philadelphia, PA: Temple University Press.

Rogers, Mark, Bamat, Tom and Ideh, Julie Eds. 2008. *Pursuing Just Peace: An Overview and Case Studies for Faith-Based Peacebuilders*. Baltimore MD: Catholic Relief Services.

Rokhideh, Maryam. 2013. "The River of Humanity: The Life and Work of Sabiha Husic of Bosnia-Herzegovina," Ed. Kaitlin Barker Davis, San Diego, CA: University of San Diego.

Ropeti, Marie. 2003. "A Biblical Basis for the Ordination of Women in the Pacific." In *Weavings: Women Doing Theology in Oceania*. Eds. Lydia Johnson and Joan Alleluia Filemoni-Tofaeono. Suva: Weavers, South Pacific Association of Theological School and University of the South Pacific, 133-139.

Ruttenberg, Tara, 2014. "If You Suffer For Doing Good: The Life and Work of Margaret Arach Orech of Uganda," Ed. Kaitlin Barker Davis, San Diego, CA: University of San Diego.

Sara Ruddick. 1989. *Maternal Thinking: Towards a Politics of Peace*. London: Women's Press.

Say, Elizabeth, A. 1990. *Evidence on Her Own Behalf: Women's Narrative as Theological Voice*. Savage, Maryland: Rowman and Littlefield Publishers, Inc.

Schimmel, Solomon. 2002. *Wounds Not Healed By Time: The Power of Repentance and Forgiveness*, Oxford: Oxford University Press.

Schüssler Fiorenza, Elisabeth, 2014. "Between Movement and Academy: Feminist Biblical Studies in the Twentieth Century." In *The Bible and Women: Feminist Biblical Studies in the Twentieth Century: Scholarship and Movement*. Ed. Elisabeth Schüssler Fiorenza, Atlanta, US: Society of Biblical Literature, 1-17.

Seedat, Fatima. 2017. "Women, Religion, and Security," *Agenda*, 30(3): 3-10.

Shani, Giorgio and Saeed, Sana. 2016. "Religion and Peacebuilding: Human Insecurity and the Colonial Legacy in Myanmar." In *Practical Approaches to Peacebuilding. Putting Theory to Work*. Eds. Pamina Firchow and Harry Anastasiou, Boulder, COLO: Lynne Rienner Publishers, 65-80.

Shannahan, Chris. 2016. "President Trump and the Christian Right," *OpenDemocracy* 14 December 2016.

Siddiqui, Mona, 2016. "Shared Norms in a Globalised World?" In *Religion, Peace, and World, Affairs: The Challenges Ahead. Berkeley Centre Ten-Year Anniversary Essays*, Ed. E. Taylor, Washington DC: Georgetown University, 84-87.

Šiljak, Zilka Spahić, 2014. *Shining Humanity: Life Stories of Women in Bosnia and Herzegovina*, Newcastle upon Tyne: Cambridge Scholars Publishers.

--- 2013. "Do It and name It: Feminist Theology and Peacebuilding in Bosnia and Herzegovina," *Journal of Feminist Studies in Religion* 29(2): 176-184.

Simić, Olivera. 2012. *Regulation of Sexual Conduct in UN Peacekeeping Operations*. Berlin: Springer.

Simoni, Alicia. 2009. "Keeper of the Soul of the People: The Life and Work of Bae Liza Llesis Saway of the Philippines," Ed. Emiko Noma, San Diego, CA: University of San Diego.

Sjoberg, Laura. 2006. *Gender, Justice, and the Wars in Iraq*, Lanham MD: Lexington Books.

Slachmuijlder, Lena. 2017. *Transforming Violent Extremism: A Peacebuilder's Guide*, Washington DC: Search for Common Ground.

Slee, Nicola, Porter, Fran & Phillips, Anne Eds. 2013. *Explorations in Practical, Pastoral and Empirical Theology: Faith Lives of Women and Girls: Qualitative Research Perspectives*. Farnham: Ashgate.

Slee, Nicola. 2013. "Feminist Qualitative Research as Spiritual Practice: Reflections on the Process of Doing Qualitative Research." In *Explorations in Practical, Pastoral, and Empirical Theology: Faith Lives of Women and Girls: Qualitative Research Perspectives*. Eds. Nicola Slee and Anne Phillips. Farnham: Ashgate Publishing Ltd, 13-35.

Snow, Deborah. 2015. "Life of Brian," *The Age: Good Weekend*, 14 Nov 2015: 10-15.

Saovana-Spriggs, Ruth. 2000. Christianity and Women in Bougainville." *Development Bulletin* 51: 58-60.

Steele, David. 2008. "An Introductory Overview to Faith-Based Peacebuilding." In *Pursuing Just Peace: An Overview and Case Studies for Faith-Based Peacebuilders*. Eds. Mark Rogers, Tom Bamat, and Julie Ideh. Baltimore MD: Catholic Relief Services 5-41.

Sylvester, Christine. 2002. *Feminist International Relations. An Unfinished Journey*. Cambridge: Cambridge University Press.

Tadros, Mariz, 2011. "Introduction: Gender, Rights, and Religion at the Crossroads," *Institute of Development Studies Bulletin*, 21(1): 1-9.

Tepedino, Ana Maria. 1988. "Feminist Theology as the Fruit of Passion and Compassion." In *With Passion and Compassion. Third World Women Doing Theology*. Eds. Virginia Fabella and Mercy Amba Oduyoye. Maryknoll, NY: Orbis Books, 165-172.

The Sister Fund. 2008. *Healers of Our Time: Women, Faith, and Justice. A Mapping Report*. New York, NY: The Sister Fund.

Thomas, Scott. 2010. "Living Critically and 'Living Faithfully' in a Global Age: Justice, Emancipation, and the Political Theology of International Relations." *Millennium* 39 (2): 505-524.

Tickner, Ann J. 2014. *A Feminist Voyage Through International Relations*. New York NY: Oxford University Press.

Tohiana. B. 2006. "Weaving Bougainville Together: Rebuilding Broken Communities: Restoring a Shattered Society." In *Lalanga Pasifika Weaving the Pacific: Stories of Empowerment from the South Pacific*. Ed. Arlene Griffen Suva: University of the South Pacific, 164-188.

Tomlinson, Matt. 2015. "Gender in a Land-Based Theology," *Oceania* 85 (1): 79-91.

True, Jacqui. 2016. "Explaining the Global Diffusion of the Women, Peace and Security Agenda." *International Political Science Review* 37(3): 307-323.

---. 2012. *The Political Economy of Violence against Women.* New York: Oxford University Press.

Türk, Volker, Riera, José and Poirer, Marie-Claude. 2014. *UNHCR Partnership Note: On Faith-Based Organizations, Local Faith Communities and Faith Leaders,* Geneva: UNHCR.

Tutu, Desmond, 2016. "Grasping the Need for Each Other." In *Religion, Peace, and World, Affairs: The Challenges Ahead. Berkley Centre Ten-Year Anniversary Essays,* Ed. E. Taylor, Washington DC: Georgetown University, 101-104.

Trggestad, Torunn, L. 2009. "Trick or Treat? The UN and Implementing of Security Council Resolution 1325 on Women, Peace and Security," *Global Governance,* 15(4): 539-557.

UN Action. Nd. *Stop Rape Now.* http://stoprapenow.org/uploads/aboutdownloads/1282162584.pdf accessed 27 September 2016.

UN Office on Drugs and Crime (UNODC). 2014. *Global Report on Trafficking in Persons 2014,* New York: UN.

UN Security Council. 2000. "Resolution 1325 on Women, Peace and Security", 31 October 2000, S/RES/1325 (2000).

UN Security Council. 2008. "Resolution 1820," 19 June 2008, S/RES/1820 (2008).

UN Security Council. 2009a. "Resolution 1888," 30 September 2009, S/RES/1888 (2009).

UN Security Council. 2009b. "Resolution 1889," 5 October 2009, S/RES/1889 (2009).

UN Security Council. 2010. "Resolution 1960," 16 December 2010, S/RES/1960 (2010).

UN Security Council. 2013. "Resolution 2106," 24 June 2013, S/RES/21016 (2013).

UN Security Council. 2013. "Resolution 2122," 18 October 2013, S/RES/2122 (2013).

UN Security Council. 2015. "Resolution 2242," 13 October 2015, S/RES/2242 (2015).

UN Security Council. 2016. "Resolution 2331," 20 December 2016, S/RES/2331 (2016).

UN Security Council. 2019a. "Resolution 2467," 29 April 2019, S/RES/2467 (2019).

UN Security Council. 2019b. "Resolution 2493," 29 October 2019, S/RES/2493 (2019).

United States Institute of Peace. 2015. *Charting a New Course. Women Preventing Violent Extremism.* Washington DC: United States Institute of Peace.

UN Women. 2016a. "Facts and Figures: Ending Violence Against Women," http://www.unwomen.org/en/what-we-do/ending-violence-against-women/facts-and-figures accessed 27 September 2016.

UN Women. 2016b. "Women at the Forefront of peacebuilding," http://www.unwomen.org/en/news/in-focus/women-peace-security accessed 17 March 2017.

Valji, Nahla. 2010. "Gender Justice and Reconciliation." In *Building a Future on Peace and Justice: Studies on Transitional Justice, Peace, and Development.* Eds. Kai Ambos, Judith Large and Marieke Wierda. Berlin: Springer-Verlag, 217-236.

Verveer, Melanne, 2016. "Countering Violent Extremism's Subjugation of Women." In *Religion, Peace, and World, Affairs: The Challenges Ahead. Berkely Centre Ten-Year Anniversary Essays,* Ed. E. Taylor, Washington DC: Georgetown University, 105-108.

Vltchek, Andre. 2014. "Christianity, Imperialism, Capitalism: Christian Dogma Should Be Questioned," *Transcend Media Service*, 29 December 2014.

Vogt, Anna. 2015. "Columbia: Power in Peacebuilding," *The City Paper, Bogotá,* July 21, 2015

Volf, Miroslav. 2015. "Religions, Identities, and Conflicts." In *Religion and Identity in Post-Conflict Societies.* Eds, Regina Ammicht Quinn, Mile Babić, Zordan Grozdanov, Susan A. Ross & Marie-Therese Wacker. London: SCM Press, 21-28.

Walker, Rebecca and Clacherty, Glynis. 2015. "Shaping New Spaces: An Alternative Approach to healing in Current Shelter Interventions for Vulnerable Women in Johannesburg." In *Healing and Change in the City of Gold*, Eds. Ingrid Palmary, Brandon Hamber and Lorena, Núñez, Berne: Springer International Publishing, 31-58.

Wandita, Galuh, 2015. *Enduring Impunity: Women Surviving Atrocities in the Absence of Justice.* Jakarta: Asia Justice and Rights.

Welch, Sharon D. 2012. "Beyond Theology of Religions: The Epistemological and Ethical Challenges of Inter-Religious Engagement." In *The Oxford Handbook of Feminist Theology.* Eds. Mary McClintock Fulkerson and Sheila Briggs. Oxford: Oxford University Press, 353-370.

Wibben, Annick, T.R. 2011. *Feminist Security Studies. A Narrative Approach.* London: Routledge.

Willett, Susan. 2010. "Introduction: Security Council Resolution 1325: Assessing the Impact on Women, Peace, and Security," *International Peacekeeping*, 17(2): 142-158.

Wilson, Shamillah. 2005. "Feminist Leadership for Feminist Futures." In *Defending Our Dreams. Global Feminist Forces for a New Generation.* Eds. Shamillah Wilson, Anasuya Sengupta and Kristy Evans. London: Zed Books, 224-239.

Wulan, Lisa, R. nd "Enhancing the Role of Women in Indonesia to Counter Terrorism," Asia Pacific Center for Security Studies http://apcss.org/wp-content/uploads/2015/01/AP-Women-Indonesia-CT-final.pdf

Woodward, Maia. 2005. "One Women's Life, One Thousand Women's Voices. A Narrative of the Life and Work of Mary Ann Arnado of the Philippines," Ed. Emiko Noma, San Diego, CA: University of San Diego.

Woolley, Alison. 2013. "Silent Gifts: An Exploration of Relationality in Contemporary Christian Women's Chosen Practices of Silence." In *Explorations in Practical, Pastoral, ad Empirical Theology: Faith Lives of Women and Girls*. Eds. Nicola Slee, Fran Porter and Anne Phillips, Farnham, Surrey, Ashgate, 147-159.

Young, Iris Marion. 2011. *Responsibility for Justice*. Oxford: Oxford University Press.

Yuval-Davis, Nira. 1997. *Gender and Nation*. London: Sage.

Žarkov, Dubravka. 2015. "Reflecting on Faith and Feminism." *European Journal of Women's Studies*, 22(1): 3-6.

Zine, Jasmin. 2006. "Between Orientalism and Fundamentalism: The Politics of Muslim Women's Feminist Engagement." *Muslim World Journal of Human Rights* 3(1): 1-24.

Significant Organizations

Asia-Pacific Women's Alliance for Peace and Security, https://ap-waps.net/

Association for Women in Development, https://www.awid.org/

Berkley Center for Religion, Peace and World Affairs, http://pluralism.org/women/

Charter for Compassion, http://www.charterforcompassion.org/

Defying Extremism, http://www.defyingextremism.com/

Ecumenical Women, https://ecumenicalwomen.org/

Elders, http://www.theelders.org/

Forum on Women, Religion, Violence, and Power at The Carter Centre, http://forumonwomen.cartercenter.org/.

Gender Action for Peace and Security, http://gaps-uk.org/

Global Women of Faith Networks, https://rfp.org/connect/global-women-of-faith-network/

Global Peace Initiative of Women, http://www.gpiw.org/.

Global Women of Faith Network, http://www.religionsfor-peace.org/who-we-are/global-women-faith-network

Institute for Inclusive Security, https://www.inclusivesecurity.org/

International Alert, https://www.international-alert.org/

Medica Zenica, http://medicazenica.org/uk/

NGO Working Group on Women, Peace, and Security, http://www.womenpeacesecurity.org/

PeaceWomen, https://www.peacewomen.org/

Pluralism Project, http://pluralism.org/women/

Religions for Peace, https://rfp.org/

Rwandan Stories, http://www.rwandanstories.org/index.html

Tanenbaum: Combating Religious Prejudice, https://tanenbaum.org/

Tanenbaum Peacemakers in Action Network, https://tanenbaum.org/peacemakers-in-action-network/meet-the-peacemakers/

United Methodist Women http://www.unitedmethodist-women.org/

University of San Diego Women Peacemaker Programme, https://www.sandiego.edu/peace/institutes/ipj/women-peace-security/narratives/.

UN Women, http://www.unwomen.org/en

Vision of Humanity's Global Terrorism Index, http://visionofhu-manity.org/indexes/terrorism-index/

Women in International Security, https://www.wiisglobal.org/

Women's International League for Peace & Freedom, https://wilpf.org/

Women in National Parliaments, archive.ipu.org/wmn-e/classif.htm

Women Waging Peace Network, https://www.inclusivesecu-rity.org/experts/

Women Without Borders, http://www.women-without-borders.org/projects/underway/42/.

World Council for Churches, https://www.oikoumene.org/en

www.ingramcontent.com/pod-product-compliance
Lightning Source LLC
Chambersburg PA
CBHW032123020426
42334CB00016B/1052